STREET MATTERS

PITT LATIN AMERICAN SERIES

Catherine M. Conaghan, Editor

STREET MATTERS

A CRITICAL HISTORY OF TWENTIETH-CENTURY URBAN POLICY IN BRAZIL

FERNANDO LUIZ LARA AND ANA PAULA KOURY

University of Pittsburgh Press

Published by the University of Pittsburgh Press, Pittsburgh, Pa., 15260

Manufactured in the United States of America
Printed on acid-free paper

10 9 8 7 6 5 4 3 2 1

Cataloging-in-Publication data is available from the Library of Congress

ISBN 13: 978-0-8229-4713-4
ISBN 10: 0-8229-4713-7

Cover design: Joel W. Coggins

TO OUR CHILDREN, OLIVIA, HELENA, AND BEATRIZ;

AND TO OUR PARTNERS, LETICIA MARTELETO AND RENATO ANELLI.

CONTENTS

ACKNOWLEDGMENTS

This book took almost a decade to evolve from its inception to its final form. The collaborative work of Fernando Lara and Ana Paula Koury started in 2012 with her first visit to Austin, leading to a research project funded by the University of Texas and Fundação de Amparo a Pesquisa de São Paulo (FAPESP) in 2014–2016 and fostered by the Fulbright grant in the fall of 2016 at CUNY. The main hypothesis was that planning and participation were not irreconcilable dimensions of Brazilian urban society. As we finalized our research proposal, the Brazilian streets exploded in protest in June of 2013, a watershed event with acute repercussions in Brazil to this day. This book was born from our struggle to understand June of 2013 in light of the previous history of urban policy and public protest, two long scholarly literatures that we thought should be stitched together.

This decade-long project would not be possible without the support of FAPESP and University of Texas Office of the Vice President for Research, which allowed us to organize events in Austin in 2014 and 2015 and in São Paulo in 2016. We would like to acknowledge our colleagues in Austin and São Paulo, such as Fritz Steiner, Charlie Hale, Michelle Addington, Fernando de Mello Franco, Carolina Heldt D'Almeida, and Paula de Vincenzo Fidelis Belfort Mattos, who have supported this project since its inception. We have had the privilege of interacting personally with many scholars upon whose work we build our analysis, and we need to thank Alexandre Barbosa, Arturo Escobar, Carlos Eduardo Dias Comas, Clara Irazábal-Zurita, Felipe Hernández, Fernando Guilherme Bruno Filho, Marta Gutman, Nabil Bonduki, Patricio del Real, Sarah Feldman, and Steven Moore. The four anonymous reviewers also need to be acknowledged because their attentive and rigorous criticism was fundamental to making this book better.

Our research and our discussions do not exist outside of teaching, which has always been a powerful source of energy and hope for us. We thank all the students at the University of Texas at Austin and São Judas University who have participated in our studios, seminars, and debates and also the students and colleagues at the Instituto de Arquitetura e Urbanismo of the University of São Paulo and HafenCity University, especially Michael Koch, Martin Wickel, and Martin Kohler.

At the University of Pittsburgh Press we are very grateful for Josh Shanholtzer, who believed in the project from the beginning and guided us gently and firmly through five external reviews and the editorial process, for the careful copyediting of Sarah C. Smith, and for the beautiful design of Joel Coggins.

We are also very privileged to have partners who are inspirational scholars that have supported and influenced our thoughts in very deep ways. Renato Anelli and Leticia Marteleto are secret coauthors of this book. We owe them everything, and we dedicate this book to our children, Vítor Olivia, Helena, and Beatriz. Their awareness of an unjust world and their energy for changing it keep reminding us of how much streets matter.

STREET MATTERS

INTRODUCTION

In June of 2013 millions of Brazilians took to the streets to protest a variety of causes, sparked by a transportation tariff hike and fueled by perception of widespread corruption and misguided priorities, particularly those of the upcoming FIFA Confederations Cup. "We want hospitals and schools with padrão FIFA," shouted the young Brazilians, referencing the expensive stadiums, airports, and hotels built according to the soccer association guidelines.[1]

Corruption and deficient infrastructure are old problems in Brazil—as are street protests—but the pervasion of these issues in 2013 was somewhat unexpected given the narrative that Luiz Inácio Lula da Silva's government (2003–2010) had found the formula for income distribution with strong economic growth and political stability, pushing the country to close its modernization gaps. International media fueled this image of a rising power, and a number of books such as *Brazil on the Rise* by *New York Times* correspondent Larry Rother and *Brazil: The Troubled Rise of a Global Power* by *The Economist* regional director Michael Reid were celebrating just that. Of the states comprising BRICS (Brazil, Russia, India, China, and South Africa),[2] Brazil seemed to have it all: democracy, natural resources, no border conflicts, no ultra-nationalist movement, plenty of room to grow, and a positive international image. The country's economy had survived the 2008 crisis with minimal damage and was surfing the global branding wave of hosting the 2014 FIFA World Cup and the 2016 Summer Olympic Games. The historical income inequality was shrinking, and the country's Gini coefficient, a gauge of income inequality, fell from 0.65 in 2002 to 0.50 in 2013.[3] Unlike Hugo Chávez in Venezuela and Cristina Kirchner in Argentina, Lula da Silva and Dilma Rousseff promoted liberal leftist policies that embraced economic growth and had strong support from local capitalists. All eyes were on Brazil and it was, at that point, a case of success.[4]

That could explain why the 2013 protests were described by the Brazilian mainstream media as a surprise. "The giant has awoken," the news said in unison. This was far from reality. Since Brazilian society had initiated its process of rapid urbanization, the streets had been a stage for social movements; protests big and small happened rather frequently throughout the twentieth century.

This book explores the idea that we should interpret urban transformation through the lens of the relationship between street protests and urban policy, making explicit the conflict between popular democracy and economic interests in the production of the space at the periphery of capitalism. The tension of street protests is the foundation on which Brazilian democracy conflicts has been based. By analyzing the historical changes at such moments, we can derive important lessons on urban policy in Brazil. Following the tracks of the pioneering works of David Harvey (1976) and Manuel Castells (1984) in their classics "Labor, Capital, and Class Struggle around the Built Environment in Advanced Capitalist Societies" and *The City and the Grassroots*, we seek the Brazilian engine in which "urban forms and functions are produced and managed by the interaction between space and society" (Castells 1984, xv).

Brazilian urban inequality produced the framework for the intensive pattern of economic exploitation in the peripheral capitalism, and in that sense the subsequent urban protests challenged the governance in the Brazilian cities. The framework of this book tries to foster an understanding of the relationship between urban planning and governance in Brazil through a historical perspective. We depart from Harvey's and Castells's theoretical analysis of this relationship, but we cannot imply direct causality between urban plans and street protests. Cities are way too complex to be shaped by any group of variables, as we elaborate further with our "theoretical tripod." What this book does for the first time in the scholarship of Brazilian urban history is to tell those histories in a parallel narrative, highlighting their strong convergences and sometimes their divergences without implying that one directly causes or induces the other. It is our hope that it may therefore be useful to address a more stable urban democracy and city governance in the future.

Is this such a radical proposal as to deserve a book? Has it not been done before? Does it help us understand what happened between 2013 and 2020? One hypothesis for why the history of urban plans has never been properly connected to the history of street protests is that these scholarships developed in opposite directions. As discussed by Clara Irazábal (2008, 26), "the literature that links public space and public sphere rarely takes a spatial angle." Setha Low (1999, 113) reminds us that we need a "theory of lived spaces in which spatial practices elude the discipline of urban planning." In summary, this book is a contribution to theorize spatial consequences of social practices under different historical patterns of urban planning in both the industrial and neoliberal periods of the Brazilian economy.

The historiography of social movements represents a shift in the most important explanations and theories regarding Brazilian society, moving away from its rural roots. The most stressed issues in the narrative about social movements were climate and race determinism in the nineteenth century, later adding Marxist approaches translated into the Brazilian rural and colonial economy. Even the most fruitful and modern theories that arise in the 1930s mainly focus on rural issues (Freyre 1933 and 1936; Holanda 1936). The first analyses on the specificity of Brazilian cities arise exactly from this tradition, as interpreted by Sérgio Buarque de Holanda, as part of Iberian heritage in "O Semeador e o Ladrilhador," a famous chapter of his book *Raízes do Brasil* (Holanda 1936). This is the case of the earlier books *Formação de cidades no Brasil colonial* by Paulo Santos (1968) and *Cidade Brasileira* by Murilo Marx (1980).

The shift from an interpretation based on cultural specificities of Iberian heritage to one focused on urban and economic problems should be considered a second step in the interpretation of the urban issue in Brazil. Urban geography had already produced major contributions such as Caio Prado Jr. ([1935] 1983) and Aroldo Azevedo (1956) when two books were published in 1968 analyzing the Brazilian urban evolution. The books *Contribuição ao estudo da evolução urbana do Brasil, 1500 a 1720* by Nestor Goulart Reis and *Desenvolvimento econômico e evolução urbana* by Paul Singer set the benchmark for future interpretations of urban and socioeconomic issues in Brazil.

A specific pattern of underdeveloped city growth, however, was addressed by *Urbanismo no subdesenvolvimento*, written by Jorge Wilheim in 1969, contemporary with the famous books of Henry Lefèvre, *Le droit à la ville* (1968), and Manuel Castells, *La question urbaine* (1972). These books were published concurrently with the institutionalization of urban sociology in Brazil, influenced by Antony Leeds, who came to the country to study favelas in 1968. He was followed by a range of scholars inside and outside the country in the establishment of an entire field of knowledge based on favelas in Rio de Janeiro, as we discuss in chapter 3 of this book. Leeds returned to Brazil in 1969 to teach in the recently created master's program in anthropology at the Federal University of Rio de Janeiro (Valladares 2000). Students of Leeds at that time included Gilberto Velho and Carlos Nelson Ferreira dos Santos, who would help disseminate his theories of urban sociology in the early 1980s (Velho 1980; Santos 1981).

In São Paulo, the creation of the Brazilian Center for Analysis and Planning (CEBRAP) greatly improved the understanding of Brazilian urban society. The center was created in May 1969, just after the military dictatorship had restricted civil rights in Brazil, brutally repressing movements against the regime. The center was directed by Cândido Procópio Ferreira Camargo and initially supported by a Ford Foundation grant. The main research focused on population studies led by Paul Singer and Elza Berquo. The original team also included Juarez Brandão Lopes, Fernando Henrique Cardoso, José Arthur Giannotti, Octávio Ianni, and Lúcio Kowarick, who joined the original group some years later. Many of those working at CEBRAP were professors persecuted by the dictatorship who had lost their teaching positions.

Part of this team contributed chapters for the book *Imperialismo e Urbanização na América Latina*, edited by Manuel Castells in 1973. The book proposes a theory of urban marginality in Latin America (Sorj 2008; Arantes 2009; Castells 1973), which influenced Ruth Cardoso and Eunice Durhan, who in 1973 published the article "A investigação antropológica em áreas urbanas." This paper is considered by Teresa Caldeira (2011, 19) the birth of urban anthropology in Brazil. The Brazilian Center for Analysis and Planning team of researchers grew when archbishop Dom Paulo Evaristo Arns commissioned a large study on urban poverty called "São Paulo crescimento e pobreza" in 1975.

Meanwhile, in Bahia, geographer Milton Santos was examining inequality and segregation as main explanations for underdevelopment. Away from the centers of São Paulo and Rio de Janeiro, and as a Black scholar in an overwhelmingly white Brazilian intelligentsia, Santos was acutely aware of the racial variable in these issues. Arrested by the military dictatorship in 1964, Santos was able to move to France in December of the same year and developed most of his important theories while teaching there. He was visiting professor in Toulouse, Bourdeaux, and in Paris at Institut d'Étude du Développement Économique et Social Sorbonne where he conducted urban planning research. In that capacity Milton Santos was able to locate Brazilian spatial inequalities in the broader context of the global south. In 1971 he moved from Europe to North America and as visiting professor at MIT, Toronto, and Columbia he wrote *O Espaço Dividido*, published in 1979. The book brought a spatial perspective challenging the idea that modernization inevitably brings well-being. His idea of a dual economic circuit—superior and inferior—anticipates the modernity/coloniality framework that Arturo Escobar used to implode the concept of developmentalism twenty years later.[5]

These books brought new perspectives to the theory and practice of urban planning in Brazil that were followed by José Alvaro Moisés (1978), Eva Blay (1978), Lúcio Kowarick (1979), Lícia Valladares and Ademir Figueiredo (1981), Maria da Glória Gohn (1982), Teresa Caldeira (1984), Sidney Chalhoub (1986), and Pedro Jacobi (1989).

All of this scholarship on Brazilian urban history stemmed from urban movements and improved the interpretation of urban society in Brazil by introducing new perspectives. Authors such as James Holston (1989), Jaime Benchimol (1992), Joel Outtes (1994), Flavio Villaça (1998), and Telma Correia (1998) pointed out the selective pattern of Brazilian urban modernization. These authors consider state entrepreneurship of major importance in the unequal modernization of Brazilian society. A second generation of Brazilian urban history scholars fostered the pioneering book by Flavio Villaça (1998), which was a significant turning point for one generation in its examination of spatial patterns of Brazilian cities.[6]

In 1999 Maria Cristina Leme organized a broad network of scholars and put together a large number of case studies to paint a fuller picture of Brazilian urban history. Working closely with experts in urban design, urban law, and planning, these authors drew on the work of the previous generation to systematize broader theories about how Brazilian cities had been built. Their significant effort consolidated a history of the institutionalization of planning in Brazil, highlighting the importance of state initiatives in the struggle toward urban improvement and modernization.

On the opposite end of the spectrum—and an indispensable reference to be included among this contemporary group—is the research on housing built by public and private capital. This research was led by Maria Ruth Amaral de Sampaio, who had participated in surveys on housing in peripheral areas with Carlos Lemos in the 1960s. The research she led in the 1990s filled an important gap in the literature about the investments made by public and private sectors to house the middle classes in Brazil, resulting in the publication of several books on affordable housing in Brazil.

Recent scholars from abroad have contribute to add different analyses such as Browdyn Fischer (2008) and Bryan McCann (2014), focusing on specific case studies that allow us to go deeper into the issues at large, less on developing broad theories and more on the gears of urban inequalities.

Despite the richness and diversity of the debate on the urban issue in Brazil, few works have crossed the boundary between social movement and urban policy or urban planning and city history, exploring the multiple interchanges of space and society. Kathleen Bruhn (2008) compared urban protests in Mexico and Brazil with a focus on how organize labor induced street manifestations. Her book gave us many insights into the relationship between protest and labor rights. But by focusing exclusively on newspaper reports as primary sources the author misses the political nuances that are not published in the daily "police" pages focused on public disturbances only. An interesting study published by Jessica Rich in 2019 uses the Brazilian public policy around HIV/AIDS to propose an approach in which social movements are capable of both protesting and negotiating with state actors to achieve their goals. We believe that has been the case throughout the twentieth century, and the dichotomy of state bureaucracy versus civil society is insufficient to explain urban development in Brazil. A few years ago, Lúcio Kowarick (2012) moved further in his analysis of the social components of the land issue with powerful results, despite not quite including urban planning variables. Other pioneering work by Michael Conniff ([1981] 2006), documenting research from 1972, inaugurated an interpretation focused on how the complex relationship between the state bureaucracy and its public and political support. Kowarick and Conniff were very close to economics and sociology and quite distant from urban planning. One notable outlier is the work of Carlos Nelson Ferreira dos Santos (1981), who in the 1960s and 1970s understood the strong parallel relationship between urban plans and social movements.

In this book we attempt to stitch all this scholarship together. Having explored hundreds of relevant publications, we find that street protests, urban policy, urban planning, and history have always been intertwined. Apart from a few pieces that highlight this relationship, however, there has been no full narrative connecting them, the main motivation behind this book.

For instance, there is significant political science and sociology scholarship on all major protests that happened in 1894, 1904, 1909, 1923, 1930, 1947, 1954, 1963, 1979, 1982, 1991, and 2013. Hundreds of other smaller protests in which the Brazilian people took to the streets have also been documented and analyzed, some but not all of which are available in English (Moisés 1978; Conniff [1981] 2006; Fausto 1984). Despite social conflicts being an integral part of city history, they have been always portrayed in the media as exceptional, something outside the norm of "lovely people" that is part of the Brazilian identity (Kowarick 2012, 23).

Quite separately, the historiography of Brazilian urbanism has devoted significant efforts to the analysis of the main urban plans implemented throughout the last 150 years. The narrative spans from Belo Horizonte (1894–1897), Pereira Passos reforms in Rio (1903–1906), Plan Agache again in Rio (1929), Plano de Avenidas in São Paulo (1930), Brasília (1956–1960), Plano Doxiadis in Rio (1964), Curitiba (1965), the closing of the National Housing Bank (1986) Estatuto das Cidades (2001), and finally to Plano PAC (2007–2013).

Meanwhile, the analyses of contemporary dilemmas and the criticism that arose from the frustration of the leftist architects engaged with urban policies have been disseminated and consumed without proper historical contexts. We hope this book contributes to reestablishing a critical and material history of urban conflicts that could be useful for cross-fertilization of urban planning and political democracy toward a critical history of twentieth-century urban policy in Brazil.

THE DOUBLE TRIPOD AS A THEORETICAL DIAGRAM

To understand the social and spatial dynamic of the main Brazilian cities, we propose a double tripod. Formed by three rods united in the middle and separated at the ends, this tripod creates two triangles at each edge. The triangle for the wealthy minority is composed of landownership, availability of cheap labor, and relative security due to repressive policing. The triangle for the poor majority is composed of housing without property rights, availability of informal or other low-paying jobs, and state repression. Here it is important to make explicit the modernity/coloniality conundrum as defined by Quijano, Mignolo, Dussel, and Escobar. Their theory helps us understand that every push toward modernization is sustained by some form of colonization, balancing the forces that act on our theoretical tripod.

Each rod of this tripod connects two points of those triangles. We have the labor rod, the land rod, and the public safety rod. Connecting the triangles is a precarious transportation system, or what we call the "transportation knot," which guarantees the spatial segregation between these two income groups.

We rely on an extensive literature to properly theorize this tripod diagram and test its usefulness in our analysis of urban plans placed in parallel to street protests. From Castells (1984, 336) we take the idea that "we need a theoretical perspective flexible enough to account for the production and performance of urban functions and forms in a variety of contexts." Our tripod is therefore inspired by Castells's search for patterns in the history of social movements and elites battling to control urban space such as in Castile in 1520s, the Paris Commune in 1871, the Glasgow strikes in 1915, and the US civil rights movement of the 1960s.

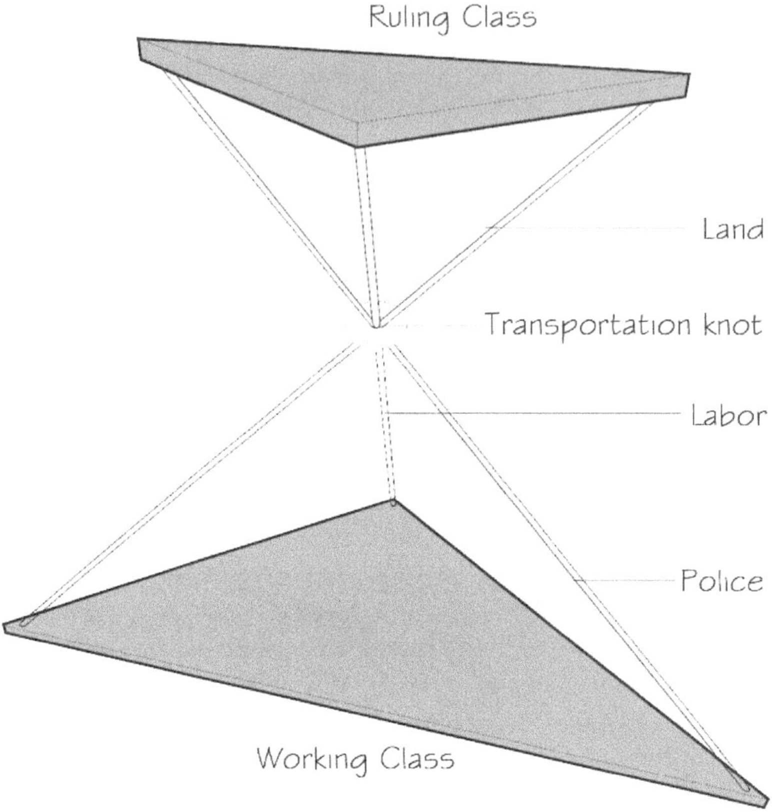

Figure I.1. Theoretical tripod. Tripod created by the authors, art by Bruno Santana de Oliveira.

As inspiring as Castells's work is, however, it seems to us insufficient with regard to the post-colonial layer that is needed to understand societies at the periphery of capitalism. From Setha Low (1999) and Anthony King (1990) we learn that the modernist city is often theorized as the colonial city. This is an added difficulty in our case because Brazilian literature has rarely discussed colonialism, arguing that because independence happened in 1820—or even before in 1808, as we discuss in chapter 1—such concepts do not apply.

Arturo Escobar's (1995) *Encountering Development* is the key to unlocking this dilemma. Escobar was the first to demonstrate that there is no modernization without colonization. The very process of modernizing implies the colonial practice of imposing values and beliefs of ruling elites onto large swaths of the population.

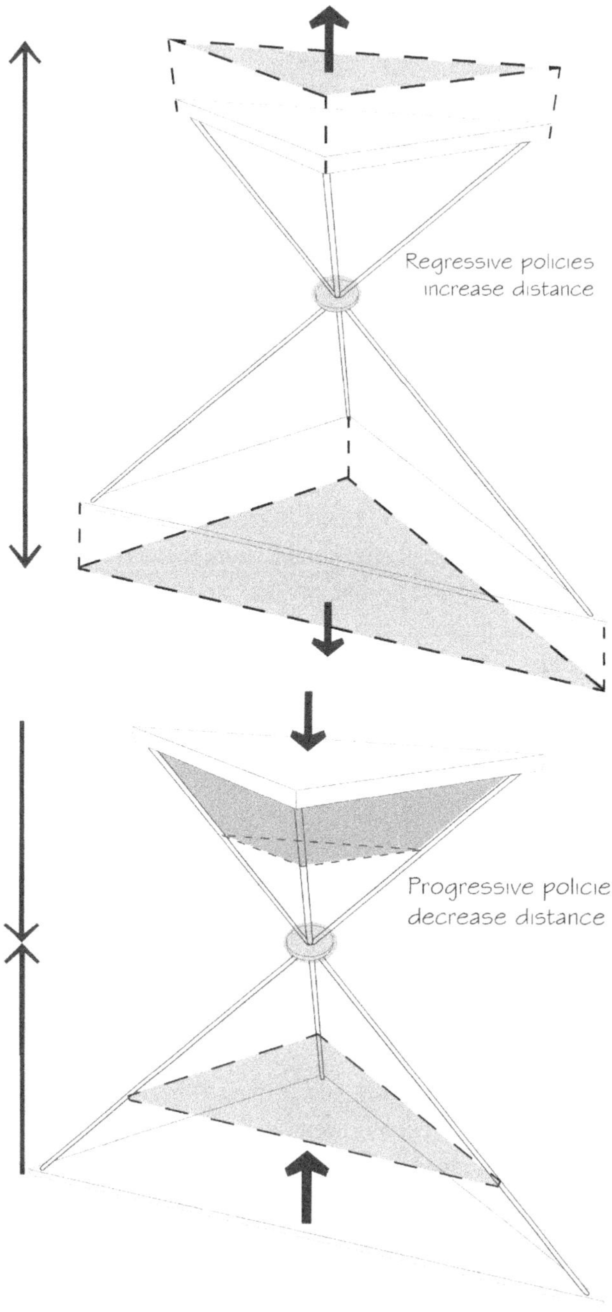

Figure I.2. Regressive and progressive movements on the theoretical tripod. Tripod created by the authors, art by Bruno Santana de Oliveira.

Our tripod diagram encompasses the modernization/colonization mirror in its very structure. Every action taken by the ruling elites from the top down in the name of modernization has an effect on the working classes below. The opposite is also true: social movements' political pressure and protests (their more radical form) push for changes in societal structure that impact the stability of those at the top of the social strata.

Castells (1984, 292) is again the one to clearly state that "any theory of urban change must account for both the spatial and social effects resulting from the actions of the dominant interests as well as from the grassroots alternative to the domination." Our tripod diagram illustrates this dynamic. Regressive policies enacted by the ruling elite have the effect of augmenting the distance between those above and the working class below.

Improvements in labor laws and wages have the opposite effect, shortening the distance. Both create instability. The former stresses the majority of the population by forcing them to live in worse conditions; the latter threatens the privileges of the elite by forcing them to pay more to obtain the same services. The push and pull of social movements and state policies affect the tripod structure and are felt on either end of the diagram. Later we discuss the position of the middle class, but before we get there allow us to discuss the three individual rods.

Take, for instance, the labor rod. Its structure assures that those on the bottom of the tripod will be subjected to high degrees of informality in their work arrangements, always serving as an excess (and therefore cheap) labor force. Fernando Haddad (2017), former mayor of São Paulo (2013–2016) and minister of education (2007–2010), summarized it well when he wrote that "the real shopping mall of the Brazilian middle class has always been the job market. Plenty of cheap labor guaranteed them nonexistent privileges in the hard core of the system. The cheap maid, the cheap nanny, the cheap driver. The lack of quality public services was largely offset by inexpensive household services."

A significant driver of the protests in Brazil throughout its history has been labor rights and labor conditions. In the tripod, we hypothesize that the labor rod had the most changes in favor of the working class throughout the twentieth century. This is sometimes a direct result of street protests, like the labor laws that followed the 1917 strike, and sometimes the result of intense lobbying and negotiations, as when the rules that applied to other workers were expanded to encompass maids by the Estatuto das Domésticas of 2015. Other times, such as in the dictatorships of 1937–1945 or 1964–1985, the suspension of strike laws and the regressive nature of governmental policies oper-

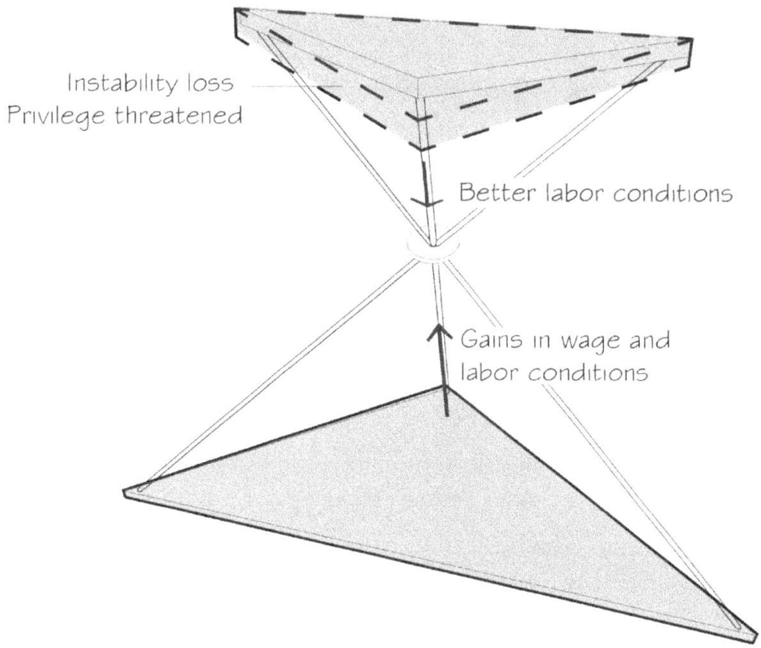

Figure I.3 Improved labor rights on the theoretical tripod. Tripod created by the authors, art by Bruno Santana de Oliveira.

ated in the opposite direction, suppressing rights, affecting the cost of living, and creating significant stress on the working class.

The public safety rod explains the inconsistent behavior of the Brazilian police: extremely docile with wealthy white people, extremely rude and violent with poor brown/Black people. In this book, we cannot even scratch the surface of serious issues like demilitarization, neighborhood policing, or the Unidade de Policia Pacificadora (UPPs) implemented in Rio de Janeiro in the early 2000s. It is apparent, however, that the binary of police protection/police repression is part of the very design of this system and a fundamental component of our tripod.

As asserted by Teresa Caldeira (1999, 87), "the most serious element in the increase of violence in São Paulo [after the 1980s] is police violence." Police repression and the struggle for rights are intrinsically connected to space. According to Don Mitchell's (2003, 29) *The Right to the City*, "the struggle for rights is one aspect of the struggle to resist the hegemony of abstract space." This struggle is a constant in Brazilian history and, as discussed by Browdyn Fisher (2008), the lack of well-defined rights is itself a strategy of control

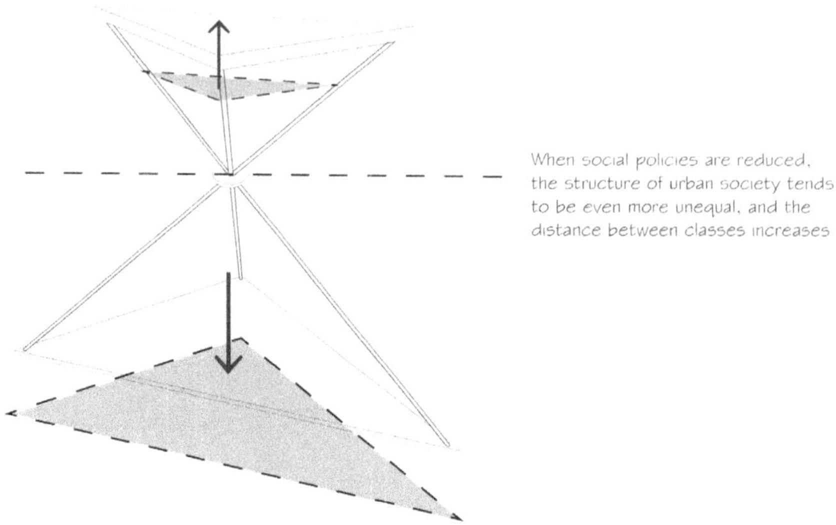

Figure I.4. Improved land rights on the theoretical tripod. Tripod created by the authors, art by Bruno Santana de Oliveira.

by the elites, who always find a way to deflate social tension with minimal concessions.

Throughout the book we discuss many instances in which Brazilians gained land rights and labor rights. Police repression however is a constant feature in Brazilian low-income society. Important improvements were realized in the twentieth century, but in 2021 the country is experiencing a sharp backslide toward police violence as state policy, forcing the regression of labor, social, and civil rights.

The third rod is the most relevant to our analysis. Land-ownership structure was built over centuries, and our first chapter explains how. This is not uniquely Brazilian, as Martinez Estrada ([1933] 1996, 52) reminds us in his classic *Radiografia de la Pampa*: Latin America has historically had a development model that exploits the people rather than exploiting the land. Concentrated landownership means that it was used less to produce wealth and more as an instrument of social control of the labor force, both in the cities and in the countryside.

Our tripod helps frame the land concentration in terms of a gradation of rights, from full property ownership to various degrees of occupancy rights. As elaborated by Don Mitchell (2003, 27), "a claim of right, no matter how contested, establishes the framework within which power operates." For the Brazilian working class, increasing security of tenure is a major component of well-being. Nevertheless, on the opposite edge of the land-ownership rod, the elite are fully aware that part of their well-being depends on the fragility of working-class housing tenure. The tripod metaphor fits well here, for stability is desired by both those residing above and those below.

This structure, and the desire for stability, assures that while a minority of Brazilian society owns a tremendous amount of land, urban or rural, the majority of the population does not have full property rights. When statistics say that 70 percent of the 210 million Brazilian citizens live in their own homes, they mean that these citizens are not paying rent. The process of planning and occupation of Brazilian cities, however, where 180 million people—86 percent of the population—now live, was such that a large number do not have the proper title and registration of their land. Avila and Ferreira (2016) calculated that 26 percent of the urban households in Minas Gerais—a state that can be used as a summary of the socioeconomic conditions of the country—do not have full documentation of their land (title and registration). That amounts to approximately fifty million people when applied to the whole country.

The uniqueness of the Brazilian land and labor conundrum was summarized by Francisco de Oliveira (2003, 131), arguing in *Ornitorrinco* that "the self-built explains the paradox of the Brazilian case in which the poor becomes owners of their homes—if you can call home the horror of the favelas—helping depress the cost of their own labor force." All this is part of Brazilian conservative modernization, a productive revolution without bourgeois revolution in the words of Florestan Fernandes ([1974] 1987). Or in the words of Arturo Escobar (1995), never stressed enough, there is no modernization without colonization. Throughout this book, we try to determine who got the bulk of the benefits of modernization, who got the bulk of the burden of colonization, and, most importantly, the conflicts embedded in different city spaces.

Urban plans have frequently stopped short of challenging landownership. In fact, the majority of the plans discussed here had disappointing results in terms of ameliorating inequalities; they have indeed exacerbated processes of exclusion that in one way or another have been in place since the Portuguese took control of the land in the sixteenth century. The institutionalization of the planning system and housing policy in Brazil were not of minor importance for the development of Brazilian cities. They managed to include a parcel of middle classes in the formal urban system, even if those plans did little to curb the huge inequalities inherited from the early republican period.

Kowarick (2012, 14) summarizes the interconnection of these issues by arguing correctly that "the capitalist expansion acquired such salvage features expressed in low wages, deficient transportation and inadequate housing." We chose this tripod image to illustrate the connections between these issues and convey that any change in one of the rods of our diagram creates instability in the whole city structure.

Are these changes and the consequent instability what drive the Brazilian people to protest in the streets? Does this urban instability affect the political process? We believe so, and this book aims to discuss this relationship, considering cities will be more stressed in the future by environmental issues and the lingering effects of the COVID-19 pandemic.

This book stitches together the history of plans for urban land with the protests that Brazilians organized to fight for their land. Between street protests and their resonance in the general public, we discovered that civil society applied a range of pressure points to the state bureaucracy and that even in the authoritarian periods public opinion influenced planning decisions. Our theory allows us to embed the history of civil society within the history of planning and its institutionalization. It is impossible to dissociate issues of wages and cost of living that are also always present at the root of urban protests, but our attempt is to shows how urban and regional planning played a key role in the management of the social conflicts around landownership. If sometimes urban and regional planning benefited the expansion of civil rights, it quite often worked on behalf of class exploitation, deepening spatial inequalities, as we discuss in subsequent chapters.

Chapter 1 conceptualizes these issues and sets up the roots of the fight for urban equality in Brazil, discussing trends in landownership related to Portuguese occupation and the dawn of urban improvements in the nineteenth century. These improvements were mostly focused on facilitating agricultural production, a system in which the cities were subordinated to the rural economy. This sets the tone for the next four chapters, which focus on the twentieth century, dissecting changes around the time of the 1889 military coup that ended the monarchy and established the First Brazilian Republic under the leadership of Brazilian bourgeoisie.

Chapter 2 focuses on the dawn of industrialization in Brazil and how urban plans and social movements responded to the challenges of the first three decades of the twentieth century. The main labor strike of 1917 helps us understand the issues at stake at that time, inaugurating the state response that would soon become standard.

Chapter 3 analyzes the Getúlio Vargas years (1930–1945), a time of intense transformation on many fronts such as the creation of the Consolidação das Leis do Trabalho (CLT; 1943 labor laws) and insufficient investment in urban infrastructure due to a unique stalemate between urban and rural political forces. Such a delicate balance of controlled modernization would lead to massive protests in the late 1940s, setting the tone for housing and transportation policies in the 1950s that were at best partial responses to structural inequalities. Later in the 1950s the demands of the periphery of Brazilian cities—not at all addressed by Juscelino Kubitscheck's accelerated developmentalism—exploded as an urban crisis, fueling the polarization that triggered the military coup of 1964.

Chapter 4 focuses on the responses to urban crises outlined in the previous section. The demands of the periphery—swept under the rug of Brazilian politics until the 1960s—were front and center in national discourse with the election of Jânio Quadros. The political crisis after Quadros resigned in 1961 dragged on for three years, culminating on the military coup of April 1, 1964. The military government recognized the importance of the urban crisis and responded by creating the SERFHAU (Federal Housing and Urban Planning Service) and the BNH (National Housing Bank). Infrastructure was indeed built at that time, easing pressure on the transportation knot that ties our conceptual tripod together. The authoritarian state changed the lengths of the rods affecting inequalities for the urban middle class, worsening conditions for the urban poor who were swelling peripheral areas of the main cities. It exacerbated structural inequalities by repressing social organizations and labor unions, imposing a twenty-year freeze in the social contract.

Chapter 5 follows with a look at the economic crisis of the 1980s, triggered by the foreign debt crisis of 1981–1982 that threatened the middle-class checkbook with stagnant wages, annual inflation of 100 percent, and increased labor demands by unions that were finally breaking away from the control of the military regime. Social movements were again protagonists in the nascent democracy that was established after the fall of the military government, culminating with the new constitution of 1988.

The last chapter proceeds to analyze the rise and fall of Fernando Collor de Mello (1990–1992), the interregnum of Itamar Franco (1993–94), and the Fernando Henrique Cardoso years (1995–2002). This dramatic decade saw significant changes in infrastructure (privatization of telecommunications and interstate roads) and land management (Favela-Bairro and Estatuto das Cidades), few gains in labor conditions, and slight relaxation of the police repression apparatus as a result of successful pressure by human rights groups since the 1970s. The low level of protest in those years would continue into the Lula presidency (2003–2010), coupled with significant gains in wages and consumption, and the consequent drastic fall of inequality as measured by the Gini coefficient (from 0.65 in 2002 to 0.50 in 2013). This final chapter, however, was written within the framework of the massive protests of June 2013, a development that made explicit all rods and knots of our tripod, prompting us to write this book.

Indeed, the main goal of this book is to stitch together the historiography discussing all these protests as the result of social struggles; a mainstream media that tends to register the protests of the working class as radical manifestations and only give value to the struggle of the middle class, and an urban history so far quite disconnected from it all.

The Brazilian working class took to the streets in 1879, 1904, 1910, 1917, 1922, 1930, 1947, 1956, 1959, 1967, 1968, 1973, 1979, 1981, and 1987. On all occasions, the reason to protest was increase in transportation costs, labor conditions, forced relocation, or police brutality. The four causes were often present at the same time.

1

IN THE BEGINNING, THERE WAS LAND

It is about land. It has always been about land. We know a little about how this land was managed before the arrival of the Portuguese in 1500 (Smith 1999). But let us start from the first European economic activity in Brazil, which was to convince the natives to cut a redwood tree—brazilwood—and ship it across the ocean. The land was renamed after a process of deforestation. Tamar Herzog (2015, 37) has called attention to the fact that one of the conditions for possession of the land according to Portuguese law was the absence of protest or opposition on the part of previous occupants. We know that native Brazilians did protest the invasion of their land and that such protests had to be buried for the sake of the occupation. As elaborated throughout the book, protests have been suppressed ever since.

The following centuries witnessed a system of economic exploration based on the power of patriarchal families controlling the land to make sure the majority of its people could work on it but never own it (Freire 1933; Prado [1942] 2006). Or as Darcy Ribeiro (1995) said poetically but sadly, Brazil has always been a people's grinding machine. That is the law of the land.

Allow us to start way back in time. We do not know much about how the original inhabitants of Brazil managed their territorial limits. From the heavily biased accounts of the first Europeans to arrive, we learn that there was indeed land conflict between different ethnicities. People fought for land. We learn the same from the communities that survived isolated in the remote corners of the Amazon. There has ever been dispute for the best land, the best fisheries, the orchards that yielded more protein content in nuts or attracted the birds that provided meat and feathers (Smith 1999; Neves 2006).

The dramatic process of land grabbing started, in the case of the Portuguese territories, in 1494 (Russell-Wood, 1992). On a warm summer day in Tordesillas, Spain, Pope Alexander VI signed the Treaty of Tordesillas, effectively dividing the world in two halves, one belonging to the king of Spain, the other belonging to the king of Portugal. The line dividing the planet was set to run north–south 370 leagues west of Cape Verde.

This was not the first treaty of its nature. In 1479 the Treaty of Alcáçovas had already given all land south of the Canary Islands to the Portuguese crown. When we consider that the Portuguese first "officially" arrived in the Americas in 1500, we realize that Brazil was "owned" even before it was "discovered" (Herzog 2015). Patricia Seed's (1995) "Ceremonies of Possession" explained how the Portuguese created a system of abstracted points (padrões) that would soon be incorporated into the world-system as elaborated by Anibal Quijano (Quijano and Wallerstein, 1992).

There is one important caveat to all the lands "given" to the Portuguese and Spanish crowns: the lands to be legally owned by them were the ones "not occupied" and "not cultivated" by other Christians. Interestingly enough, nobody bothered to convert the natives to Christianity before taking their land, only after.

CAPITANIAS HEREDITÁRIAS

Hereditary captaincies were the vehicle for the transfer of occupation and development rights from the king of Portugal to his noblemen, with the understanding that these noblemen would control, develop, and populate the land for the benefit of the kingdom. These occupation rights were bound by the Ordenações Manuelinas (after Manuel I of Portugal, ruler of Portugal from 1495 to 1521) and the Ordenações Filipinas (after Felipe II of Spain, ruler of Portugal after 1580). According to the Manueline law, all land belonged to the king. The right of occupation was given to anyone who cultivated such land for two years, provided that all possible previous heirs were notified (Herzog 2015, 7). In Portugal, a kingdom of only thirty-five thousand square miles, the law dictated that no single person should own more land than was "reasonable." Of course, the king decided what was and what was not reasonable.

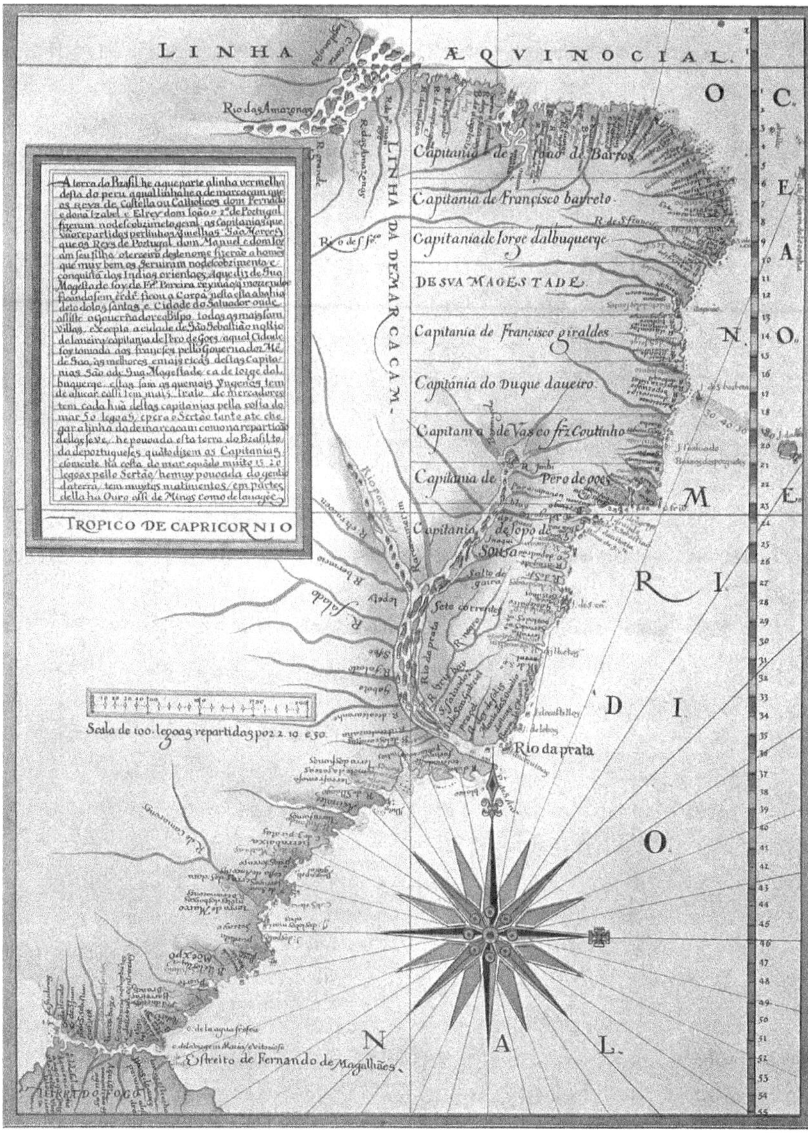

Figure 1.1. Map of *capitanias hereditárias*, 1574. Public domain, Biblioteca da Ajuda, Lisboa.

Such disposition was made flexible after the arrival of the first governor-general, Tomé de Sousa, in 1548, to facilitate control over this vast territory. Indeed, only the wealthy were called to own land in Brazil. Tamar Herzog (2015, 25) explains that the ordinance was ambiguous by design, to make sure the force of violence would prevail over the force of law.

Latifundia was the Portuguese strategy for Brazil. Faced with the task of occupying and defending this enormous territory in the South Atlantic, the Portuguese donated vast amounts of land to a few noble families, binding them to the colonial enterprise. This was quite a change for the Portuguese administration overseas. In Africa—and as far as Goa, India, and Macau, China—the Portuguese strategy was to control the port and impose a trade monopoly, enforcing some kind of agreement with the local lords. In Brazil the Portuguese crown initially implemented this system in the sixteenth century, but after Portuguese restoration in 1640 (Portugal was under Spanish rule between 1580 and 1640), the crown encouraged full territorial control.

Territorial policy shifted from fortified ports to full occupation when Portugal realized that trading with the Natives was not as profitable as the new business of sugar plantations being tested in the Atlantic islands.

In addition, several northern European nations attempted to take control of parts of the Brazilian territory during the troubled period of Spanish control over the Portuguese crown. The French were the most frequent invaders, having taken hold of Rio de Janeiro from 1555 to 1560 and the island of Maranhão between 1594–1615 (to this day called São Luís after Louis XIII). The Dutch also held control of Pernambuco between 1630 and 1654. The threat of losing the Brazilian territory to their northern rivals prompted the Portuguese crown to enforce the *capitanias hereditárias*, strongly encouraging territorial occupation by Portuguese subjects. The Sesmarias laws of 1395 dictated that land must be cultivated (to make sure the population had enough to eat) and gave the king the power to expropriate land that was not being used for food production. Under this legal system, and worried about full control of the land, the Portuguese crown donated huge parcels of land to its noble beneficiaries, giving them the right to explore the land as they saw fit, with the caveat, of course, that the king maintained property rights.

The issue of property rights versus occupation rights would come back to the forefront in the beginning of the eighteenth century when gold was discovered in Minas Gerais. The *paulista* explorers who found gold there in 1697 should have had exclusive rights over these lands as the first Christians to occupy them. Instead, they would soon be forced out by the Portuguese crown, which used the Sesmarias law of 1395 to justify the military control over the mines. The dispute exploded into the Emboabas War of 1707–1709, which settled the issue in favor of the Portuguese gold miners (Romeiro 2008).

The hereditary captaincies lasted until 1769, when they were revoked by the Marquis de Pombal, a reformist Portuguese prime minister of the late eighteenth century. The Pombaline reforms of 1769, called Lei da Boa Razão (law of good reason), strongly encouraged property rights for those who occupied and cultivated the land. This law used "immemorial occupation," or the fact that nobody else knew how long such a family had occupied and cultivated those lands, as legal justification for full property rights.

This would be the land law of Brazil until decades after independence. In 1842 the conservative government led by Bernardo Pereira de Vasconcellos wrote Bill 601, aiming to legalize the private property of land (not only private occupation) in Brazil. The bill moved slowly through Congress and was only approved in 1850 after an even more conservative cabinet (the Saquaremas) stripped the articles about territorial tax and government expropriation. Signed into law by the emperor on September 17, 1850, the Lei de Terras (land law) in effect gave full property rights to all legal occupants at that time. After that moment all *terras devolutas* (empty land) became property of the state and could only be acquired by public auction, paid in cash. The Lei de Terras established conditions for the transformation of old *sesmarias* (land rights as a consequence of cultivation) into new properties that included measurement, confirmation, in addition to cultivation. It is no surprise that neither measurement nor confirmation was ever properly enforced. Regina Gadelha (1989, 39) reminds us that the registration of property titles in the church archives (church and state were still joined in Brazil) was obligatory under penalty of losing the property while maintaining occupation rights, which in practice is no penalty. No efforts were made to survey and document the land boundaries. Gadelha analyzed the 1850s Lei de Terras in detail and concluded that properly surveying the existing lands would limit the power of the elite landowners.

The scholarship on the Lei de Terras agrees that it was implemented mostly to keep land concentrated in the hands of a minority of powerful landowners who controlled the ministerial cabinet. The law was influenced by the Wakefield colonization system and specifically worded to prevent immigrants from becoming landowners immediately upon arrival in Brazil (Motta 1998, 83). Funds from the sale of land by the state were used to finance travel of immigrant workers, but prices were kept artificially high to make it difficult for newcomers to become landowners. According to James Holston (1993) the Lei de Terras brought new conflicts and no new solutions because it legalized the practice of *grilhagem*, or illegal occupation of land for sheer speculation and not cultivation. Simonsen and Gudin ([1945] 2010, 12) stated back in the 1930s that while the United States embraced a strategy of agriculture with industrialization very early on (Alexander Hamilton, report on manufactures 1791; U.S. Tariff Act 1816), Brazil opted to reaffirm the model of large rural properties for agricultural exports based on slavery.

It is therefore not a coincidence that the Lei de Terras might have helped spark one of the early popular revolts in Brazil in 1851–1852. On September 6, 1850, a week before signing the Lei de Terras, the Brazilian emperor signed the Lei do Registro Civil (Law of Civil Registry). The first version of this law still mandated that people's births, marriages, and deaths be registered in the church archives. The following year, 1851, saw the creation of civil registry offices, run by the municipalities. Sidney Chalhoub (1996) explains that when the civil registry law was disseminated into the provinces, rumors equated the new mandate with the idea that all people of color would be enslaved; revolts erupted between December 1851 and January 1852 in Sergipe, Pernambuco, Paraíba, and Ceará.

Those, however, are hardly the first major revolts in nineteenth-century Brazil. There were slave revolts in Bahia in 1807, 1808, 1809, 1813, 1822, 1823, 1826, and 1830. In Maranhão a rebellion (known as Balaiada) of Blacks and peasants erupted in 1838. Three years earlier, a revolt in the northern province of Grão-Pará installed a provisional government with the participation of peasant leaders that resisted for years, the death toll rising to 30,000, or 30 percent of Pará's population. The year 1857 would see the first strike of 600 textile workers (150 of them slaves) at Ponta d'Areia, in the state of Rio de Janeiro. Two decades later, the Movimento Quebra-Quilos in Paraíba was a full-scale revolt against the military draft (for the Paraguay campaign) and the introduction of the metric system. The long list of popular revolts in the nineteenth century also includes Revolução Pernambucana (1817), Confederação do Equador (1823–1824), Revolta dos Mercenários (1828), Noite das Garrafadas (1831), Cabanada (1832–1835), Federação do Guanais (1832), Revolta dos Malês (1835), Sabinada (1837–1838), Motim do Fecha-Fecha (1844), Motim do Mata-Mata (1847–1848), Insurreição Praieira (1848–1850), Revolta do Ronco de Abelha (1851–1854), Levante dos Marimbondos (1852), Motim da Carne sem Osso (1858), Revolta dos Muckers (1868–1874), Guerra das Mulheres (1875–1876), Revolta do Vintém (1880), and República de Cunani (1895–1900).

All of these rebellions fit the idea that stress and trepidation on the socioeconomic tripod as presented in the introduction help us understand the broader picture. Changes in the relationship between the people and the power might not seem enough to push the population into full rebellion until we reconsider how fragile that equilibrium has always been. In the absence of full citizenship rights, any minor threat to the precarious balance of unspoken rules and petty favors that governed daily life of the Brazilian population could spill into full street protest (Fischer 2008). Nowhere was this more visible than in the country's capital at the time, Rio de Janeiro.

The city had grown tenfold, from 50,000 in 1808 when João VI moved his court there, to 150,000 by the mid-nineteenth century, and to 500,000 in 1890. Rio de Janeiro was famous—or infamous—as a hotbed of tropical disease due to deficient infrastructure. Until the 1850s water distribution was insufficiently managed by the government through public fountains. Slaves carried water barrels from the public fountains to the houses of the elite and carried human excrement back to be discarded into the waterways (Benchimol 1990, 65; Russell-Wood 1992, 52).

Lúcio Costa offers a famous explanation for the deficient infrastructure of the city as late as the early twentieth century: slaves had been the water mains, the power source, and the sewage system of Rio de Janeiro throughout its history. To give the readers an idea of how limited this system was, Gilmar Machado (2011, 10) estimates that by 1850 there were thirty public fountains in Rio, for a population of 150,000.

The liberal reforms of the 1850s that gave Brazil the Lei de Terras also set up the framework for the privatization of city infrastructure services. In 1864 a sewage company began operating: Rio de Janeiro City Improvements Company, funded by the Gleen and Mills Bank. Water was still the responsibility of the state, and a two-year drought in 1869–1870 left the city's water sources depleted. Two engineers—Francisco Pereira Passos and André Rebouças—struggling with the water issue, laid out plans that would dominate discussions for decades.

Francisco Pereira Passos studied engineering at the Escola Militar in the 1850s and later in Paris, where he saw firsthand the works of Eugène Haussmann. Pereira Passos proposed to channelize all waterways to control flooding and facilitate the drainage of sewage to the ocean. For Pereira Passos, water was one more resource to be controlled by efficient engineering. The city should be rectified, hills demolished, swamps drained, and infills built over the ocean to help facilitate circulation and development. In the 1870s and 1880s, new residential areas were being developed in the south (oceanic) parts of Rio, and there was a significant need for increasing the supply of water.

ANDRÉ REBOUÇAS AND THE LAND CENSUS

André Rebouças was born in Bahia in 1838 and studied engineering in the 1850s at Rio's Escola Militar. The positivist teaching of the nineteenth-century Brazilian military dominated urban development debates and actions of the time, and Rebouças worked on a series of infrastructure projects built by the empire.

The first major project under his supervision was the improvement of the Port of Rio in the 1860s. The following decade he was put in charge of addressing Rio's water crisis. Both of these endeavors were quite successful despite facing fierce opposition from the city's elite. Rebouças was able to triple the supply of water downtown with his intervention at Tijuca.

The Tijuca waterworks were part of Rebouças's ambitious plan to privatize the distribution of water, based on the protection of the springs and creeks. This project encountered strong opposition from members of the elite who profited from private water distribution (using slave labor) and were interested in neither public nor private modernization (Trindade 2011). The fact that Rebouças was Black in a country that still had slavery added a roadblock to the campaign, and his business proposals never got the necessary support of the government, which preferred to run its "business with no risk," with the state paying for the infrastructure as if the whole population could benefit. This would later evolve into a kind of capitalism with no risk that is inherently Brazilian. Again, however, only a few benefited from the little infrastructure built by the imperial government.

Being close to the emperor and Black, Rebouças was also an important counselor on the issue of slavery. Time and again he wrote to Emperor Pedro II (and we can only assume that they talked at length) that abolishing slavery should be just the first step on the emancipation of Afro-Brazilians. Economic integration was tantamount, and in an agricultural country that means owning land. Rebouças argued, correctly, that landownership was a murky business in Brazil and that modernization could not take hold without the proper rule of law governing who owns what (Carvalho 1998).

Slavery was abolished on May 13, 1888, and soon afterward Rebouças started lobbying the emperor to contract a nationwide land survey to help modernize contracts and the economy by improving the finance sector that was stunted by the frailty of land titles. The powerful landowners that controlled Congress and most of the Brazilian economy were not interested in such a survey. Besides, Rebouças defended the use of vacant land (meaning land not properly owned and registered) for settling ex-slaves and immigrants. Rebouças finally got the approval of the emperor to include the survey as part of the 1890 census. The law approving funds for such a survey was signed in October 1889. The oligarchy, with support of the military, staged a coup and took power the following month, on November 15.

It would be too simplistic to state that the coup that installed republican rule was a direct consequence of the contracted land census, but it is too much of a coincidence that it happened a few weeks after to be discounted.

Slavery had formally ended in 1888, but slave-like labor conditions and racist culture die hard in Brazil. When Brazil became nominally independent in 1822 about half of its population consisted of slaves. In 1888 the percentage of slaves was down to 5 percent of the population. Our point is that while slavery was slowly dismantled throughout the nineteenth century, racism persisted. Freed slaves were only nominally free.

Rebouças went into exile with the imperial family and ended up killing himself in Funchal, Ilha da Madeira, in 1898. His land survey was never carried out. His plans for Rio de Janeiro's waterways were never implemented (Carvalho 1998).

Rebouças's idea of private investment in city infrastructure was only partially realized, the Brazilian way. All development of land on the south beaches of Rio was based on public concession of public transport. The government financed the construction, private companies operated the facilities and reaped the profits, while the public paid for insufficient services (Benchimol 1990, 90).

The problem of insufficient infrastructure, housing, and transportation would only become more acute in late nineteenth-century Rio de Janeiro. Benchimol (1990, 128) links the aggravation of housing problems with the slow and gradual end of slavery between 1850, which saw the passage of the first law prohibiting Atlantic traffic of slaves, and 1888, the year of full emancipation. As we explained before, the Brazilian empire (and the soon-to-be Brazilian republic) did not prepare for the demographic transformations that were happening at the time (Carvalho 2003). While most of the traditional narrative frames it in terms of "lack of planning," we would rather discuss it as a purposeful project, designed by the oligarchical elites to keep their privileges.

This not-so-subtle shift in the framing of the problem is important for two reasons: it exposes the cruelty of part of the local elite that was never able to think beyond slavery (unfortunately this resonates to this day, as we discuss later in the book) and gives proper agency to the social movements—some of them led by progressive members of the elite—that worked hard to push real modernization of Brazilian society. Using our theoretical tripod to explain this, we would highlight that the "lack of planning" was rather a deliberate strategy to keep a flexible system that allows full control by a small minority of landowners and political leaders. Most of the pressure from below to shorten the distance between rich and poor was made invisible and dismissed as "mob rule," while elite proposals were carefully devised and implemented to make sure progress would happen without changing the structure. The abolition of slavery, for instance, was done in a context of no land rights, no labor rights, and increasing police repression: the three rods of our theoretical tripod.

In the case of Rio's urban crisis of the 1870s–1890s, the capital was under pressure from both more people coming to live there and the collapse of the slave economy that had previously run all city systems, including water, sewage, and power.

Up until the 1870s, most poor inhabitants lived downtown in tenement houses called *cortiços*. A *cortiço* was usually a long row of single rooms, each occupied by one or more families, with a single bathroom somewhere in the complex. The fact that most *cortiços* were built behind old townhouses made them relatively invisible to the official street life of the city, although everybody knew where every single one of them was. The demolition of a large *cortiço* called Cabeça de Porco ("pig's head") in 1893 signaled the beginning of a decades-long campaign of city cleansing carried by the authorities.

Benchimol (1990) again reminds us that it was a consensus among Rio elites that their society would benefit from building houses for the poor, known as *casas populares*; the debate was whether to do so downtown or in the outer periphery. As has almost always happened in Brazilian urban history, the argument for moving the poor to the outskirts ended up winning the day, for there was as much money to be made in land deals as in construction itself (163). The strategy of pushing the poor toward the periphery made a lot of land available for development downtown, therefore rewarding the landowners of both the center and the periphery. It also gave the general public the illusion that poverty was being addressed, when in fact it was only being dislocated. Moreover, the early sprawl of the late nineteenth century introduced an important variable to the urban equation: public transportation.

Throughout the colonial period and almost all of the nineteenth century, slaves and horses were the main modes of transportation for the elite; this would change drastically as new motorized transportation arrived, allowing and encouraging profit from the territorial expansion of the city. In the 1850s Rio had a couple of lines of trams pulled by donkeys. The first electric tram would be installed in 1872, and in 1879 we would see the first protest against fare increase in Rio de Janeiro. The following year, fifty thousand people (about one in every ten) marched against the rise of tram fares in Rio, marking the Revolta do Vintém, the first full-city revolt based on transportation deficiencies.

A new tax of twenty cents or one *vinten* would be charged to every passenger on January 1, 1880. On December 28, 1879, five thousand people took the Largo de São Cristóvão to protest against the new tax. The revolt continued into the first days of 1880, with three people dead and hundreds hurt when the police, unable to contain the crowd, called the army to intervene. The rebellion was dispersed, but the tax was canceled and the treasury secretary resigned. The leader of the revolt, journalist Lopes Trovão, had been writing furious editorials demanding improvements for Rio's periphery, and the cause continued to gain momentum.

Historian José Murilo de Carvalho (1987, 15) discusses extensively the transformations the city of Rio was undergoing at the turn of the twentieth century, calling it the most turbulent time of the city's history. First and foremost, it was a city of immigrants; only 45 percent of its half-million inhabitants were born there, with 26 percent born in other parts of Brazil and 28 percent foreign born. It was not a democratic city, as only 2 percent of its inhabitants had full political rights (44). And it was a deadly city, with malaria and yellow fever claiming fifty-two lives for every hundred thousand inhabitants every year.

The urban crisis briefly discussed above was acute. In 1890 city council was dissolved and an authoritarian intendancy was created, imposing a new building code that was intensely fought by property owners, especially the landlords. It is not hard to imagine the results of such forces imposed on a structure (our theoretical tripod) that was already stressed.

One must understand that 50 percent of Rio's population was composed of domestic workers, formerly enslaved people who lived in pretty much the same conditions as before emancipation. Foreigners controlled properties and finance, imposing rent barriers by demanding that an established business owner cosign every lease agreement. A report from the Portuguese legation in 1893 estimated that their citizens controlled 70 percent of real estate and commercial capital in Rio.

Such levels of inequality and lack of civil rights created the hotbed for revolts to erupt, every single one of them, including the Revolta do Vintém in 1880, the Quebra de Lampiões in 1882, and the Quebra de Bondes 1901, resulting from a combination of high rent prices, low wages, police repression, and inadequate public transportation: the three legs and the knot of our theoretical tripod.

CANUDOS

The first revolt to capture the attention of the whole country was the Canudos rebellion in Bahia from 1893–1897. In the impoverished area of the *sertão*, as the northern backlands were called, a holy man named Antônio Conselheiro started attracting crowds of followers to his sermons against modernization. Born in 1830, Antônio Vicente Mendes Maciel had walked the arid lands of Ceará and Bahia since the early 1870s, preaching against the oppression of peasants and small subsistence farmers, attracting the alarmed attention of both the church and the justice system. In 1882 the archbishop of Bahia excommunicated him for being a false prophet and forbade him from entering any property of the church (Ramos 1974). By this time he was already attracting a crowd, and the number of his followers would grow exponentially after slavery was abolished in 1888 and landowners simply expelled the freed slaves from their property, adding chaos and misery to an already-impoverished region.

In 1893 Conselheiro decided to settle in a place called Canudos, building a city that his followers, now numbering eight thousand, called Belo Monte (beautiful hill). Tension with local landowners was frequent as more and more destitute peasants chose to join the community in Canudos and participate in its collectivist means of production.

In 1886 the mayor of Juazeiro called on the Bahia state government to rein in a conflict between Conselheiro's followers and the city elite over a lumber contract. Officials dispatched to control the Canudos population reported to the state government that they were against the separation of church and state and therefore enemies of the newly installed republic. A force of thirty policemen was sent to discipline them, only to be massacred by hundreds of Conselheiro's supporters bearing rifles, machetes, and knives. The defeat of the local police demanded the attention of the federal government in Rio de Janeiro. Aware of the heavy costs of the nineteenth-century rebellions in Pará, Maranhão, and Paraíba, President Prudente de Moraes sent a punitive expedition of one hundred soldiers in November of 1896. This second expedition was also defeated by Canudos's scarcely armed militia, leaving 150 dead on the battlefield.

By now there was a national outcry fueled by reports of savagery on the part of Canudos inhabitants. The army came back twice, in January and March of 1897, with five hundred soldiers, but fierce resistance forced them to retreat both times. A full military campaign with over three thousand soldiers was prepared, encircling the city in September 1897 to suffocate it. Malnutrition and hunger, prevalent in Canudos since its creation, were now rampant. Conselheiro died of dysentery on September 22. Leaderless, the crowd of more than twenty thousand resisted for two more weeks, until the final attack on October 2. Only 150 women and children survived (Monis 1978).

The tragedy of Canudos would be another footnote in Brazil's long history of oppression if not for the publication of *Os Sertões* in 1902. Written by Euclides da Cunha, war correspondent for *O Estado de São Paulo* newspaper, *Os Sertões* starts with the hegemonic narrative of the civilized republic fighting the barbaric rebels and gradually shifts toward an intense analysis of the land, its inhabitants, and the forces that built such a society. Recent scholarship has read the Canudos campaign and *Os Sertões* as a land distribution movement as much as a missionary movement, which was the narrative at the time, and we must stress this point (Martins and Lage 2004).[1]

Interesting still is the temporal coincidence between the destruction of Canudos's Belo Monte in October and the inauguration of Minas Gerais's new

Figure 1.2. Church of Belo Monte, Canudos, after the destruction of 1887. Museu da República, Acervo. Photo by Favio de Barros, Brasiliana Fotográfica.

capital of Belo Horizonte in December of the same year. The issues at stake here are very different—a semi-urban missionary and land rebellion whose agents are the poorest of the poor versus a new capital to forge a new political consensus by the elites. However, together they mark the consolidation of the republican coup, the implemented powers of which would dominate the country until 1930.

If the protests were usually a reaction to imposed urban transformations, the case of Belo Horizonte was precisely the opposite. A whole new city was built in response to what the republican oligarchy perceived as "monarchist" support in Ouro Preto. The construction of the new capital was written into state law in 1891, shortly after the republican coup. The goal was very clear: much like Haussmann's vision in Paris, a new positivist urban design would allow plenty of development (meaning public land being sold to generate private profits), while at the same time organizing society in terms imagined by the local empowered elite. The very growth of Belo Horizonte before the 1940s, with large swaths of land remaining empty close to the commercial center while the periphery densified rapidly, speaks to the same process of land speculation and control that is one of the main pillars of our theoretical tripod.

The situation was the same in Santos, which, by the turn of the twentieth century, was the main port of São Paulo and already a rival to the Port of Rio in terms of tonnage and value. Sidney Bernardini (2016) discusses in detail a series of urban plans for Santos, such as the Municipal Plan of 1896, the plan by José Rebouças (brother of André Rebouças) in 1903, and the plan by Saturnino de Brito in 1905.

Santos was the main port of coffee export. Its original purpose was to link to the economy of São Paulo; despite being only fifty miles apart, the two cities are separated by geography that runs from sea level to 3,000 feet before dropping to 2,500 feet, where downtown São Paulo sits. The impact of this vertical disparity shrank considerably after the construction of the railway in 1867.

Despite its importance, Santos was a place of endemic tropical diseases such as yellow fever, smallpox, bubonic plague, malaria, typhoid fever, tuberculosis, cholera, and others. The city was avoided by foreigners but also by Brazilians. We do not have precise numbers for mortality rates, but reports from the 1860s say that the death rate was higher than Rio's 52 per 100,000.

The catastrophic sanitary conditions of Santos were improved after 1892 with improvements made concurrently with the construction of the new pier. The original plan was presented by Estevan Fuertes, who had been in charge of public works in Puerto Rico and New Orleans. His plan was not deployed because of the high costs of the infrastructure proposals.

At the beginning of twentieth century, in 1905, Saturnino de Brito was invited to lead the sanitary commission. He presented a radical solution which included the substitution of the former sewage and wastewater treatment systems. He applied the new technology of electric pumps (Telles 1984, 328) with automatic controls to lift the sewage to upper stations. The treated sewage was then dumped into the sea through an emissary, a huge iron pipe supported by a pencil bridge.

The drainage system was innovative too. Brito constructed channels using precast concrete elements produced in a factory deployed at the building site. To avoid water getting stuck in the channels, he planned a system to be cleaned by tidal movements.

As was the case of every major Brazilian city, however, these improvements benefited a few (mostly the elite who owned the businesses) and ended up forcing the poor out to the periphery of the city (Bernardini 2016, 234). In 1894 the revolting population broke the public fountains and the light posts at the main plaza (Praça dos Andradas), enraged about fare increases for gas and public transportation. The stage was being set for larger revolts, and the perfect storm gathered in Rio de Janeiro in the first years of the twentieth century.

PEREIRA PASSOS AND THE VACCINATION REVOLT

When elected president in 1902, Francisco de Paula Rodrigues Alves inherited a capital in turmoil. Yellow fever ravaged the city and the poor, with nowhere to live, cluttered themselves in *cortiços* downtown. To curb the yellow fever epidemic, Alves gave full powers to Oswaldo Cruz, the sanitarist in charge of public health campaigns, and Francisco Pereira Passos, who was named mayor of Rio de Janeiro. In the first few weeks of his term, Pereira Passos was able to concentrate power under his own office and limit those of Congress and city council to implement his plans based on circulation and sanitation.

Pereira Passos had attended the Military Engineering Institute in Rio (1952–1956) and the École Nationale des Pont et Chaussées in Paris (1958–1960). In Paris he took classes in railroad construction but witnessed firsthand the transformations taking place under Eugène Haussmann. In 1860 having returned to Brazil, Pereira Passos initiated work on railroads all over the country. In 1875 he was part of a team that designed a plan for improving the central areas of Rio. The proposal considered opening large boulevards, draining swamps, land-filling mangroves, and demolishing hills as solution to the congestion and epidemics that were inhibiting the development of the Brazilian capital city. According to Pereira Passos, nature had to be tamed and controlled; hills and mangroves were seen as impediments to an ordered and progressive city.

Contrary to the Portuguese empirical approach to urbanism, which was pragmatic and piecemeal, Pereira Passos's plan was grandiose, idealistic, and highly symbolic, but it was not new. In the 1880s André Rebouças proposed the integration of forests and waterways into the city fabric, an idea very different from Pereira Passos's imposition over the old town. The most visible facet of Pereira Passos's plan entailed opening a large boulevard to connect the newly developed areas of Botafogo, Glória, and Flamengo (to the south) with the old center of town, Avenida Central. To do so, 1,225 buildings were demolished in 1904 alone.

Two other avenues were built. One followed the ocean to the southwest and consolidated the expansion of bourgeois residential areas to the south. In the words of Maurício Abreu (1987, 43), Rio was a city "squeezed" between the bay and the mountains, and the stratified society of the early twentieth century decided to open connections so that the wealthy could move south and the poor move north.

The other, northbound avenue helped connect the expanded port to the nascent industry deeper within Guanabara Bay. Asphalt pavement was used in Brazil for the first time, but the new avenues were about more than circulation. They included gardens and public squares that were the spaces of excellence on par with Rio's new republican elite. The new avenues facilitated occupation of the southern beachfront, including the previously too-distant Copacabana.

If the new boulevards did improve circulation and change Rio's center of gravity, the sanitation component was addressed mostly by the choice of what to demolish (Abreu 1987, 66). The bulk of the structures demolished were occupied by low-income Brazilians. The old Portuguese way of selling lots by *testada* or width-at-street resulted in narrow properties extending deep into the hilly terrain of its cities, as in Lisbon, Salvador, Rio, Goa, or Macau. Population growth led to densification, and the deep and narrow backyards were then divided into dozens of rooms, each rented to an entire family, often with a single latrine and water source for all. At that time, with the favelas still in their infancy, the *cortiços* were to blame for the constant epidemics in the city. Very often the living conditions of the poor were also blamed for their moral values (or lack thereof). The positivist response to these issues was to eradicate them from existence, the metaphor of a tumor on the city fabric being an apt description of this point of view. Extirpate the bad tissue and the body of the city will heal.

It seems absurd in hindsight, but Pereira Passos's grandiose plan for downtown Rio had no provision for housing those displaced by demolitions. Since most *cortiços* inhabitants were renters, they received no compensation and were told to find housing elsewhere. The growth of self-built houses in steep hillsides, now commonly known as *favelas*, was certainly fueled by the large-scale demolitions in 1904–1906, which displaced an estimated four thousand people (Chalhoub 1996).

In parallel to this urban surgery, epidemiologist Oswaldo Cruz was named director of public health in 1903 and began working with city and federal authorities to eradicate mosquito-borne illnesses, such as malaria and yellow fever. Federal agents were hired to fumigate the entire city and had the authority to enter any property. The population, terrified by the demolitions and aware of the authoritarian ways of both Pereira Passos and Cruz, revolted against the idea of the mandatory smallpox vaccinations decreed by law on November 5, 1904. Five days later the city witnessed widespread chaos. Life in central Rio came to a halt with barricades, stoning of storefronts, destruction of urban rail lines, and general attacks against the police. By the time the government

Figure 1.3. Cartoon depicting Revolta da Vacina, 1904. Revista O Malho, October 22, 1904. Public domain, courtesy of Fundação Oswaldo Cruz.

declared a state of siege on November 16, fifty people had died. The event was named Revolta da Vacina ("vaccination revolt").

However, the label Revolta da Vacina is misleading (Needell 1987; Carranza and Lara 2014). José Murilo de Carvalho (1987, 136) reminds us that the enemy here was not health campaigns but state repression. The vaccine obligation challenged the principle of individual freedom, an argument that is still very much alive, as we now know. However, different from the immunization struggles of 2021, the yellow fever vaccination campaign of 1903–1904 was the last drop in a very full bucket of conservative transformations that were being imposed on the population of the Brazilian capital. The positivist ideas behind sanitation, circulation, and beautification were part of a larger project of Europeanization or "whitening" of Brazilian society (Schwarcz 1993). The selective immigration that would "whiten" the country was the latest iteration of the centuries old settler-colonial project in which land is taken from indigenous and/or impoverished peasants to anchor a financial capitalist project of the world economy.

Rio de Janeiro, the capital and still the most important city of the nation (soon to be surpassed by São Paulo) had to be seen as a tropical offspring of European modernity. Brazil had been under pressure to abolish slavery since the 1850s, which finally happened in 1888. By the turn of the century the macroeconomic goal was to attract foreign investment and foreign labor force. The urban transformations of Pereira Passos addressed both by creating a European façade while tackling the epidemics that tainted the image of the city. The old Rio had to be obliterated, and that included the poor, pushed to the northern suburbs or the hillsides.

Here we have instability in two rods of our theoretical tripod: occupation rights were steamrolled by a municipality eager to demolish houses and push "undesirables" out of downtown, and police repression was blatantly used in order to make that feasible. The result, once again, was a full-force revolt that paralyzed the city for ten days and left more than fifty people dead.

2

URBANISM OF CORONÉIS, TENENTES, AND BACHARÉIS

In Brazil the oligarchy of the first three decades of the twentieth century is called República do Café com Leite ("coffee with milk republic") for the strong alliance between São Paulo and Minas Gerais. Worthy of note is the agricultural emphasis of these economies, the two largest in Brazil at that time. After the exhaustion of the gold mining economy of Minas Gerais in the early nineteenth century, the state became gradually more rural and its economy more agricultural, but it still had the largest population and therefore maintained important political power. São Paulo, meanwhile, saw the coffee plantations expand from the Paraíba do Sul Valley (the hilly area between São Paulo and Rio de Janeiro) to the flatter but no less fertile region to the west. By 1830 coffee was already the main export of the country, and by 1850 Brazil was the largest producer of coffee in the world.

In the 1910s a strong alliance between the oligarchical elites of these two states formed, with elected presidencies subsequently alternating between former governors of Minas Gerais and São Paulo: *mineiros* Afonso Penna (governor 1892–1894, president 1906–1909), Venceslau Brás (governor 1909–1910, president 1914–1918), and Arthur Bernardes (governor 1918–1922, president

1922–1926) and paulistas Prudente de Morais (governor 1989–1990, president 1894–1898), Manuel Ferraz Campos Sales (governor 1986–1987, president 1902–1906), Francisco de Paula Rodrigues Alves (governor 1887–1888 and 1900–1902, president 1902–1906). Together they cemented the power of rural landowners despite fierce opposition from urban professionals.

The first ones to rebel were the sailors in November 1910. This rebellion was known as Revolta da Chibata ("revolt of the whip"). While the main issue of the rebellion was the fact that the Brazilian navy still used whipping to punish sailors, it is impossible not to draw connections between this cruel form of punishment and the fact that slavery was legal in Brazil only twenty-two years before. In fact, the most senior leader of the Revolta da Chibata to be punished was João Cândido, a black official immortalized as Almirante Negro ("black marshal").

Born in 1880 to former slaves, João Cândido Felisberto entered the navy at age thirteen. Between 1909 and 1910 Cândido lived in England as part of a crew being trained to operate the dreadnought *Minas Geraes*. Having observed a society without slavery (although certainly not without racism), Cândido got back to Rio de Janeiro to work on the new vessel with progressive new ideas. The flogging of a sailor with 250 strokes sparked the Revolt of the Whip, with João Cândido as one of its leaders. He was released after being arrested and tortured but lived in poverty until his death in 1969, age eighty-nine. One of the pillars of our theoretical inverted tripod—police repression for the poor below and police corruption for the wealthy above—was made stronger by the facade of liberalism in the first three decades of the twentieth century.

A decade later another rebellion would spark right in the middle of the armed forces, but this time it was led by officers, not by rank-and-file soldiers or sailors. Called *tenentismo* because it was basically a revolt of young lieutenants (*tenentes*) against their senior colonels and generals, the movement was conceptualized for years before erupting into a rebellion at Forte de Copacabana in 1922.

This revolt was against corruption and personalization of government nominations, in defense of Brazilian industry and economy against foreign beneficiaries, in defense of universal education, and against widespread election fraud (still very common in the 1920s). The tenentes were suppressed in 1922; several of them died trying to hold the Copacabana fort, but their cause only grew, culminating in the movement that brought Getúlio Vargas to power in 1930. Unlike the sailors of 1910, the tenentes who survived the rebellion were neither tortured nor died in poverty. All of the rebellious young officers were soon pardoned, many held leadership positions under the Vargas regime, and some reached the highest offices in the nation, such as Eduardo

Gomes (twice commander of the air force), Protógenes Guimarães (navy commander, congressman, governor of Rio de Janeiro), and Ernâni do Amaral Peixoto (congressman, governor of Rio de Janeiro, ambassador to the United States, and son-in-law of Getúlio Vargas).

In July of 1924 this group rebelled again, this time led by retired general Isidoro Dias Lopes. Still alarmed by corruption back-door deals of politicians of São Paulo and Minas Gerais, they also fought for secret balloting (a major tool of *coronelismo* was the rewarding or persecution based on who people voted for—and they had the records to do so); public education for all and the end of judiciary fees that kept the poor out of courts completely. On July 5, 1924, the revolting officers stormed the residence of the São Paulo governor, forcing him to abandon the city. For three weeks the city of São Paulo was under the control of the rebellion, with support of worker unions and the federal government controlling all the surrounding areas and access points. Between July 15 and July 27 the federal government dropped bombs on working-class areas of the city such as Mooca and Brás in an effort to punish the labor movement support of the rebellion. On July 28 the revolting officers abandoned the city toward the west, being surrounded by federal forces at the border between São Paulo and Mato Grosso. In that confrontation several rebels were killed. In the city of São Paulo, the civilian deaths amounted to five hundred (Linhares 1977; Batalha 2000). As with previous revolts, the army and navy officers were all pardoned by Getúlio Vargas once he took over the federal government in 1930.

URBAN AND RURAL POLICIES UNDER CORONÉIS

Victor Nunes Leal and Raimundo Faoro, among others, have extensively analyzed the República Velha (old republic) (1889–1930). Faoro, in the seminal work *Os Donos do Poder* ([1958] 1991), discusses how politics have always controlled economics in Brazil. Such predominance of the state as capitalist inductor, indeed generating private profit, is labeled "patrimonialist," a term still fit for the Brazilian economy to this day.

Leal (1997) discusses the power shifts inside the República Velha. In the early years of the republic, power was concentrated in the hands of the *marechais*, army and navy leaders in Rio de Janeiro such as Deodoro da Fonseca (president from 1889 to 1891), and Floriano Peixoto (1891–1894). These two men, also leaders of the military academy in Rio, were protagonists of the coup against the emperor that instituted the republic in 1889. Their military style of government was heavily centralized in Rio de Janeiro and both had trouble dealing with the regional oligarchies (Carvalho 1987).

After power was handed back to civilians with the election of Prudente de Morais in 1894, the regional bosses (*coronéis*, from *coronel*, or "colonel," referencing the military rank directly below general) gained more and more control over their jurisdictions. Back in 1831 the minister of justice of the imperial government, Diogo Antônio Feijó, created a National Guard comprised of civilian volunteers to help keep control of smaller cities and rural areas that, as discussed in the first chapter, exploded in a plethora of rebellions. Landowners who volunteered to lead the National Guard were given the coronel title. The honorific is not equivalent to the active-duty coronels of the army, but the oligarchy loved the titles and used them to impose their power over the peasant population in return for "representing" the emperor in the backlands. By the end of the nineteenth century, every landowner worth his name and honor had the title of coronel, basically the layman's equivalent of a nobility title.

Back in the early years of the twentieth century the coronéis exerted full control over the political processes in their areas of influence. By bribery or by violence the coronéis made sure that an overwhelming majority of the population voted for the candidate of their choice. In return, the federal government in Rio de Janeiro did nothing to threaten the power of the provincial coronéis, much to the contrary their weak position was in fact supported and legitimized by a veneer of democracy that was in reality controlled by the coronéis themselves.

By the second decade of the twentieth century this political structure stared to crack, not in the rural areas still under the stronghold of the coronéis, but in the cities where new ideas of political participation and revolution were gaining traction. The revolt that really scared the oligarchical government of the República Velha was the general strike of 1917 in São Paulo.

The state that had pushed ahead with a strong agricultural economy was by now investing its surplus capital in early industrialization. The policy of attracting white European immigrants to replace formerly enslaved workers brought two million Europeans to São Paulo (Schwarcz 1993). The argument of the paulista elite was that there was a need for workers in the growing coffee economy. But while two million white peasants went to work in São Paulo's agricultural sector, four million black Brazilians were unemployed or underemployed at the time. The immigration policy was a disguised attempt to whiten the Brazilian population, devised by an elite that was ready to accept eugenic ideas of white superiority (López-Durán 2018).

A direct goal of this policy was to depress the wages of rural workers as much as possible. While some immigrants prospered and were able to purchase land, many left the rural economy because the living conditions (and expectations for the future) there were not much better than in the poor areas of Italy, Portugal, Spain, Armenia, Syria, or Japan they had left behind. The nascent industrialization and improved opportunities in the city of São Paulo worked as a strong magnet for immigrants and Brazilians alike. The city population grew almost tenfold in thirty years, from 64,000 in 1890 to 579,000 in 1920.

Working conditions in the factories were not much better. Going back to our inverted tripod, we are reminded that one of the main rods is the informality of the work arrangements for the majority of the population, which keep wages low for the masses at the bottom, benefiting the wealthy few at the top.

Work in a factory should signify escaping this informality, but in the first decades of the twentieth century, that was not the case. Men, women, and children submitted themselves to ten or twelve hours per day, seven days per week. If such working conditions were better than plowing fields and picking coffee it was because, in the city, the poor at least had hopes of a better future.

These hopes hinged on the possibility of joining forces to demand better wages and working conditions. Organizing was made easier by density and city anonymity, at least in comparison to almost-total control imposed by landowners in rural areas. Immigrants also brought ideas from socialist and anarchist movements that were gaining momentum in Europe.

Boris Fausto (2016) reminds us that large organized strikes had happened before. In 1907 there was a major coordinated strike in four main industrial centers of the state—São Paulo, Santos, Ribeirão Preto, and Campinas—in demand of eight-hour workdays (146). In response to a strike at Santa Marina glass plant in 1909, workers were given houses alongside the factory property in which to live, with the implicit threat that they would be evicted if they ever went on strike again (117). The issues of labor rights and housing rights were therefore tied by their umbilical cords at the birth of rapid Brazilian urbanization.

At this point we must go back to our tripod diagram to explain that it represents the urban Brazil of today, not the rural Brazil of the 1900s. However, the seeds of contemporary structures that maintain and profit from outrageous inequality were already visible in the first decades of the twentieth century. The reader might remember that a pillar of the current structure is the lack of property rights at the bottom of the social pyramid and the majority of landownership at the top. Such explicit land concentration was not created by the coronéis, as it was inherited from the colonial and the post-independence imperial regimes, but it was very much exacerbated during this time (Fischer 2008). In the República Velha, landownership corresponded squarely with political power, the coronéis holding both tightly.

The public safety rod of our conceptual tripod creates a dichotomy of police repression at the bottom and law evasion at the top. This is a consequence of any stratified unequal society but, as in landownership, the disparity was exacerbated during the República Velha. In a system in which landowners retain not only the economic and political power but also a title of colonel, giving them full authority over the police, one can imagine how such police would operate and who they would protect.

The knot of our conceptual diagram points to the transportation system as a structure that today keeps the poor away (in time and space) from the infrastructure and opportunities concentrated in wealthy areas. This was not at all a problem in rural areas because peasants walked to and from work and their shacks, which were built on the worst land available, inside or at the margins of the farms. However, the strategy of isolating the working poor on the worst land without full property rights would not only continue but would mushroom in the decades ahead.

To the impoverished masses of underemployed and illiterate formerly enslaved and their descendants, the only land available was the smallest possible plot of steep terrain at the back of each property where the elite allowed servants to live, in exchange for eternal gratitude and twenty-four-seven availability to work. The infamous favelas were not built overnight but little by little, with the convenient permission of the elite and their functionaries. The strategy was exactly the same for rural and urban poor.

TENENTES AND BACHARÉIS FIGHTING FOR URBAN POLITICAL POWER

The issue in the early years of the twentieth century was that such misery did not fit the picture of modernization that an enlightened elite was keen on developing. Or, according to the works of Arturo Escobar (1995, 2018), there was too much coloniality and not enough modernity. If in the rural areas the coronéis reigned supreme, in the cities the elite had to deal with young rebels, tenentes (young army officers), or bacharéis (lawyers). This proto-progressive alliance lambasted the rural elite for maintaining the country as a large plantation, exporting primary goods (coffee, rubber, sugar, dried meat) and importing everything else, from textiles to nails to furniture. The tenentes and the bacharéis would be the first to defend incentives for industrialization and basic labor regulations that could eventually create an internal market for Brazilian products. They were, however, decades away from power (partially achieved only in 1930), and the ruling elite of the 1910s thought and acted like coronéis despite running a growing city.

In 1912 the mayor of São Paulo, Antônio Prado, was intent on beautifying his city and ordered the demolition of several low-income housing agglomerates (*cortiços*) downtown. That sparked a demonstration on May 1 and a general strike after May 15.[1] We know little about the 1912 strikes, but according to Fausto (2016, 150) the demolitions and a widespread shortage of rental units were among the main complaints of the striking workers.

In 1917 a much larger strike would paralyze São Paulo. The movement started in June 1917 at the textile factories (specifically Cotonificio Crespi and Estamparia Ipiranga), where women workers protested against bad food and sexual harassment, for change in wages for children and women (who were paid less for the same work), and for improvement in overall working conditions. On July 7 a large beer company (Cervejaria Antártica) stopped production, and on July 9 the marching workers clashed with the police. A shoemaker named Antonio Martinez was killed in the conflict when the strike reached fifteen thousand workers (Fausto 2016, 192).

The commotion created by Martinez's death expanded the movement to forty-five thousand workers at its peak, around July 12. While clashes with the police became widespread, a committee was formed to negotiate in the name of all striking workers. Their formal demands were to raise the minimum wage, institute eight-hour workdays, adopt the freedom to unionize, secure immunity from persecution for strike leaders, and implement rent control. Each group and each factory negotiated individually after July 15, and by the end of the month most workers had returned to the factory floor, with only a few demands addressed by their bosses.

The first general strike of 1917 moved the government and employers away "from its dogmatic dream of peaceful society" and triggered measures to face social conflicts. In 1918 the São Paulo government instituted a commission on social legislation which conducted the first studies for a work code focusing on labor accidents (Street and Moraes Filho 1980, 78). Governor Washington Luís also created *feiras livres*, organizing street vendors to connect small farmers to urban consumers that needed fresh inexpensive food. Some years later the Communist Party was created and the following year saw the approval the first retirement and pension law, the Eloy Chaves Law.

Despite great pressure for social reform from the workers as well as some employers and government advisers, the mainstream of politicians, linked with the liberal agrarian sector, insisted on denying the pervasion of social problems in Brazil. Social historians record the famous words spoken by Washington Luís in his campaign to be governor of the state of São Paulo in 1919:

> The workers agitation is an issue that matters most to public order than social order. The social order is the spirit of some workers . . . men from other

Figure 2.1. General strike, July 1917. Public domain, Biblioteca Nacional.

> climates, they are used to having other laws, they were martyrized by suffering unknown by us, they were exacerbated by evils that do not thrive here, they are agitated in a suitable moment of the high cost of living . . . produced by European war. They're claiming by rights that have not been denied to them. They're complaining about situations that do not exist here in Brazil.
>
> There is a lack of hands to work . . . leagues of fertile lands that are throbbing waiting for workers. (Washington Luís quoted in Egas 1927, 21)

Such was the position of the last president of the first Republican period. Social issues were a matter for the police, an attitude that fits squarely with our theoretical tripod.

Police repression was (and unfortunately still is) one of the main pillars of Brazilian inequality, protecting a few wealthy families at the expense of basic rights for a majority of the population that is poor, does not own land despite living on the periphery, and has precarious jobs; these two conditions form the other two rods of our theoretical tripod.

It is interesting to note that while most elite Brazilians thought this way, Europe, devastated after World War I, included a labor charter in the Versailles Treaty. Provisions for labor issues in chapter six of the Versailles Treaty fit squarely with the demands of the Brazilian strikers in 1917: right to free association, end of child labor, eight-hour workdays, a minimum wage for dignified life, and gender equality in wages.

Paradoxically, the same Brazilian elites who denied even the existence of social issues were convinced that industrialization was the way of the future. Ruy Barbosa, the first minister of finance in the republican period, stated that "the Republic will consolidate among us on solid foundations only when the regimen builds a democracy based on industrial labor. . . . The industrial development is not an economic question but a political question" (Barbosa quoted in Carone 1978, 79).

In the 1920s the Brazilian elite lived this paradox. A few educated individuals experimented with modernity while the majority of the population worked like eighteenth century Londoners: without any protection and absolutely at the periphery of modernity. Nestor Garcia-Canclini (1995) calls this a modernism without modernity, a critique of how artificial the explosion of modern poetry, modern music, and modern art was in a country where 70 percent of the population was illiterate.

Arturo Escobar (1995) taught us that development as we know it in the Americas brings with it a dark side of coloniality and inequality that we have not yet fully addressed. No place embodies this contradiction better than São Paulo. It was here, not in Rio, that the avant-garde found space to flourish. The Semana de Arte Moderna ("modern art week") of 1922 was the mythic foundation of Brazilian modernism. And while Rio was shaken by a rebellion of young military officers (*movimento tenentista*), São Paulo was grappling with worker's demands galvanized by anarchists. In 1924 young tenentes and union leaders aligned in support of the military revolt, with working-class neighborhoods taking the brunt of the federal government repression. Their brief alliance would come back stronger in the 1930s under the Vargas regime.

JORGE STREET AND VILA MARIA ZÉLIA

It was in this scenario of extreme inequality and early unionization that Jorge Street started his career as an industrialist in the textile business. Jorge Luis Gustavo Street was born in Rio de Janeiro in 1863 to a family of Scottish and German ancestry. Before and after graduating as a medical doctor in Rio, Street lived for some years in Bonn, Berlin, and Vienna. He practiced medicine in Rio in the 1890s but by 1904 was devoting most of his time to the São Paulo textile factory he inherited from his father at the turn of the century. Using modern management methods and with Germanic industries as inspiration, Street knew that the success of his factory depended on the well-being of his workers. For him,

> [to] deny the existence of a social issue in Brazil was a mistake. It is true that between us [Brazilians] the problem does not have the same gravity that it has for other people. Indeed it happens. Among us the workers never

> had—after the abolition of slavery—a tragic life such as described by reports on the social conditions in the industrialization of Europe. However, there are, undoubtedly between, us abuses and injustices against children, women, and even men—workers regarding the minimum age allowed; the limit of work hours; minimum wage. These are the most frequent abuses. As you know I speak from my experience, for more than 25 years I drove factories with thousands of workers and I know well what I am telling you about. I'd employed children with 10 or 12-years of age, maybe because his parents lied to the recruiters. The normal journey of work was 10 hours but frequently they work 11 or 12 hours. What do you say about pregnant woman who worked until the eve (of childbirth). What about that? . . . Those examples are to show you that the social problem exists between us. (Street quoted in Morangueira 2006)

In 1912, in response to all the issues Street recognized as major problems, he started to build his social experiment. His company purchased a large site in Belenzinho neighborhood (from the Tietê River to Celso Garcia Avenue) and hired French architect Paul Pedraurriex to design a workers' village, which he named Vila Maria Zélia, after his daughter, who died as a teenager. The complex was to include amenities such as childcare, comfortable houses, and cafeterias for workers and their children. North American readers (and Brazilian ones too) will be surprised to learn that Street started building his employee housing complex seven years before Henry Ford did the same in Dearborn.

In fact, industries providing housing for their own employees was already an old idea, having been first implemented in eighteenth century Spain in the town of Nuevo Baztán. In nineteenth-century England the number of housing complexes built for industrial workers exploded in conjunction with the Industrial Revolution, Trowse (1805) and Blaise Hamlet (1811) being the first ones. The most famous of these initiatives are the ones built by Robert Owen, who identified himself as a socialist, in New Lanark as early as 1813 and in New Harmony, Indiana, in the 1820s. In Chicago George Pullman had been building houses for his workers since the 1880s.

Continuing to seek the best for his factories, Street endorsed the 1917 general strike: "I had already given the increase of 20 percent in the workers wage (the main request in the strike). The factory was working powerfully and in high order when I was asked by a commission of striking (represented by workers from Crespi, Matarazzo, etc.) to grant clearance to the workers so they could express their solidarity to their colleagues who were fighting for better wages. I gathered the workers in the factory courtyard and communicated the committee's request and granted the clearance requested" (Street and Moraes

Filho 1980). Street was not alone in his progressive views. In the 1920s Berta Luz and Carmen Portinho were leading the suffragist movement for women to have the right to vote. The tenentes in the armed forces were fighting for meritocracy. Intellectuals were redefining the meaning of Brazilianness. It is worth noting—and we discuss this in more detail in the next chapter—that all of the social actors named above, including Jorge Street, would be co-opted by the Vargas regime and work for the federal government in the coming decade.

But as the exception that proves the rule, Jorge Street's initiative to build Vila Maria Zélia would be the pilot to a special kind of patronage, a new relationship between capital and labor that worked as a precursor for the Institutos de Aposentadoria e Pensão (retirement and pension institutes) of the 1930s and 1940s.

In 1912 Street purchased several acres in the Mooca neighborhood to expand his textile business. Mooca at that time was the immediate periphery of São Paulo, with plenty of inexpensive land available, but already serviced by rail lines connecting the city to the port of Santos. Between 1912 and 1916 Street built his Companhia Nacional de Tecidos de Juta. *Juta* is a Brazilian plant that can be transformed into a sturdy fiber, used to make hundred-pound (fifty-kilo) coffee bags. Street was building a textile business, designed by a European architect, to serve the coffee boom. A modern industry attached to an archaic oligarchy. Adjacent to the factory he also built a housing complex for his employees.

Vila Maria Zélia became a legend of the paulista industrialization narrative. Vila Zélia was not the first nor the largest in Brazil at the time. In 1892 a similar initiative had already been built in Salvador by Emporio Industrial do Norte. And in Sorocaba, one hundred miles inland from São Paulo, the Votorantim industries had already built three hundred employee houses by that time.

However, Vila Maria Zélia became iconic because Jorge Street was very vocal with his proposals in defense of Brazilian industry. Despite going broke after the crisis of 1929 that brought coffee exports to record lows, he carried on as an important industrialist and politician, joining the Ministry of Labor in the mid-1930s to advise the Vargas government on national policies. As reminded by Teixeira (1990, 33), Street fought on two fronts to defend the nascent Brazilian industries: international tariffs to protect local production from cheaper imports and labor regulation.

Looking at a map of Vila Maria Zélia inserted in the São Paulo of today provides hints on how it was developed more than a century ago.

About 170 row houses (*sobrados*) are organized in a five-by-four grid of urban blocks, surrounded by industrial warehouses. The houses, intended to

Figure 2.2. Aerial photo of Vila Maria Zélia, 1918. Public domain, Associação Comercial de São Paulo.

shelter a thousand people (family size among the Brazilian working class in the 1910s averaged seven persons), were served by a church, daycare, general store, and elementary school. It was probably the most complete response to the general strike of 1917 (although construction of Vila Maria Zélia had started in 1912) in trying to provide better living conditions for industrial workers.

However, it is hard to avoid the interpretation that better conditions on these terms meant tight social control. One must ask why the industry did not use the same amount of capital to improve the wages of the workers and give them the choice of living anywhere. The answer is quite obvious. The villa was a property of the industry and as such could be used as collateral for loans.

Another important consequence of this solution was the social control that it imposed on the workers. There was a hygiene component to the housing complex. Workers were required to allow visits from factory inspectors in order to live at Vila Maria Zélia. These inspections were sold as health visits, and indeed they had a role in preventing illnesses that could disrupt work productivity. But it is beyond doubt that many layers of social control and routine systematization were imposed on workers who lived at Vila Maria Zélia (Teixeira 1990, 69).

Children were forbidden to play in the streets. Workers were forbidden to run alternative (labor-oriented) publications. And the largest looming threat over everybody was losing the job and the house at the same time. One can only imagine how effective this threat was in the 1920s, fifteen years before comprehensive labor legislation was enacted in Brazil.

Nabil Bonduki (1994, 715) summarized it thus: "the tendency of the state and the ruling elite during the Old Republic has always been to regard working-class villages as a model initiative to be stimulated, as it guarantees decent living conditions, overcoming the insalubrity of tenements (*cortiços*), without requiring the intervention of public power, and still providing ideological, political and moral control to the workers, a desirable outcome against the fear of workers revolts." Important to note here is the direct relationship between Street and the workers. Palmira Teixeira (1990, 96) interviewed people who had heard the stories of Jorge Street, the factory, and Vila Maria Zélia from their parents. She documents quotes such as, "he was not our boss, he was our father." A typical father of the 1910s, Street was against paid vacation and one day off per week (they disrupt the labor routine) and against limiting child labor (162). On the contrary, a ten-year-old was "invited" by factory management to drop out of school and join the work force, and as a "prize" the family was relocated to a larger house.

The main ideology behind Vila Maria Zélia was one in which its six thousand workers were mere extensions of their main living purpose, to produce *juta* sacks for the coffee plantation. The liberal government of the so-called Old Republic was enchanted with the idea that every industry should have its own housing villa, providing better conditions and exercising full social control over its workers and their families.

In this sense, the destiny of Jorge Street and Vila Maria Zélia in the decades ahead is ironic but very telling. Street left the presidency of the textile company in 1923 when he was forced to sell most of his shares to keep the business afloat. His remaining shares would evaporate during the crash of 1929 that brought the coffee business to its knees. Street at that time was already working for the São Paulo state government, first at the Union of Textile Industries and later at the secretary of labor.

Vila Maria Zélia had an even more telling future. After the Wall Street crash of 1929, most business associated with coffee production went bankrupt. In 1931 the Companhia de Tecidos de Juta was foreclosed by the federal government, to whom the company owed in taxes more than it was worth. Vila Maria Zélia was then managed by Instituto de Aposentadoria e Pensões dos Industriários and was even used as a prison after the Vargas government turned into a full-force dictatorship in 1937. Political prisoners such as Paulo Emílio Sales Gomes and Caio Prado Jr. labeled the prison Universidade Maria Zélia.

The fact that the vila and its creator ended up as part of the government apparatus in the 1930s is ironic. The liberal policies of the Old Republic (1889–1930) were a disaster for the well-being of the population. The emphasis on financial orthodoxy kept the country an exporter of commodities, namely coffee at that time. Nascent industries were either satellites of the coffee business—such as the textile factories of Jorge Street—or were left to their own devices.

After the 1930 coup the role of the state would be magnified to the point of all-encompassing. Under Vargas the federal government recruited all modernizing forces, from intellectuals on the left to entrepreneurs on the right, and imposed itself as the great mediator between capital and labor. The role of benefactor and controlling boss once played by Jorge Street was absorbed by the state.

In the case of our theoretical tripod the now-powerful federal government positioned itself as the support that would allow the lower rods (informal labor, lack of ownership, and police repression) to continue holding up the upper structure without much stress. There was indeed a spatial consequence for that change. If earlier in the twentieth century elites were debating whether the working classes should live downtown close to employment but in dense conditions, or live on the outskirts on cheaper land but dependent on lengthy commutes, the 1930s settled the dispute for the latter. Small (and always insufficient) improvements to public transportation allowed Brazilian elites to claim downtown areas for themselves, close to all kinds of infrastructure, pushing the working poor further and further out (Kowarick and Ant 1994, 67).

There would be no more Vila Maria Zélia in proximity to downtown and employment opportunities. Instead, the Institutos de Aposentadoria e Pensões would purchase cheap land at the immediate periphery of all large cities and build housing for their members there, providing shelter for current workers and pensions for future retirees.

For this scheme to work it was important that the state build the necessary infrastructure of roads, water, and electrical grids. The Vargas government took upon itself the task of spearheading the second leap of Brazilian industrialization, investing in steel, electricity, oil exploration and refinery, heavy mechanical, and chemical plants, all between 1937 and 1945.

The next chapter details how these industries changed the urban landscape in Brazil while simultaneously feeding the Institutos de Aposentadoria e Pensões that built houses for those they employed while abandoning the large majority not employed by those sectors.

One final issue is how the Vargas government responded to the challenges of the 1920s in Brazil. Going back to the coronéis, the Vargas regime did not challenge them directly but took away their autonomy. The República Velha had adopted a structure of federalism very close to the US model, in which states have a high degree of independence. That structure of state autonomy coupled with the political control of the coronéis ensured that the rural oligarchy had absolute power over their territory in each state.

The agreement between the oligarchy of São Paulo and the oligarchy of Minas Gerais assured them both full control not only of their regions but also of the federal government to make sure they reigned supreme with no opposition whatsoever. It is important to note that Vargas himself was schooled in the conflicts of his native state of Rio Grande do Sul in the 1920s (Neto 2012). A political dispute between Antônio Borges de Medeiros and Joaquim de Assis Brasil (both lawyers, positivists, and landowners) became a bloody fight between their supporters with a series of violent encounters that resulted in ambushes and assassinations. The federal government had to mediate an agreement, and in 1928 Getúlio Vargas was elected as a leader palatable to both sides.

Once Vargas assumed the presidency after the 1930 coup, he attempted to address the problem by centralizing power in Rio de Janeiro, something that he only achieved in 1937 with the dictatorial powers of Estado Novo. His 1934 constitution sharply diminished the autonomy of states vis-à-vis the federal government. Vargas curtailed the power of the state governments but not that of the local coronéis, allowing his government to maneuver around local demands but holding the power of decision within his inner circle.

Meanwhile, urban inhabitants were experiencing a different set of issues. The suffragist movement took to the streets in the 1920s, obtaining localized victories in the courts. Women in Rio Grande do Norte were able to vote after one of them, Celina Guimarães Vieira, successfully sued the government in 1927. Vargas captured the spirit of the moment and settled the issue in 1932, giving all women the right to vote in Brazil.

Before that, intellectual circles were strongly invested in modernism (even before actual modernization, as extensively discussed in existing scholarship). Vargas responded by bringing several of the intellectual leaders of the Semana de Arte Moderna to work in his government. In summary, Vargas put in motion a negotiated modernization that would improve the lives of some urban workers with the introduction of labor legislation, pander to the educated elite by embracing modernism, and keep landowners happy by not challenging their absolute powers in rural areas.

In terms of our theoretical tripod, we see the Vargas regime improving labor laws for urban workers and investing in housing estates but doubling down on police repression and censorship to compensate for the concessions in the other two structural rods of society. Also, wages did not rise under Vargas, and union participation was low. Brazilian urban workers paid the mandatory *imposto sindical* (mandatory union fees) but did not take the additional step of signing up to a specific union. This created a unique Brazilian scenario of wealthy unions with very low membership numbers, or a *pelego* machine of union leaders closely aligned with the Vargas government.[2] Moreover, Brazil was still 70 percent rural in the 1930s, and most of Vargas's concessions in labor rights and housing investment benefited a minority of the urban inhabitants, less than 15 percent of the total Brazilian population.

Nonetheless, Vargas's housing and urban development policies constitute an important and quite understudied component of his fifteen consecutive years in power (from 1930 to 1945) and set the tone of Brazilian urbanism and its relationship with social movements for decades after that. The next chapter distills Vargas's urban initiatives and their relationship to urban protests.

3

URBAN POLICY UNDER GETÚLIO VARGAS

Following the tracks of the struggle of poor people to achieve the right of landownership in Brazil, we find a history of an agrarian economy led by a patriarchal culture. The oligarchical families of landowners were very powerful in Brazil after the colonial period (1500–1822), and with military support they overthrew the Brazilian empire (1822–1889), leading the country through the first republican period from 1889 to 1930. Landowners and the military were two forces that led the modernization process (or lack thereof) during this period.

At that time the cities were beautified and improved according to the interests of Brazilian cosmopolitan and rural bourgeoisie, as discussed in chapter 2. Thus, it was not of minor importance that the modernization process in the first Republican period set up the conditions for the rise of a non-rural bourgeoisie and a significant number of urban workers. These social classes would have an active role in the upcoming political changes, which were born of a widening and complex urban society and economy. Thus, from the 1930s onward, the Brazilian political dispute would lead to the overthrow of the first rural elite leadership concentrated in São Paulo and Minas Gerais.

The aftermath of this political shift was the 1930 revolution under Getúlio Vargas's (1882–1954) command. In this well-known moment of the history of Brazil, social issues would take the stage. The transformations under Vargas leadership shaped the Brazilian urban society toward more skilled groups of workers such as the new bureaucracy, the unionized workers, and the communist party as discussed by the literature (Rodrigues 1968; Harding 1973; Levine 1982; Castro Gomes and D'Araújo, 1989; Hall and Garcia 1989; Wolfe 1993). The aim of this chapter is to show how urban management and housing policy played a key role in the political agenda from this period onward.

Once in power, Vargas embraced a labor strategy in which the bureaucratic state framed an urban social policy. It explored the impact of the demographic transition in the 1940s, reducing the political impact of popular protests during that time. Under Vargas the Brazilian state was quite successful in intermediating the social conflict as framed by our theoretical tripod.

URBAN ISSUES IN THE 1930 REVOLUTION

Brazil was a predominantly rural country in the 1930s, and coffee was still its main export product. The coffee economy had grown supported by a finance and commerce system that was concentrated in urban areas. The city of São Paulo is the most dramatic case of growth due to the coffee plantation economy, but the same is also true for secondary cities like Campinas and other state capitals like Porto Alegre and Belo Horizonte in the first Republican period. Rio de Janeiro was by far the largest Brazilian city in the 1872 census, twice the size of Salvador and Recife, both important Brazilian cities that had grown in the realm of sugar industry.

Between 1890 and 1900, São Paulo had exponential growth and became the second-largest city in the country, solely behind Rio de Janeiro. São Paulo's growth, driven by the coffee economy, did not mean that other Brazilian cities had stagnated. On the contrary, the republican period was responsible for the urban modernization of many cities, such as Salvador. After the crisis of sugar exports, the state of Bahia experienced a phase of economic diversification with the prevalence of the textile industry and the export of cocoa and tobacco. Like Rio de Janeiro and São Paulo, the turn of the century in Salvador was marked by a series of works related to the port modernization and the improvement of the city (Azevedo 1990; Vasconcelos 2016). Belém, capital of Pará state, and Manaus, capital of Amazonas state, were also enhanced by the rubber economy in the early republican period.

The relationship between Brazilian cities and the export economy is not exclusively related to the coffee economy in the republican period, but the specificity of it triggered a different urban phenomenon, characterized by a

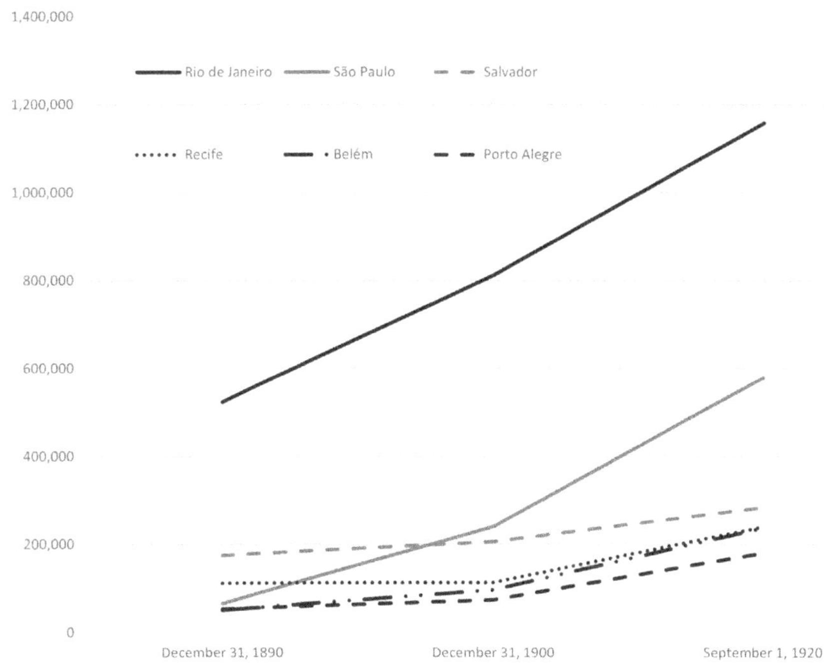

Figure 3.1. Population of the largest Brazilian capitals between 1890 and 1920. Table composed by the authors with data from Brazilian Census (IBGE 1930, 1997, 2001).

fast and huge growth of the city of São Paulo, as shown in Figure 3.1. It happened while the majority of the population was still living and working in rural areas.

The rural economy guaranteed the political grip of some families of landowners called *coroneis*. The Republican period was characterized by the political dominance of the oligarchies linked with the interests of these families, as discussed in chapter 2. As the following events prove, the presence of a non-rural bourgeoisie (the industrialists) and a working-class movement was not of minor importance. The immigration policy that brought many European workers to the Brazilian labor market joined the cosmopolitan bourgeoisie to change the culture of work and industry in the ongoing modernization process. This was part of the conflict at the foundation of capitalist society in Brazil.[1]

The 1930 revolution marks an important change in Brazilian society toward an urban economy and faster industrialization as the result of national policies. Those policies were triggered by 1929 international crises that increased the living costs and resulted in widespread dissatisfaction among the population. The international crises made clear the need, by part of former

Table 3.1. Economic sectors, 1872–1940, percentage of total employed population

SECTOR	1872	1900	1920	1940
Agriculture	64.1%	53.4%	59.7%	66.4%
Industry	4.9%	3.4%	13.8%	10.3%
Services	31%	43.2%	16.5%	23.3%

Source: Data from Malloy 1979, 177.

leadership, for a shift in the ongoing rural centered set of policies. They accelerated new political alignments and gave space for the emergence of a new movement boosted by generalized hope of deeper transformations in the social and economic structure of the country.

A broad factual description of 1930 events including the political articulation and the outbreak of conflicts was written by Alzira Alves Abreu (1984). Despite not fitting the ideal typology of social revolution as pointed out by Lucia Lippi (1984), the movement is the landmark of Brazilian modernization, and it is indeed of great importance for urban modernization in twentieth-century Brazil.

The 1930 revolution was politically led by Getúlio Dornelles Vargas and militarily supported by the tenente-coronel Pedro Aurélio de Góis Monteiro. The army movement prevented elected president Julio Prestes from taking office. Prestes was supported by the departing president, Washington Luís, both from São Paulo state. The movement was triggered by the breach of an agreement regarding presidential succession in which São Paulo and Minas Gerais would alternate leading the federal government. The breach of that agreement reorganized the political forces that supported the movement.

The revolutionary movement accused the government of defrauding the polls and capitalized on the assassination of Paraíba governor João Pessoa Cavalcanti de Albuquerque, vice president candidate of Getúlio Vargas ticket. Pessoa's assassination was framed as a political revenge at national level, when in fact it was motivated by a local dispute: Pessoa had exposed an extramarital affair of a local opponent, João Duarte Dantas. Nonetheless, the death of João Pessoa on July 26, 1930, galvanized the opposition to the government of Washington Luís and his presidential candidate Julio Prestes. The opposition leaders of Rio Grande do Sul, Paraíba, and Minas Gerais found support in sectors of Brazilian bourgeois ostracized by the oligarchy agreement and in the military sector. A long political articulation occurred before the insurrection went public on October 3, 1930.

The conflict broke out in Porto Alegre, in the southern state of Rio Grande do Sul, where Vargas was governor (1928–1930), and in Belo Horizonte, Minas Gerais, soon followed by Paraíba and other northeastern states. It lasted one month, until Vargas was nominated the chief of transitional government on November 3.

In the first week of the conflict the revolutionary group boarded several railcars on a journey from the south toward the republican capital of Rio de Janeiro. The movement led by Vargas was an opportunity for the urban workers in São Paulo to demand higher wages. Since the beginning of the century, they were suffering with the ruthless working conditions in the factories and the treatment given by the state to the social issue, which included immigrants' deportation and police brutality.[2]

A few days prior to the arrival of the revolutionary convoy in the city of São Paulo, droves of rioted workers invaded the Cambuci prison where union's activists were jailed.[3] The furious people made a bonfire with everything they found ahead and the building was "devoured by flames" (Wolfe 1993, 50, quoting the British consul). The aftermath was known as the Bastille of Cambuci (50–51). On October 31, the revolutionary convoy reached the city of Rio de Janeiro and was received by three thousand soldiers from Rio Grande do Sul, showing the military support for the 1930 revolutionary leaders.

CITY GOVERNMENT AND SOCIAL ISSUES

Vargas's challenge after taking power was to break the engine of oligarchies' political support and to keep on his side both urban classes: workers and bourgeoisie. City governments were strategic for the rural oligarchy's political support. Managing little towns' municipal budgets, the landowners' representatives were able to control the exchange of votes for personal favors, keeping their grip on the democratic system. As a result, local governments were the locus of power in the old republican period. Control of the municipal government was a daunting task imposed after the beginning of the revolutionary government. From 1930 to the constitution of 1946, municipal governments were the responsibility of the Departamento das Municipalidades, a technical assistance agency to support the implementation of municipal budgets and plans. The agency was created to keep municipalities under control, even with mayors appointed by federal government.[4]

To further resist the rural classes, the new government also needed to keep under control the urban classes, workers, and bourgeoisie. Vargas regulated the workers and patronage association under the supervision of the Ministry of Labor, Industry, and Commerce from the start. The ministry was created on November 26, 1930 (Decreto no. 19.433), and a few months later the Act of 19 March 1931 (Decreto no. 19.770) allowed just one union per sector of employment and disbanded the majority of existing workers' associations.[5] It deeply changed and weakened the former workers' movement in Brazil, which relied on the anarcho-syndicalism heritage. The wave of rural migrants that would be integrated in the labor market in the 1940s would complete the changes started by the Act of 19 March 1931. However, this would not happen without protests.

The streets of São Paulo were the battlefield in which Vargas needed to affirm his control of the social issues. In July of 1931 seventy thousand industrial workers marched from Largo São José to the center of São Paulo, protesting abuses committed by their bosses. Vargas refused to negotiate with a non-official movement demonstrating to the whole nation that labor conflicts were under his government's control (Wolfe 1993, 54–56).[6]

After controlling the local governments and sponsoring the workers' movement, Vargas's revolutionary government started to plan the transition to a constitutional democracy. The electoral code was established in 1932, a new constitution was approved in 1934, and Vargas was elected president by Congress in a constitutional regime.

The new constitution restored the election of mayors and expanded municipal budgets, reinforcing local governments even though they were still controlled by the Departamento das Municipalidades. The same principle drove the control of the social issue through the union's legislation. Despite the plurality and autonomy stated in the new constitution, in reality the ministry "expanded its specific control over union activities" (Harding 1973, 110). The new constitution also highlighted the role of the state in resolving social issues and limited individual rights in favor of collective rights, as was the case with the property rights of urban landowners.[7] They were now obliged to pay a contribution for urban improvements. This fee, paid by owners for using public works, was intended to refund to the state a small part of the real estate appreciation accrued by the private owners.[8]

Despite the importance of social rights in the 1934 constitution, as pointed out by Robert Levine (1982, 316), the constitution failed to bring social peace, and it was adopted amid a new wave of labor conflicts. There were twenty-nine riots in the city of São Paulo in 1934 (317). In Rio de Janeiro workers also went on strikes organized by maritime workers and post office workers demanding better wages (Rodrigues 1968, 42). Actually, the new constitution endorsed the engine of social control that the revolutionary government established since 1931 but at the same time bounded the repressive system under its legal corpus.[9] It gave space for the protests for better work conditions.

Act 38 (Lei de Segurança Nacional) of April 4, 1935, closed any political freedom loopholes in the constitution. It prevented the increase of communist groups, which were growing,[10] especially the Aliança Nacional Libertadora, organized one month before the act to rally the communists' support in the national political arena. The Aliança Nacional Libertadora worked for the expansion of social rights[11] and was involved in a failed military uprising called Intentona Comunista in Natal, Recife, and Rio de Janeiro. The aftermath served as an excuse to persecute the communists' organization and to start an era of increased repression that would be formalized two years later by the Estado Novo dictatorship. Aside from the details of the 1935 communist uprising, this event makes clear that social issues were kept under strict control of the national government.

The 1937 Constitution was drafted in the context of crises of liberal democracy worldwide. This constitution extended the Vargas term in office, suppressed the principle of eligibility of mayors, and reduced the share of municipal budgets. The Estado Novo (1937–1945) established the Vargas dictatorship and provided permission for political persecution, undermining once again the former social leaders from the communist party, from anarcho-syndicalist heritage, and from rural movements.

The state was responsible for abominable episodes of violence against popular leaders. Such was the case of Jewish German communist leader Olga Benário Prestes, companion of the Brazilian communist leader Luís Carlos Prestes. Both of them were arrested in 1936 as leaders of 1935 communist uprising, and Olga Benário Prestes was delivered to the Nazi regime, taken to a concentration camp, and executed in 1942. In rural areas the leaders of the Cangaço movement were also punished in 1938. The couple Lampião e Maria Bonita were persecuted, maimed, and killed by the Alagoas state police. Cangaço was a sect rural movement such as Canudos was forty years before.

Vargas contended with the former popular and workers' leadership, squeezing labor to provide a cheap work force for the ongoing industrialization of Brazil. Concurrently he supported controlling the price of coffee, proving once again the centrality of land and the export economy in the Brazilian urban society. He also became the main character linked with the defense of popular rights ruled by the urban labor legislation. The social security system played an important role in that goal, and housing was a sensitive case in the formation of the Brazilian urban society.

THE SOCIAL SECURITY SYSTEM AND THE BRAZILIAN URBANIZATION PROCESS

Under the Ministry of Labor, the former social security system created in 1923 for workers from each private company was reorganized into institutions for the main employment sectors. Unified by professional categories instead of by private companies, the administration of pension funds and the responsibility for the benefits were transferred to the state.[12] The Ministry of Labor created to manage the labor policy took control of the funds, widening significantly the coverage of the employment sectors by creating a powerful and well-endowed system to implement Vargas's social and economic policy.

The benefits guaranteed by the social security system for the insured workers were health insurance, retirement by age, and disability and maternity aid. The system also guaranteed the insured family funeral assistance and pension upon death or detention of the insured. For both the insured worker and their family, the social security system provided health care and hospitalization, social service, and rental insurance. Those were the primary benefits guaranteed for the workers to be distributed from the funds through the institutions of retirement and pensions, called Institutos e Caixas de Aposentadoria e Pensões. Beside the primary benefits these institutions also supported emergency home-care service, popular canteens, and food supply (Sussekind 1955, 162).[13]

The institutos and caixas created after 1930 were:

Instituto de Aposentadoria e Pensões dos Marítimos (IAPM)—sea services workers, 1933, Act 22.872;

Instituto de Aposentadoria e Pensões dos Comerciários (IAPC)—commerce workers, 1934, Act 24.273;

Caixa de Aposentadoria e Pensões dos Trapiches e Exportadores de Café (CAPTEC)— warehouse workers, 1934, Act 24.274 (became IAPTEC in 1938 with Act 627);

Caixa de Aposentadoria e Pensões dos Estivadores (CAPE)—dockers, 1934, Act 24.275 (became IAPE in 1938 with Act 627);

Instituto de Aposentadoria e Pensões dos Bancários (IAPB)—banking workers, 1934, Act 24.615;

Instituto de Aposentadoria e Pensões dos Industriários (IAPI)—industry workers, 1936, Law 367;

Instituto de Aposentadoria e Pensões dos Servidores do Estado (IPASE)—state servants, 1938, Act 288;

Instituto de Aposentadoria e Pensões dos Ferroviários e Empregados em Serviços Públicos (IAPFESP)—railway and federal service workers, 1960–1966.

The surplus gathered in the expansion of the security system was invested to increase the resources of the institutions. The managers considered these investments of fundamental importance to face the future when the benefits to be paid by the system would be greater than the security collection. The capitalization of the security system initially was provided from mortgage loans for house purchase and also from short-term loans for the workers. The construction of housing estates for the workers was included in the portfolio

Table 3.2. Social Security system revenue

YEAR	AMOUNT COLLECTED	PERCENT OF 1928 BASELINE
1923	13.592:960$500	22.40
1927	30.466:011$150	50.10
1928	**60.808:597$100**	**100**
1932	92.883:425$214	152.70
1933	101.973:282$535	167.70
1934	127.878:717$400	210.30
1935	226.202:071$000	372.00
1936	308.245:201$000	506.90
1937	359.445:403$000	591.10
1938	**558.328:524$900**	**918.20**

Before 1945, Brazilian accounting systems used a method of representing currency such that 13,592,960,500.00 in modern figures would have been written as 13.592:960$500.

Source: Rego 1942, 144–45. The same author also pointed out the patrimony realized until 1937 by the security system reached 940.396:830$500, and two years later it had increased to around 1.500.000:000$000.

Table 3.3. Urbanization and industrialization in Brazil

	POPULATION OF INDUSTRIAL CITIES			INDUSTRIAL CENSUS RESULTS		
DATE	S. Paulo	Guanabara	TOTAL	Number of factories	Employed persons in industry	% FROM POPULATION OF INDUSTRIAL CITIES
1900	239,520	691,505	**931,025**	—	—	—
1910	409,427	624,718	**1,034,145**	3.258	—	—
1920	576,633	1,157,873	**1,734,506**	13.336	313,156	18%
1940	1,337,644	1,781,507	**3,119,151**	40.053	815,041	26%
1950	2,130,626	2,377,451	**4,508,077**	82.154	1,309,614	29%
1960	3,700,274	3,223,403	**6,923,677**	110.339	1,796,537	26%

Source: Table created by the authors, based on Rodrigues 1968, p. 66.

of investments, even though they were made by direct initiative of the institutions and were affordably rented (Sussekind 1955, 131, 162).

The social security system supposedly would guarantee the political support of the urban workers through benefits of pensions and social assistance and also provided a huge amount of capital, managed by the state, to foster the urban base needed for the ongoing industrialization process.

The funds were regimented by workers', states', and companies' contributions at a time of industrial economy expansion. As pointed out by Wilson Suzigan (1986, 90–91), from 1936 to 1939 new investments in the manufactur-

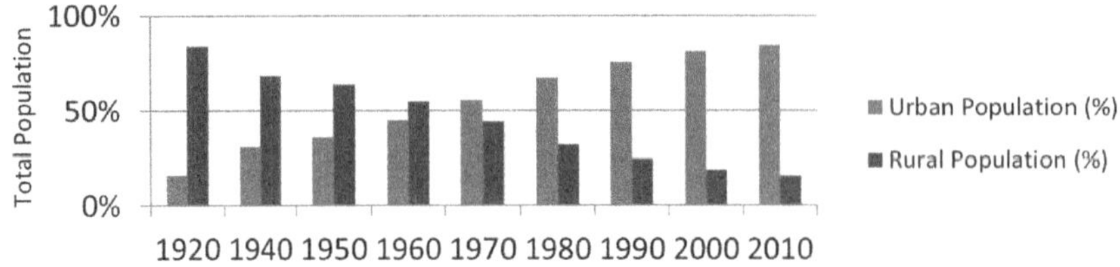

Figure 3.2. Rural and urban population. The urban population would surpass the rural in Brazil in 1966. Table composed by the authors with data from Brazilian Census (IBGE 2007, 2011).

ing sector resulted in the expansion and diversification of Brazilian industry, which explains the significant increase in the security system collection in the same period.

The capitalization of the funds was made by investments in housing supply. There were three modalities of investments. The first was housing estates produced by initiative of the institutes to rent units for their associates (Plan A). The second was a mortgage system available for the associates (Plan B). The third was investments in the real estate market (Plan C).

According to the government report made in 1953 by Rômulo de Almeida, the second Vargas government's head of economic advisory for the National Social Welfare Commission, the "appearance of prosperity in the large Brazilian cities" had attracted workers from poor regions.[14] The widening of the industrial labor market overlapped with the crises of the agro-export economy of that time, encouraging the rural exodus and boosting the housing shortage and the real estate market demand in the big cities.

The new urban society that emerged from the Estado Novo in the 1940s was quite different, mainly in São Paulo, where migrants were arriving in droves. The transformation reached its peak between 1940 and 1946, the period of the state of São Paulo's accelerated industrial development. The working-class composition represents the wider urban phenomenon. From 1936 to 1940, immigrants were the majority in the urban labor force.[15] In the next decade, the majority of urban workers came from rural areas (Rodrigues 1968, 143).

The exodus of rural workers to the big cities triggered the housing shortage and the urban crises of the 1940s. The pension funds, created primarily to provide social security and pensions for the funds' affiliates, were invested in the housing supply of the expanding real estate market in Rio de Janeiro, São Paulo, and Minas Gerais. The investments were mobilized to construct affordable housing for the workers affiliated in the system with restricted loans.[16] The security institutions rented several modern housing facilities to workers, and some of them were furnished with health-care clinics, grocery stores, green areas, and leisure amenities (Bonduki and Koury 2014).

The number of units the security institution offered its affiliates did not meet the demand but nonetheless had a significant impact on the real estate market. The presence of these units increased the costs of urban land and building materials and reinforced the real estate market and the polarized pattern of urban growth that characterizes Brazilian cities until this day.

FAVELAS AND URBANIZATION

The urbanization processes of the 1940s combined the growth of urban jobs, the improvement of real estate, and the proliferation of favelas (shantytowns). The favelas were part of a fast urbanization process based on low wages for the majority of urban workers. This was widely discussed in Alberto Guimarães's *Report on Favelas* (1953), written for the city of Rio de Janeiro, which analyzed the housing standards of those informal settlements through data collected by the 1950 census. The report contributed some important issues toward better understanding the multiplication of favelas in Rio de Janeiro.

The first issue to improve the understanding of favelas was to make its definition more precise. In 1950 favelas were understood as a group of rough units illegally settled in lands owned by others, or in non-urbanized areas next to the cities.[17] The units were built with rough materials, such as galvanized sheets and wooden planks. The streets were unpaved, and the houses were unnumbered. Access to the sanitary network, electricity, telephone lines, and piped water was also inadequate.[18]

The first favela was a settlement of soldiers that had returned from the War of Canudos and were allowed to settle at the Providência hill in the first years of the twentieth century.[19] The spread of this kind of settlement started after the 1930s, mainly in the peripheral areas of Rio de Janeiro; a few favelas were located in the hills between downtown and the northern zone, attracted by the industrial jobs in the region. By 1941 the favelas had occupied several parts of the city. The standard of living of urban workers worsened during World War II because of the high cost of goods and the inflationary process concurrent with the growth of the real estate market. All those elements contributed to a serious housing shortage and the proliferation of favelas in Rio de Janeiro (Guimarães 1953, 7).

The problem of settling an increasing number of workers in the cities was well known by the government since the 1939 report commissioned by the Ministry of Labor on mocambos and favelas in Recife,. The report verified that 40 percent of the dwellers were affiliated with some security institution. After the report, the security institutions were allowed by the ministry to invest two-thirds of its revenues in the city of Recife (Portaria MT 1939). Similar procedures were suggested to solve the problem of favelas in Rio de Janeiro (Rego 1942, 159).

In the same year, the Liga Social Contra o Mocambo (League against the Mocambos) was created in Recife and the Proletarian Parks Program was launched in Rio de Janeiro. The league was an initiative led by Agamenon Magalhães (1893–1952), state interventor in Pernambuco, to galvanize the civil society around the mocambos problem. Concurrently, the Proletarian Parks (1939–51) was a state program created by physician Victor Tavares de Moura (1892–1960), who had followed the 1939 census in Recife (Bonduki and Koury 2014, 355; R. Rodrigues 2013, 9; Diego 2008, 116–17).

The Proletarian Parks and the League against the Mocambos were organized initiatives of the state to supply housing for low-income workers. The need to improve housing supply as benefits offered to urban workers linked to the security system was pointed out by Rubens Porto as early as 1936. Porto worked in the engineer office of the Ministry of Labor and had an important role in gathering resources and technical support, which allowed the security system to contribute to producing housing estates for urban workers (Porto 1938; Almeida 2008, 35–48).

The urgency of the urban phenomenon triggered initiatives at the state level that could be implemented faster than the reform needed in the security system to face the housing shortage. Considering the difficulties of tackling the housing deficit in the short term, Vargas decreed a law to avoid evictions in 1942, the Lei do Inquilinato. Nabil Bonduki (1998, 15) affirms that in reality the law carried out the opposite, worsening the crisis in São Paulo. On one hand, landowners were able to fake the conditions necessary to get the permission for evictions. On the other hand, the law warded off private investments in real estate. These conditions induced peripheral growth, increasing the number and the size of favelas in the largest cities.

In 1948, almost one decade after the 1939 census in Recife and the security system reform of 1937, the Institute for Commerce Workers and the Institute for Industry Workers undertook a broad census with their affiliates. The report concluded that the situation of the workers had not improved significantly, and the majority of them had incomes so low that they could not buy or rent a house.

According to the census, among the 349,836 Brazilian commerce workers, 60.76 percent of them earned less than one thousand cruzeiros per month. The rate reached 75 percent among the 763,059 industry workers. These categories were considered skilled workers, and workers in other sectors of employment were paid even less. Facing the problem of workers' lower wages, Alberto Passos Guimarães (1953, 6), who introduced the favelas census in Rio de Janeiro in 1950, concluded that over 50 percent of workers in Rio de Janeiro received less than one thousand cruzeiros per month and therefore had less than two hundred cruzeiros left to rent a house. The amount was not enough to rent a 323-square-foot house for an average family of five people.

In the beginning of the 1950s, Luiz A. Pinto (1953) described with precision the situation of favelas in Rio de Janeiro. He was interested in race relations and dedicated a chapter of his book to analyzing urban ecology and the race issue. In this text he produced a comprehensive interpretation of the favelas locations in the Rio de Janeiro city. According to him Rio de Janeiro could be divided in two regions, the oriental one, with downtown, urban, and suburban areas, and the large western portion that was still rural. The oriental region beyond downtown could be divided into three sectors. The wealthy lived south of downtown. The lower middle classes and the urban poor were settled in the northwest sector. In between those two zones, the western part was occupied by a diversified sector that include middle classes, industries, and lower classes. The favelas occupied the oriental region of the city, infiltrating all three main sectors. The poorest north sector presented the largest concentration of favelas, followed by the rich south and downtown (Pinto 1953, 116–19, 123).

Pinto proved that the most favela dwellers were workers, and a majority of them were formerly enslaved and their descendants. He disagreed with the myth of a Brazilian mixed society free of racial segregation. Because the favelas were present in every sector of the oriental region of the city, a hasty look at the census data could be misinterpreted as a mixed or non-segregated urban society. His numbers alone make the case: in the city of Rio de Janeiro, 29 percent of the inhabitants were Afro-Brazilians and 7 percent were favela inhabitants, but among those favela dwellers the concentration of Afro-Brazilian reached 71 percent (Pinto 1953, 129–32). Pinto showed us clearly the connection between race, class, and urban segregation. His analyses strengthened the evidence pointed out by Guimarães (1953) and others that favelas were an urban response to the formation of Brazilian industrial labor market.

Thus, the favelas were part of an urban phenomenon historically defined in the period of fast urbanization, and popularly the term denotes a widening socioeconomic segregation of workers in the space of the city which was intensified in the 1940. The term *favelas* since then meant less a specific architectural heritage and rather a place for housing the urban poor in significant density, excluded from public investments but organically embedded in the formation of low-cost labor markets.

RIGHT TO MOBILITY AND URBAN UPHEAVALS IN THE LATE 1940S

There is nothing more representative of the urban crises in the Brazilian cities of the late 1940s than the last edition of the newspaper *Folha da Noite* covering the urban upheaval in São Paulo on August 1, 1947.

Heading the front page were impressive pictures of the destroyed trams, a crowd trying to topple a bus, a firefighter struggling to control an electric tram in flames. The headline warned: "The streets are the stage of serious events: people destroying trams and buses of the municipal company of transportation." The rebellion against the increase of the price of the tickets started in São Paulo but soon became a national phenomenon, spreading to the largest cities such as Rio de Janeiro and Belo Horizonte among others (Duarte 2005, 55).

The increase in the fare price also increased the cost of living for the workers who lived in the farthest peripheral areas and depended on public transportation to get to their workplaces. The episode in São Paulo shocked the nation both by the violence of the crowd, which depredated 25 percent of the public fleet, and the brutality of the police, who arrested 350 people (Moisés 1982, 56).[20]

The aftermath of public transportation upheaval occurred just two years after the democratic transition in 1945. The analysts who studied the event have different points of view on its political meaning. José Alvaro Moisés (1982, 53) pointed out the episode as part of the emergence of urban social movements in Brazil. Detached from the institutionalized channels of the newly democratic regime and even from the leftist parties, the 1947 movement started a new pattern of popular participation in the political debate after the long period of Vargas dictatorship (1937–1945). It is difficult not to recognize in Moisés's (1982) interpretation the enthusiastic role of urban-base democracy, which had supported the foundation of the Partido dos Trabalhadores (1980) and the fight for democracy in the 1980s. A. L. Duarte (2005, 46–50), on the other hand, highlighted the connections between the 1947 upheaval and the political debate through the political parties and organized workers' movements, contesting Moisés's (1982) interpretation. The main contribution of 1947 for urban studies at large was to make explicit in the protests the whole urban agenda:

> August 1 was not only a protest against a precarious transportation system and the increase in the tickets' price , . . . was also a manifestation against the conditions of housing, against the deficiency in public health care, against the absence of schools, against the bad conditions of urban health and the

> bad salaries and other necessities, because these were tried by the popular classes. . . . If the open conflict emerged related to the subject of public transportation, it was because all the urban demands came together from the abandoned population.[21] (Duarte 2005, 49–50)

It is also very difficult not to recognize in Duarte (2005) the urban agenda that mobilized mass protests in Brazil in 2013. The links between democracy and urban issues were fully understood by the workers after the 1947 upheaval, and urban planning was included in the political agenda of the twentieth century.

4

DARK CLOUDS OVER THE CITIES

This fourth chapter focuses on the urban crisis that developed from the late 1950s to the 1970s. It was an era of spatial contrasts between the fake impression of wealth in the metropolitan centers and the extreme poverty in the rural hinterland. Thus, regional, metropolitan, and urban planning were highly debated, tested, and applied in these controversial years of harsh transition from democracy to authoritarian regime. The pioneer experiment in metropolitan planning was Curitiba in 1966, around the same time that the Federal Service of Housing and Urbanism was emboldened by the creation of federal funds to guarantee workers' income (Fundo de Garantia por Tempo de Serviço, FGTS). On the opposite side, the federal housing policy, which should be strategic to face the political issue in large urban areas, was under the Ministry of Interior, making it difficult to deploy intra-urban innovations. In the short Brazilian 1960s (1960–1964), urban and regional contradictions stressed the conflicts between owner classes and the poor in both rural and urban sites. This era reinforced our double tripod, for there were episodes in which the upper middle class found their triangle shaking. In 1964 it was the property edge that felt threatened by João Goulart government's intention to at least discuss some kind of land reform. The president found himself entangled in the Cold War Manichean rhetoric of those times. The left and right wing polarized controversies on Goulart's reformist agenda and thus triggered the military coup on April 1, 1964.

Just six years later, in the early 1970s, the regional problems were being managed by the planning system and investments in infrastructure for basic sectors were improving the economy, but a metropolitan crisis, an oil crisis, and a sequence of urban protests exposed a significant political vulnerability of the military regime: urban policy. In response, the military created in 1974 the first institution for metropolitan planning, the Comissão Nacional de Regiões Metropolitanas e Política Urbana. Given that labor rights and political repression (two of the main rods of our theoretical tripod) had dismal hopes of improvement during the military dictatorship, the focus of the planning bureaucratic elite was to improve the efficiency of the transportation system (the knot of our diagram) and the regulation of the land market in order to make the best use of the existent infrastructure. The measures for urban land control proposed by this commission were not implemented during the dictatorship but became the basis of the urban policy chapters of the 1988 Constitution.

THE NEW TERRITORIAL DEAL IN JUSCELINO KUBITSCHEK'S PRESIDENCY

The next president was Juscelino Kubitscheck (1902–1976). In his term in office, from 1956 to 1961, the social issue was no longer organically linked to development as it had been in the Vargas period. Economic development goals were mobilizing all the president's attention, and economic success seemed to be enough for a modern, industrial, and democratic society. The economic planning was focused on sectoral programs, such as the expansion of basic factors for industrial production and the huge project of the new capital, Brasília, which resulted in a significant boost to the construction industry in Brazil.

The plan devised in Kubitscheck's term in office was called Plano de Metas "target plans" and established two lines of strategic action. The first would address the bottlenecks of five basic sectors: energy, transportation, capital goods, food production, and training of human resources. The first three were priorities. The energy sector (electric, nuclear, mineral oil) accounted for 43 percent of the goals, transportation (railways, highways, ports, merchant shipping, and air transportation) 29.6 percent, and industry of capital goods 20.4 percent (Lafer 1970, 29–50). The second line of action would produce strategic points of investment linking the supply chain in a dynamic set of economic relations. Brasília was included as the last goal of this plan and can be considered its synthesis. Built in just four years, the new capital cost about 250 billion cruzeiros in values of 1961, mobilizing 2.3 percent of the gross national product, a significant expansion of the economy based on the construction industry sector.

The Target Plan had a massive impact in the Brazilian economy due to state spending in public works and huge inflows of foreign capital. The intervention changed the industrial pattern of the country and was considered a shift toward production goods and durable consumer goods (Latini 2007, 115). In addition to the change in the industrial pattern, the Target Plan radically changed the physical-spatial configuration of Brazilian economic development through road building. The new capital Brasília was the focal point of the road plan that completed the national integration. The automobile industry in Brazil was deployed to supply the system and soon become the main face of this transformation (Ianni 2009, 155). Between 1957 and 1960 most of the production was of medium trucks and buses, being surpassed by the production of automobiles only in 1960 (Latini 2007, 151).

After 1960 the impact of individual mobility on intra-urban space and on middle-class suburbanization that would characterize the following decades was intensified and triggered severe criticism toward "the Brazilian road pattern of development." The huge boost to economic growth, mainly triggered by the Target Plan's investment in building roads and a new capital city, were deeply criticized.

Some of the critics pointed out the social exclusion. The workers who materialized the dream of national modernization were expelled from the modern city. They were driven to peripheral settlements called *cidades satélites*, showing the selective nature of the ongoing project of modernization that would crash a few years later, in 1964. A. Paviani (1987) rigorously analyzed this point of view, showing the conflicts within the urbanization process of the new capital. Another point of analyses of the critics was the intensity of the real estate market in Brasília (Medeiros and Campos 2010).

The new Brazilian capital was also useful for some authors to explain new patterns of relationships between modernism and modernization. Holston (1989) and Gorelik (2005) did exactly that, despite telling their narratives from opposite perspectives.

Created as part of a huge development program in which social issues were detached from economic aims, Brasília could not be expected to be successful in something it was never designed for. Ameliorating inequality was never the point. In this period, the social conflicts were masked by the growth of the construction sector, only to be later aggravated by the lack of effort to amplify the welfare system in Brazil. The Kubitscheck campaign's slogan, "Fifty Years in Five," clearly affirmed that the social conditions would be improved as a consequence of economic growth. The backlash of the urban issue would point out the limits of the Brazilian democracy experiment, as we discuss later.

MODERNIZING THE INNER NATION

In Brazil both the social issues and economic development were intertwined with the real estate market, as we have discussed. Industrialization, the social security system, and the urbanization process were embedded in a certain way of producing the city, led by the welfare state. The spatial concentration and the imbalance of infrastructure provided by this model remains a challenge for urban planning in Brazil.

The engine of the real estate market, led by the welfare state, was assembled in the Estado Novo period (1937–1945) and was decried as early as the 1940s by official reports.[1] The reports pointed out that the concentration of investments in urban areas threatened the expansion of industrialization aimed by the regime. Real estate in the largest cities absorbed the capital that would flow from the banking system to industrialization. In reality, the large amount of capital invested in the real estate markets of the largest cities produced a crisis in liquidity for many banks, leading to the closure in 1955 of many financial institutions that had privileged this kind of investment (Costa 1978, 207–8).

This influx of liquidity also contributed to capital flows toward smaller cities from 1956 to 1959, searching for gains in the rural economy, exploring real estate profits in such cities, and further improving the banking system, which had since 1944 spread credits and agencies through the interior of the country. The main increase of bank agencies in the period was in the states of São Paulo, Rio de Janeiro, Espírito Santo, Paraná, and Goiás (Costa 1978, 215 and 300).

The construction of the new capital, Brasília, from 1956 to 1961 followed the ongoing process of expansion (a.k.a. land grabbing) toward the interior that started with the construction of Goiânia, the new capital of the state of Goiás, in the 1930s. Certainly Brasília boosted even further the development of Brazil's interior, mainly by fostering a new economic polarization in the territorial center of the nation. But this was far from being a totally new phenomenon, inaugurated by Oscar Niemeyer's Monumental architecture, Lúcio Costa's pilot plan based on highway connections, and Juscelino Kubitscheck's ambitious Target Plans.

The ongoing economic engine of interiorization to which Brasília belonged was formalized by the effort of building the new capital city and symbolically expressed the task of modernizing Brazil from its territorial center.[2] It meant the displacement of the former territorial inhabitation pattern of concentration on the Atlantic shores that was dependent on European and US markets for the export of agricultural products and imports of manufactured goods. Brasília represented the national autonomy promised by modernization through conquering the internal market for Brazilians. Such a project was systematized by Celso Furtado (1962), the celebrated Brazilian thinker who had dreamed of overcoming deeply social inequalities linked with rural heritage by means of economic modernization.

Resources from the social security system were mobilized for the construction of some residential areas in Brasília. The social security institutions built twelve thousand housing units and spent 1.2 billion cruzeiros in 1961 (Bonduki and Koury 2014, 413; Oliveira et al. 1998, 4).[3]

Figure 4.1 displays the number of housing units produced by the social security institutions in states and capital cities between 1956 and 1959. Around 65 percent of the investment was made in smaller towns in São Paulo and Minas Gerais, and a huge concentration in Brasília.

Despite the contribution of social security system funds to building housing facilities in Brasília, in Kubitscheck's term in office (1956–1961) social welfare did not play the same political role as it had in the past. The economic development goals were very successful and mobilized the attention of the Brazilian society. Economic success seemed to be enough for a modern, industrial, democratic society. Even in the presence of an inflationary process and lack of capital, which since 1959 threatened the end of Juscelino Kubitscheck's term, he remained confident in the stable basis of democracy he would leave as a legacy.

The agreement with the unions in Kubitscheck's term was led by vice president Goulart, who had gathered the support of the labor movement as the Ministry of Labor in the second Vargas term. He was appointed in 1953 and at that time played an important role in negotiation with the mariners, who were organizing a strike. Goulart had promised to increase the minimum wage by 100 percent to cover the inflationary losses that were threatening their standards of living. He was forced to resign in February of 1954, but Vargas maintained his promise and signed a 100 percent increase of the minimum wage on May 1. The episode shaped Goulart's political profile and cemented union support.

In 1956 Goulart was elected vice president in Juscelino Kubitscheck's term as representative of the Partido Trabalhista Brasileiro, keeping his party's huge electoral base in alliance with Partido Social Democrático. He would keep this same position in the next term, with Jânio Quadros as president.

Goulart's political support in the unions was strategic for the modernization process in the Kubitscheck era (Maranhão 1981; Castro Gomes 2004b).

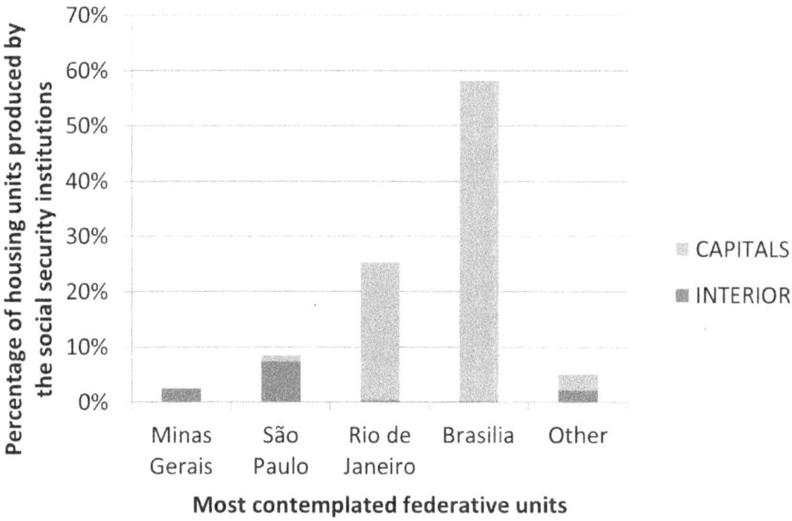

Figure 4.1. Investment in capital cities versus interior cities, 1939–1960. The authors, from data collected in Pioneiros da Habitação Social Project, led by Nabil Bonduki and Ana Paula Koury from 2000 to 2014.

Ironically it enabled the shift from the social-welfare-centered policies of Vargas to Kubitscheck's developmentalism in a relatively stable democratic regime.

At this point we need to ask why the Kubitscheck years were seen as a golden era of economic growth and stability. On the symbolic side, Brazil's soccer team won the first FIFA World Cup in 1958, bossa nova was playing all over the world, and the architects of Brasília were recognized as a genial tropical branch of modernism. The country was surfing a tide of optimism similar to Lula's best years of 2006–2010. Back to our theoretical tripod, we see a change in perception, not in substance. Police repression continued in force, and the demands of construction workers in Brasília, for instance, were responded to with batons and even bullets. Landownership and occupation rights were not any better than before, and labor rights were only inching ahead. The transportation system was consolidating around road traffic, with trolleys and light-rails being abandoned for buses and cars.

A more careful observation shows that the 1950s were not so "golden" as it seems. Several protests were carried out by the workers' struggle, supported by the inter-union apparatus created in the fifties.

In the mid-1950s, São Paulo became the most populous Brazilian city, surpassing Rio de Janeiro, then the federal capital. The industrial concentration in the metropolitan region of São Paulo, especially in the municipalities of metropolitan region called ABC (after the names of the cities Santo André, São Bernardo, and São Caetano do Sul), transformed São Paulo into the most important stage of the conflict of interest between the working class and the patronage. During this period, the working classes used the inter-union movement to pressure official unions controlled by the Ministry of Labor.

Social movements had been organizing since the early fifties to protest against the rising cost of living. The Passeata da Panela Vazia ("empty pot march") and later the Movimento contra a Carestia de Vida ("movement against life costs") had highlighted the political limits of economic growth based on underemployment and informality (Gohn 1995). These triggered union movement organization that served as a platform for both formal and informal sectors. The strike of 300,000 in 1953 is directly linked to the Panela Vazia movement and serves as an example of how the labor movement bypassed the restrictions on self-organization made by the unions law of the Vargas period. Soon the workers realized they needed economic information in order to support their cause, and created the Departamento Intersindical de Estatística e Estudos Sócio Econômicos (DIEESE) in 1955 to that end (Mendonça 2002).

The most famous conflict of this period happened on February 9, 1959, when the police entered the barracks of the Pacheco Fernandes construction company in Brasília, shooting indiscriminately. Official numbers report 9 dead and 50 hurt, while interviews with eyewitnesses counted at least 20 bodies pulled from the bloody dormitory into construction trucks. Before that, in October of 1957, a general strike in the city of São Paulo had mobilized 400,000 workers, made possible because of inter-union support. At that time Jânio Quadros was governor of São Paulo and wisely chose not to repress the union movement, consolidating his support with workers' movement, which was unsatisfied with federal policies (Maranhão 1981, 286). The inter-union movement played an important role in the political struggle for working-class rights in Brazil, making very visible and loud their claims against exploitation of urban and rural workers.

URBAN REFORM AND THE AUTHORITARIAN CYCLE

Decades later, in the second half of the 1980s, the issue of urban reform would be central to the debates around the return of democracy, attested by the inclusion of two chapters about urban policy in the 1988 Constitution. Using our theoretical tripod to explain that moment, we see that all rods—labor, repression, and landownership—were stressed to the limits during the 1970s, with planning attempting to improve life conditions by finding efficiencies without challenging the structure. Despite its centrality as a societal problem, the urban issue is seldom mentioned in the most well-known explanations on Brazilian inequalities before the 1970s.[4] This section of chapter 4 attempts to close that gap with a discussion of the planning debates of the 1950s and 1960s.

At that time, the most pressing issue to overcome poverty concentration in Brazilian society was land reform and the extension of labor legislation from urban to rural workers, and the extension of voting rights to illiterate adults. It was evident for most authors that poverty was concentrated in the rural areas and segregated from the system of rights that ruled the urban Brazilian society (Furtado 1962; Prado [1966] 1977). Again we see two main rods of our tripod occupying a central place in the political debate.

While most authors in the 1960s were focused on inequalities in rural areas, the urban issue would play a decisive role both in the succession of Juscelino Kubitscheck and a little later in the episodes that led to the military coup of 1964. Actually, it would become the most politically sensitive issue in Brazil thereafter.

According to Fausto Britto (2006), who has studied the demographic transition in Brazil, the novelty of Brazilian urbanization was the fast process of urban growth triggered by internal migration from the countryside. It was far superior to that of developed countries and reached an average of 2.3 million new inhabitants in Brazilian cities every year in the 1960s. "This massive redistribution of people changed the profile of the urban population: in 1970, more than half of the urban population was already living in cities with more than 100,000 inhabitants, and one-third of that in cities with more than 500,000 people. In the year 2000, 60% of the urban population were living in cities with more than 100,000 inhabitants, showing that urbanization and concentration of the population in large cities were simultaneous processes in Brazil."[5] Jânio Quadros's successful campaign to the presidency in 1960 was focused on urban problems at the periphery and on combating corruption scandals. His skyrocketing career outside of major political parties demonstrates the power of urban issues in Brazil.[6] Quadros was a well-known character in São Paulo's peripheral neighborhoods. His electoral stronghold was Vila Maria, at the northern edge of the city, a place that experienced a dramatic demographic increase between 1950 and 1980, combined with an acute shortage of infrastructure. The neighborhood received people from other Brazilian states such as Minas Gerais and Espírito Santo. It was not a paulista neighborhood but an amalgam of Brazilians from everywhere. Quadros was first elected councilman alternate in 1948, and in fifteen years he would reach the country's presidency. Fernando Henrique Cardoso (1980, 181–82) explains this process, highlighting that Quadros's popularity came from his ability to explore urban issues. The politician realized the importance of that claim beyond the labor agenda pushed by the traditional left: "There was a large claim from urban peripheral areas, the *vilas* without water, without sewage, unpaved, without enough public transportation that broke out in politics. Two decades of fast urban industrial development had promoted droves of internal migration arriving at São Paulo. Hundreds of thousands of people from northeast region, from Minas Gerais and from the interior of São Paulo, people who needed more attention as inhabitants even before joining a union."[7] The results of the 1960 elections brought together two different political strands, confirming the power of vice president João Goulart. The winning ticket in the 1960 election was called *jan-jan* and came from an independent movement that linked a presidential candidate from a conservative coalition of União Democrática Nacional (UDN) and minor parties with a vice president from the opposing coalition, the left-leaning Partido Trabalhista Brasileiro–Partido Social Democrático alliance.

Quadros's polemical presidency was extensively discussed by contemporary witnesses (Cabral 1962; Victor 1965) and has been debated by historians and political scientists since (Skidmore [1967] 1982; Maranhão 1981). Despite his short term of only seven months in office, Quadros centered the issues of housing policy and urban reform in his government's agenda; both these issues had been absent from Kubitscheck's years.

Before his resignation in August of 1961, Quadros launched a housing assistance plan and announced the creation of the Instituto Brasileiro de Habitação (Brazilian Institute of Housing, Act 3.139-11-07-1961). This framework was an effort to overcome difficulties inherited from the creation of the Fundação da Casa Popular (FCP), bringing back the debate started in the second Vargas term (1950–1954). The new institution was directly linked to the presidency and funded by a financing system that relied on taxes levied on consumption and real estate transactions. To increase the capacity of the construction sector, an assistance plan was also created to employ workers who had recently migrated from the countryside (Azevedo and Andrade 1982, 46). With the resignation of Quadros, these proposals were abandoned, and none of them was implemented in the early 1960s. The interdependence between political stability and urban policies, including housing and urban reform, became evident.

Vice president João Goulart took office in September of 1961 in a series of institutional crises promoted by sectors of the military adamantly against Vargas's political heritage. The deal for the maintenance of legality in Quadros's succession included the institution of a parliamentary regime to trim the powers of the new president. Goulart governed under this parliamentary regime until a referendum in January of 1963 restored his full presidential powers.

Adding to the political crisis, the government of João Goulart faced an economic crisis and frequent workers' strikes, which were stopped only by military repression after the 1964 coup. The economic situation had been worsening since the end of Juscelino Kubitscheck's term. In the beginning of the 1960s, the GDP growth had slowed, and inflation kept rising out of control.

Goulart tried to break out of the economic crisis and promote social development through the Plano Trienal de Desenvolvimento Econômico e Social (Triennial Plan of Social and Economic Development) launched in December of 1962 by the recently created Ministério do Planejamento (Planning Ministry). The economic measures defined in the triennial plan aimed at keeping inflation under control by reducing investments. However, such austerity measures only worsened the economic crisis, aggravating the political turmoil of Goulart's term (Macedo 1970, 55–60).[8]

The triennial plan also defined a set of guidelines for basic reforms that had been established in Kubitscheck's term (Ferreira 2013). In terms of social development, the plan included improvements to education and to the health system but did not mention anything on urban or housing policy (Plano 1962). Goulart's agenda was focused on the development of rural areas, most affected by extreme poverty.

In February 1963, just one month after the return to the presidential system with huge popular approval, the official magazine of the Instituto de Arquitetos do Brasil (IAB, Brazilian Institute of Architects) criticized the governmental plan (Arquitetura 1963, 2). Although recognizing the need for economic measures and the importance given to social development in the official document, the architects pointed out the lack of attention given to the housing problem. Throughout the plan, there is only one single reference to housing, included in the chapter on health policy under the item "pre-investments for the improvements of human factor." In this item, the housing problem appears as crucial in eliminating diseases that were still prevalent in the majority of Brazil's poverty-stricken communities (Plano 1962, 94).

Since the early 1960s a large-scale social crisis had been cooking, a direct result of the urban pattern of unequal growth. The architects pointed out to crowded cities and lack of adequate housing, which were threatening political stability and democracy itself. In the 1960s federal agencies that had traditionally provided units, such as the institutes of pensions and retirement and the FCP, posted an even more insignificant performance, worsening the situation (Andrade and Azevedo 1982 43; Bonduki 1998, 129; Manoel 2004, 75).

In March of 1963 a presidential message to Congress sought to correct the mistake of omitting housing and urban policy from the government plan. The text pointed out the problem of urban growth in smaller state capitals, which had surpassed the national rate of population increase. While the national average was 63 percent, cities such as Goiânia (188 percent), Macapá (128 percent), Curitiba (100 percent), Belo Horizonte (93 percent), Fortaleza (91 percent), and São Paulo (72 percent) were far above that, while Rio de Janeiro (39 percent) was significantly under the average, still recovering after the federal government's move to Brasília. The congressional message promised to create a housing policy to meet the shortage in the largest cities but also made clear the intention to regulate construction activities to avoid the real estate speculation that prevent workers' access to the housing market (Goulart 1963, 11, 134–37).

The Act 87, proposed by Floriceno Paixão, a lawyer and congressman focused on the social security system, was approved in April 1963. The act presented the same justification as Act 1911, also sponsored by Paixão in 1960, based on a comprehensive diagnosis of the housing shortage since 1950 produced by Instituto de Aposentadoria e Pensões dos Industriários employee Natexilpatri Guitton. Act 1911 proposed to create a national housing plan, a superintendence of housing, and a national housing fund, but it was not approved.

The new Act 87 presented in April 1963 mixed the former housing acts 1911 and 1960 with Act 3.139/1961, presented in Jânio Quadros's term to create the Instituto Nacional de Habitação and resulting in an important legal device focused on the housing shortage. It took from Act 1911 the concept of social interest housing linked to worker's wages. The measure aimed to correct the distortion of the former policy in the Vargas era, which had financed houses for white-collar workers only. Another important point to be corrected on the former policies was the destiny of the funds gathered for housing. They must be operated by Caixa Econômica Federal following a plan for evaluating the needs and the feasibility of the investments. The law was designed to close any loopholes in the investments, avoiding speculation in the real estate market and the flight of capital to private banks that had occurred in the banking crisis between 1955 and 1959.

Drafted by Instituto Brasileiro de Habitação, the housing policy would be linked directly to the presidency and composed by an independent council, which would be in charge of the plan and provided with specific funds. By establishing a financial system and an independent management of the housing policy, the new act attempted to correct the distortions that led to the failure of the Popular Home Foundation (1946) and finally alleviate the pressure of the urban masses on the Brazilian political process.

At this point the perception of the urban issue was limited to housing policy, and the urban reform was only included in Goulart's basic reforms agenda after a seminar organized in July of 1963 by the Brazilian Institute of Architects and the Institute of Retirement and Pensions of the State Servants (Bonduki and Koury, 2010; Francisconi 2013; Koury 2013a).

The Seminário de Habitação e Reforma Urbana (Seminar of Housing and Urban Reform) sought to introduce the urban issue in the basic reforms proposed by Goulart. The debates were split among four subjects: (1) the housing situation (moderated by Vinicius Fonseca); (2) housing and urban agglomeration (moderated by Acácio Gil Borsoi); (3) urban reform and measures to establish housing and urban policies (moderated by Joaquim Guedes); and (4) implementation of urban planning and housing programs (moderated by Jorge Wilheim).

The last group, led by Jorge Wilheim, proposed a review of Act 87. The act was originally centered in housing policy, and its revision produced a shift toward a law centered in urban policy, placing housing policy under an urbanistic umbrella. The new document instituted an urban policy superintendence in charge of the housing plan. It would be also responsible for articulating the housing policy and the urban reform. This agency would control urban growth and promote technical innovations to produce large-scale housing by adopting streamlined processes and innovative designs.

Another important observation highlighted at the seminar report was that private landownership was limiting urban growth. Consequently, the report recommended an amendment to the 1946 Constitution that would exclude the need for cash payment for expropriations in case of social utility. The suggestion aimed to compensate homeowners and urban landowners with government bonds. The same solution was proposed to compensate landowners in an agrarian reform project presented by Goulart to Congress. Both reforms, agrarian and urban, recognized the structure of landownership as a limit to Brazilian social and economic development, as hypothesized by our tripod diagram.

To tackle the problem of landownership in the housing policy as proposed by the seminar, a technological component was included. Standardizing and normalizing (by modular coordination) home designs and their components would contribute to partial prefabrication of housing units. Those could be built by the private sector or by the state, but the goal was to lower the cost of each unit, covering the deficit faster with the limited funds available. The funds allocated to housing programs would allow new experiments and innovation in industrialization, which had originated on the construction site of Brasília and now under the Seminário de Habitação e Reforma Urbana proposal would be brought to a national scale.

The organization of the meeting in 1963 and the government decision to intervene in housing and urban policy would have been strategic to social stability, but we now know it was too late. The political instability was already irreversible in 1963. Ironically, the proposals revealed its political potential and were partially adopted by the civilian-military regime that broke the legal mandate of Goulart on April 1, 1964. The main lines of the housing and planning model had been drawn. Many of the proposals for radical transformation would not be incorporated, such as the restriction on property rights and the technology push. The new housing policy pulled out productive innovations aimed at social and urban issues and implemented a conservative modernization under the authoritarian regime.

Jorge Guilherme Francisconi (2013) described and analyzed the controversial political transition and the creation of the National Housing Bank, highlighting the role of Sandra Cavalcanti, who pleaded to military president Humberto Castelo Branco to intervene in the urban issue. She was secretary of social service in Guanabara State in the government of Carlos Lacerda (1961–1964) during his controversial slum removal campaign and became the first president of the National Housing Bank.[9] In 1964 the seriousness of the urban issue led Cavalcanti to write a memorandum to president Castelo Branco, proposing an act (18/IV/1964) creating the National Housing Bank. In her memorandum Cavalcanti recommended the creation of a bank as "central institution" to guarantee the "healthy currency flowing the housing system" safety from the inflationary process. She pointed out to the importance . . . of the future activities of the bank "in basic sanitation and mass transportation" to the need to provide the housing estates with "water, energy, sewage, vigilance, and transportation."[10] Cavalcanti stressed the importance of working beyond housing units and basic urban infrastructure, incorporating public services such as mass transportation and demonstrating how this was a sensitive question in the expansion of the largest cities (Francisconi 2013).

THE FEDERAL PLANNING SYSTEM AND ARCHITECTS UNDER THE AUTHORITARIAN REGIME

In August of 1964, just four months after the coup, the military government had created the BNH and the SERFHAU with Act 4.380-21/8/1964, which also established the operational model and secured investments in the financial system. The National Housing Bank was in charge of housing policies and the Federal Service of Housing and Urbanism was in charge of urban policies. However, the understanding of SERFHAU's role in the planning system would change significantly in the period of its operation.

The creation of BNH provided political support for the military regime. In the autocratic regime deployed after the coup, the control of urban growth and reduction of the housing shortage was strategic for political stability in a country with huge rates of urbanization. As hypothesized by our tripod, both police repression and control of the labor movement were central tenets of the military regime, so the possible improvement in social conditions could only come from the housing supply and from a more efficient transportation knot.

Act 4.380 was proposed by Paulo Assis Ribeiro, a member of the team working under Minister of Planning Roberto Campos (1964–1967). Campos implemented a comprehensive ideology in the federal policy in which territorial planning (urban and regional) was widespread. He nominated as part of his advisory board two architects, Harry Cole and Luis Alfredo Stockler, and one engineer, Rubens Mattos Pereira. Harry Cole was linked with the Institute of Architects and was the representative of part of the architects' agenda in the new government system of planning (Feldman 2005, 222–28; Lucchese 2009, 268–88, 346).

The architects in the early 1960s had criticized the competition and the construction of Brasília. Between 1956 and 1964 the president of the Brazilian Institute of Architects at Guanabara was Maurício Roberto, who had placed third with his brother and partner Marcelo Roberto in the public competition for the urban design of Brasília in 1956. Their proposal was deeply detailed in terms of regional planning, the result of an interdisciplinary team. An urban design based on poli-nuclear settlements and the development of the region was embedded in the administrative center proposal. Beyond the urban area they presented land studies, rural planning, and also a financial study for the new capital (Tavares 2014, 270–83; L. Souza 2014, 217–24).

The jury of the competition chose the very simple pilot plan made by Lúcio Costa, but the debate regarding a comprehensive idea of planning reached the pages of *Arquitetura* magazine, the official publication of the Institute of Architects. In 1962 the editorial of the magazine started to advocate a new understanding of planning. It criticized the plans based on roads that shaped housing blocks and stated that good architecture could not be achieved detached from urban planning, as had happened in Brasília (Lucchese 2009, 60).

The Seminario de Habitação e Reforma Urbana of 1963 was a consequence of this debate on planning and had already shown the architects' skills on urban policies and the political centrality of the urban issue. Both elements contributed to the architects' role in the new system of planning deployed by Roberto Campos in the Ministry of Planning and by João Paulo dos Reis Velloso at Instituto de Pesquisa Econômica Aplicada, where Cole, Stockler, and Pereira would be integrated in 1965 in the sector of regional and urban development (Lucchese 2009, 277–78).[11]

Beyond responding to the sensitive popular problem of housing, the BNH found a way to incorporate in its administration the dueling proposals from the former period: namely, Lacerda's group through Sandra Cavalcanti and the architects' agenda through Campos's advisory board.

The law defined the bank as an autarchy initially capitalized with one billion cruzeiros and increased by 1 percent monthly from the wages linked with the social security system.[12] In 1966 a fund to guarantee income stability was created by a tripartite contribution. This fund would be integrated into the housing financing system and increase the capacity of BNH's operations. It happened under the presidency of Luís Gonzaga Nascimento e Silva (1965–1966), inaugurating the second phase of the BNH.[13]

Those funds financed the most important period in the history of BNH, providing finance support for housing policy that expanded to research on technologies, research on the housing deficit, planning of available land and best location for the housing complexes, evaluation of socioeconomic aspects, and assistance for municipalities to develop and deploy their master plans (Trindade 1971, 108–10).

At the same time SERFHAU attributions were defined and the service was flush with resources. The institution became responsible for coordinating between local and national planning, providing technical assistance for BNH to operate according to the integrated planning system. To achieve this goal the SERFHAU financed local development plans and urban master plans (Decree 59.917, 30/12/66; Vizioli 1988, 23; Mota 2007, 8–16; Lucchese 2009, 270).

In 1967 Harry Cole was named SERFHAU superintendent (1967–1968) in substitution of George de Almeida Magalhães (1964–1967). In this position Cole had the opportunity to advocate for comprehensive planning; promote capability workshops for architects, engineers and economists, bring planners such as Francis Violich and John Friedman from the United States to give lectures, and also write several articles in trade magazines for architects and public administrators (*Revista Arquitetura do IAB Guanabara* e *Revista de Administração Municipal do IBAM*, Instituto Brasileiro de Administração Municipal). Cole also opened a registration system to hire architects to develop urban and regional plans. The SERFHAU overhaul broadened the conditions that innovative solutions had placed in the territorial development and was formulated in a close debate with the IAB–Rio de Janeiro (Feldman 2005, 228–36; Lucchese 2009, 291–305, 346).

To foster the SERFHAU's increasing planning efficiency, Cole had also proposed a restructuration.[14] He tried to shift the institutional hierarchy in which the SERFHAU was under to the housing police of BNH. His major point was to create a specialized secretary of territorial planning at the ministry level to integrate economic and spatial development. His other points included that budgets would be approved based on the liability of the plans, housing plans and urban development plans would be integrated, and the capacity to produce better and more plans would be improved through training teams and prepared guidelines (Lucchese 2009, 272). The majority of these proposals were implemented by the SERFHAU overhaul of 1967. However, the ministry level secretary of territorial planning was not created. On the contrary, the BNH system and the SERFHAU, along with regional development banks, were transferred from the Ministry of Planning to the Ministry of Interior (Decree no. 60.900, June 26, 1967). This shows us how strategic it was for the military government to create an interior polarization of investments to overcome the political threat of the metropolitan phenomenon.[15]

Cole resigned the superintendency of SERFHAU in November of 1968, claiming that while the SERFHAU was under the BNH, implementing an urban planning policy would be impossible. His successor was Leo Serejo Pinto de Abreu. It is important to highlight that in 1969 the BNH became the second most important Brazilian bank, and the SERFHAU had increased its presence in the media concurrently with the growth of metropolitan regions.

The other featured architect who occupied the stage in the transition to the dictatorship was Jorge Wilheim. He had led the urban reform group in the Seminário de Habitação e Reforma Urbana of 1963 and had published several articles highlighting the importance of urban planning just after the publication of the official report of the seminar. His advocacy toward urban reform through the Instituto de Arquitetos do Brasil also gave him an important role as urban planner in the authoritarian period (Silva 2015). He became a central character of planning in Brazil at least until 2002, when he coordinated São Paulo's master plan under the Estatuto da Cidade principles.

Wilheim's approach as urban planner became explicit in the book *São Paulo Metrópole 65: Subsídios para o seu plano diretor*, in which he proposed guidelines for the master plan of São Paulo. He was writing in Faria Lima's first year as mayor of São Paulo (1965–1969); Lima would commission new plans for the city, the Plano Urbanístico Básico, and the plan to deploy the subway system. In this book Wilheim discusses how to connect the city, which had grown as an archipelago of neighborhoods linked by roads opened in the colonial times. He criticized former plans by Prestes Maia (1930) and Robert Moses (1950), in which the transportation system was detached from social urban life, once again supporting the pivotal role of the transportation knot in our theoretical diagram (Anelli 2011, 23–25).

For Wilheim the former plans' deceptive idea of a centralized city led to mistakes, and as a consequence the city remained poorly connected. Beside his theory of social integration through transportation systems, he incorporated a deep knowledge of the geomorphology of the city and its anthropic occupation, allowing him to present significant proposals for a better-connected city (Wilheim 1963, 18–19, 95–96).

Urban transportation had a central role in this thinking on the city of São Paulo, and it would be transformed into a method that he applied to several master plans developed for many Brazilian cities throughout his prolific life. It is no coincidence that our theoretical tripod has transportation as the knot that connects it all. Despite Wilheim's intention to contribute to the master plan of São Paulo, his methods were first tried in Curitiba and Joinville in 1965.[16]

Curitiba was growing faster than many state capitals in the 1960s. Its master plan was contracted by a call for proposals sent to planning consultants. The winning consulting company was Serete Engineering, with Jorge Wilheim's proposal. It was the same company that had presented the guidelines for the call for proposals. After the SERFHAU overhaul in 1967, the role of consultant companies would increase. They became the main producer of plans for SERFHAU instead of academic or public institutions created to plan at the municipal level in the former period (Feldman 2005, 228–33).

Irã Taborda Dudeque (2010) has analyzed the history of planning in Curitiba, pointing out that the greatest achievement of the master plan proposed by Wilheim was the interpretation of the territory overlapping with the geomorphologic characteristics of the city and its occupancy along the time. This interpretation allowed him to choose the best option to overcome the traffic problem. According to Dudeque, Wilheim realized that the main traffic line "followed the path northeast-southeast and that the most populated neighborhoods of the city . . . were concentrated in this urban strip." Wilheim proposed to densify this strip and to transform it into the main axis for the connection between the centralities, therefore ordering the city's growth (124–27).

After Joinville and Curitiba (1965), Wilheim would develop plans for Natal (1967), Osasco (1966), Goiânia (1968), Guarulhos (1969), São José dos Campos (1969), Paulínea (1970) and Campinas (1970). In all those cities Wilheim had the chance to test in different situations the planning approach which he started to develop on the *Seminário* of 1963. Those plans triggered his career as urban planner and urban thinker in the next decades, when the authoritarian regime deployed a robust system of comprehensive territorial planning.

In 1968 Wilheim was in charge of two positions in the Instituto de Arquitetos do Brasil (IAB). He was director of the National Division of Housing and Planning (1968–1969) and member of the Superior Board (1968–1973). In this period, the Instituto de Arquitetos do Brasil was advocating changes in the National Housing Bank policies. The summary of the IAB positions regarding housing policy was introduced by J. R. Serran (1976), who gathered the results of several meetings in which the institute had participated from 1954 to 1975. The work was required by the institution "to examine the issue of the relationship between IAB/BNH" (Serran 1976, 1). He highlighted the importance of architects' critical approach in improving the debate on housing policies. He divided the history of their participation in three phases. The first was the fight to implement the housing policy (before 1964); the second was the fight to change the housing policy (after 1964); and his conclusion enthusiastically announced his perception of an ongoing change in the participation of architects in the political decision in the third era of this relationship between the architects and the planning system. He pointed out that until 1963 architects were on the fringe of housing policies. Serran was writing after Jorge Wilheim was appointed São Paulo State secretary of planning in 1975, and the role of architects in the military regime would prove him right, despite Cole's criticism.

In the early 1970s SERFHAU hired Wilheim to develop a method for urban planning as part of a new overhaul of the service. This happened after the 1970 decree (No. 66882, July 16, 1970) that had centralized the development of municipal master plans at the federal level. Master plans were initially made by the national service of municipalities, created in 1961 during Quadros's term, and would be integrated in the SERFHAU system by law only in 1970. The restructuration proposed by Wilheim actually did not occur, and the SERFHAU was formally closed in 1975 (Decreto no. 76.149, August 22, 1975; Mota 2007, 7).

At the beginning of the 1970s, while Jorge Wilheim was on the Superior Board of Instituto de Arquitetos do Brasil, he developed studies for other public institutions of metropolitan planning, such as the Executive Group of Planning the Great São Paulo (GEGRAN) in 1970 and the Metropolitan Plan of Belo Horizonte (Plambel) in 1971.

Since 1969 the Ministry of Interior has been trying to tackle the lack of infrastructure in urban areas deploying combined sewage and housing programs. The program, called PAC (Concentrated Action Program, or Programa de Ação Concentrada), defined a time of great activity in the SERFHAU with the production of integrated local plans of development (*planos de desenvolvimento local integrado*) and the organization of integrated system of information to subsidize the plans. This was triggered by the territorial studies developed by the Brazilian Institute of Geography and Statistics in an attempt to identify the deficiencies of the urban network (Motta 2007, 11–16).

Concurrently with local development plans, which were focused on the urban network, the Instituto de Pesquisa Econômica Aplicada started to study the problems of infrastructure in the intra-metropolitan space with regard to their integration in the metropolitan economic system. Soon after, in 1971, the

BNH would be transformed into a public company, widening its role in providing urban infrastructure and housing in the peripheral neighborhoods of largest metropolitan areas (Vizioli 1988, 28–37; Lucchese 2009, 299).

The engine of how to finance urban development started to become a central issue in the following years. Beside specific funds for urban development divided by region, the surplus of urban plots after the public investments were accounted as a way to finance urban renewal. The BNH launched Projeto Cura (Urban Community for Accelerated Recovery, or Comunidade Urbana para Recuperação Acelerada) in 1973 to apply this concept. Projeto Cura was drafted by Harry Cole as private consultant. The project aimed to improve urban efficiency by fostering development in some neighborhoods to correct real estate market distortions. This urban design experiment would be applied in Vila Valqueire in Rio de Janeiro. The main idea of the program was to invest in a middle-class neighborhood with infrastructure and a high incidence of vacant plots. The real estate market would lead the local development and increase the housing supply for the growing cities (Lucchese 2009 110).

The program did not have further consequences, but it was a first symptom of the great future challenge in the planning system: the metropolitan regions. The SERFHAU faced severe difficulties to intervene in the metropolitan scale because of its origins in the financial system of the BNH. Metropolitan policy demanded supra-municipal jurisdiction and political articulation, something that was never implemented during the SEFHAU years (1966–1975). The development of the metropolitan issue and the growth of urban poverty would mark the next phase of Brazilian planning history.

The lack of workers' protests since the 1964 military coup was interrupted in 1968, when two large workers' strikes broke out in the industrial regions of Osasco and Contagem, located in the metropolitan regions of São Paulo and Belo Horizonte, which mobilized six thousand and fifteen thousand workers, respectively. These strikes express the deterioration of working-class living conditions during the military period and were considered a break in populist heritage of the Brazilian trade union movement (Weffort 1972).

METROPOLITAN POVERTY

Housing and mobility were the main struggles of urban dwellers. Violent protests against urban transport services called the Quebra-Quebra de Bondes ("vandalizing trams") occurred in Rio de Janeiro in 1956, and two years later in São Paulo a protest against the increase in bus tickets resulted in five persons killed by police. The Movimento de Associação de Moradores ("movement of association of residents," 1954–1964), Movimento pela Casa Própria ("movement for homeownership," 1961–1962), and Movimento dos Loteamentos Clandestinos ("movement of clandestine allotments,"] 1972) show the climbing of urban crises in the path of Brazilian urbanization process.

Clandestine allotments had met the housing needs of the migrants arriving in the city who were not eligible for public housing financing. The impossibility of regularizing the properties in these allotments, which did not respect the urban rules or offer any utilities infrastructure, triggered protests and public visibility to a problem of significant proportions. The measures adopted to curb this type of allotment also denied homeowners' self-construction, which in the absence of other means was the solution adopted by the migrants in São Paulo. According to Gohn (1995, 113), the housing movements in the eighties "have, as one of their causes, the disappearance of the self-construction as a solution for popular housing."

In the beginning of the 1970s, the precarious living conditions in the peripheral areas of the city were worsening, increasing the organization of urban movements for sewage, paving streets, and further public services such as waste management and transportation (McCann 2014). Henceforth the political importance of the metropolitan region and the difficulties of SERFHAU under the Ministry of Interior to deal with the huge phenomenon of metropolitan concentration were clear.

Since the mid-1960s the demographic transition had been taking place in Brazil, and concurrently within metropolitan regions, informal settlements were growing fast and would become an even more sensitive political problem. This would give space to another kind of political leadership in the architectural field: activism supporting informal settlements focused on social problems instead of economic development.

Carlos Nelson Ferreira dos Santos was the first to occupy this position when he described his own activities in the favela Brás de Pina in Rio de Janeiro in 1965. He was still an undergraduate student of architecture at Universidade do Brasil (Rio de Janeiro) when he was called to make a plan for the urbanization of the neighborhood. Some of the inhabitants had decided to resist the eviction ordered by Carlos Lacerda, governor of Guanabara State. The governor's intention was to remove the favelas, transferring the dwellers to housing projects such as Vila Kennedy and Vila Aliança, recently built by BNH far from the city center. Part of the families supported by the church and by the Association of the Favelados of Guanabara State decided to stay and to improve the living conditions in the Brás de Pina neighborhood.

Carlos Nelson Ferreira dos Santos and some colleagues of him were called to design the plan. Santos (1981, 32–57) remembered the process in transforming the marginal initiative in an institutionalized policy. It began in 1967 during Francisco Negrão de Lima's term as governor (1965–1971), when the

Guanabara State created a group to plan the urban industrial development of the state (which was actually the metropolitan region of Rio de Janeiro) and address the problems caused by the transference of the capital to Brasília. In this group, there was a secretary of urban renewal for the favelas. Santos and his group were invited to be part of this secretary in the Housing Research Center. The center was an operator of the BNH funds, and its main work was to produce a report on infrastructure, urban amenities, and housing conditions in the favelas of the state. To carry out the research, the center created a community development company, Codesco, also integrated in the BNH system. Codesco had an interdisciplinary team and operational funds for the urbanization of favelas. The company existed until the early 1970s, and its achievement was recognized as an alternative of urban development in poverty-stricken neighborhoods to avoid eviction and urban segregation.

One year before Codesco started to work, another institution under federal control was created: the CHISAM (Coordination of Social Housing of Rio de Janeiro Metropolitan Area), with a totally different orientation. It was tasked with creating reports on favelados' living conditions, but its aim was to support the removal of them to free land for housing estates built by the BNH system. To face this policy and to affirm their right to stay near the center of the city, the favelados created the FAFEG, Federation of Associations of the Dwellers of favelas in Guanabara State, the same year CHISAM started to operate (Ramsdell 1990; Valladares 2005).

In the 1960s São Paulo became the largest city and the most polarized metropolitan region in the country. The precarious living conditions in the poorest peripheral settlements had mobilized left-wing student organizations, public sanitation activists, and representatives of the Catholic church (Jacobi 1989, 155). The church deployed a humanitarian agenda for the Brazilian society, mobilizing public opinion to face urban poverty and the brutality committed by the military regime against human rights. According to Claudete Soares (2000, 25–34) this was a guideline adopted in Latin America since the Second General Conference of the Latin American Episcopate held in Medellín in 1968, which brought the church closer to social issues. This agenda was developed following the directives given by the Second Vatican Council (1962–1965), held under the papacy of John XXIII. The Second Vatican Council broke with some hierarchies of the church for prioritizing social action, which led some sectors of the church to associate with the left-wing movements in Latin America. This movement was known as liberation theology and had a great importance in the organization of urban movements in Brazil in the 1970s. Inspired by liberation theology, Catholic clergy implemented the

Movement of Basic Ecclesial Communities, which worked with the most deprived populations, initially in rural northeastern Brazil.

The Catholic church also participated in the youth movement of the Juventude Universitária Católica (Catholic University Youth), the Juventude Operária Católica (Catholic Workers' Youth), and the Juventude Agrária Católica (Catholic Agrarian Youth). According to Gohn (1995, 96), "the church's work with young people had the same repercussion as the work developed in the seventies to the poor people in the peripheral areas of large urban centers." In 1972 the National Bishop's Confederation, led by Don Paulo Evaristo Arns, published a report on the violation of human rights by Latin American dictatorships and soon after launched a "peripheral operation" to improve the living conditions the poorest region of the city. To meet this goal the archdiocese invested US$5 million to build 1,200 community centers to host the base ecclesiastic communities. These communities would play an important role in engaging civil society in the transition to democracy in the following decade.

Singer and Brant (1980, 73) have explained the method applied by the base ecclesiastic communities. They used the assembly and the vote to organize work for day-to-day life in the communities. In the absence of public policies to meet their needs for housing and public services, the residents managed common life themselves by joint efforts. The regular assembly attendance and the vote were strategic to strengthen communitarian ties and to guarantee individuals' commitment to the collective work. In addition, the organized community was strengthened to pressure public representatives to meet their needs.

To improve knowledge about the peripheral areas of São Paulo, the archdiocese hired researchers from the Brazilian Center of Analyses and Planning to produce a report called *São Paulo 1975 Crescimento e Pobreza*. The study strengthened ties between Catholic church representatives and some left-wing intellectuals. The articulation was of great importance for the political organization of social movements and also to promote the struggle for democracy. Left-wing intellectuals argued that Brazilian society was not amorphous, and that the poor people living in the peripheries were able to organize and fight for their interests, legitimizing through urban popular movements the democracy "expropriated" by the brutality of the military repression. Actually, the social movements linked with urban demands believed the shift to democracy would bring the expansion of their access to housing, urban amenities, and basic public services such as transportation. Bryan McCann's (2014) *Hard Times in the Marvelous City* details this process, with favela dwellers organizing to petition for improvement in small increments, one water tap or electrical connection at a time, and achieving it. Again, protesting for small infrastructure improvements was the only recourse possible at that time since labor rights, police repression, and land rights, the rods of our theoretical tripod, were stiffened during the military dictatorship.

Unlike housing and day-to-day life, which could be improved by individual effort, public transportation depends entirely on the state and was even in worse condition. In Rio de Janeiro in 1975, the number of passengers in the Central do Brasil, the railway system that connected the periphery of the metropolitan region with downtown, had increased almost 50 percent in the past decade, but the investments in the system were minimal. There had been no new railcars since 1964, and half of them were undergoing maintenance in 1975. Thus, around 560,000 workers and 140,000 people were suffering every day to commute to work in the metropolitan region of Rio de Janeiro. In the metropolitan region of São Paulo, a local newspaper estimated that almost 15,000 workers were not able to attend to their industrial jobs every month due to transportation problems (Moisés and Alier 1978, 24–25).

Concurrently with the growth of metropolitan regions through peripheral neighborhoods, the worsening conditions of public transportation annoyed the population. In July of 1974 many upheavals against the precariousness of urban transportation systems broke out in in the main metropolitan region of the country, namely, São Paulo, Rio de Janeiro, and Brasília (Moisés and Alier 1978, 13–63).

The revolts ended in depredations of train stations and buses, exposing the political fragility caused by the lack of more efficient planning for the metropolitan agglomeration. The explosive concentration of poverty in the metropolitan regions had drawn the attention of Ernesto Geisel's government (1974–1979), which finally created a commission to deal with the administrative problem of the metropolitan conurbations, just one month before the public transportation upheavals. The Comissão Nacional de Regiões Metropolitanas e Política Urbana was created in June of 1974 (Decree no. 74.156), and next year the SERFHAU was extinguished (Decree no. 76.149, August 22, 1975; Reis 1996, 46).

The measures clearly indicated the recognition of the military government regarding the role of the metropolitan regions in the political process, signaling a shift in power of the urban planning system from the Ministry of the Interior and its effort toward decentralization. Back to our theoretical tripod, all three rods, landownership, labor rights, and police repression, were strong pillars of the military movement. With the transportation knot failing further in the 1970s, the solution was to invest all efforts in planning efficiencies in an attempt to improve life conditions and hold on to eroding popular support. The aim was to achieve greater efficiency to control (note that we deliberately use the word *control*, not *eradicate* or *ameliorate*) urban poverty. When that failed, small concessions were made to labor demands and political freedoms.

THE COUP, THE FRAGMENTATION OF THE LEFT, AND URBAN AND COUNTRYSIDE GUERRILLAS

A great discussion on rural workers organization in the 1960s can be found in Manuel Correa de Andrade's (1963, 241–55) book that describes Brazilian peasant leagues' formation in 1955 and the role of lawyer Francisco Julião in the fight for rural workers' right to property. If in the city the option available for organized workers was the formation of a union structure parallel to the state, in the countryside the absence of regulation in workers' rights created an independent movement that threatened the forms of external market accumulation. Conflicts over landownership in Brazil follow the country's economic and social history. The social organization of rural workers happened late compared to the organization of urban workers. The Confederação Nacional dos Trabalhadores na Agricultura (National Confederation of Agricultural Workers) was organized in 1963 and represented Brazilian rural unionism, according to Gohn (1995, 103). Like their urban counterparts, rural workers' organizations were persecuted by the military after the 1964 coup. In 1975 the church supported rural workers through the Pastoral da Terra, which reached mainly the south of the country. A decade later, in 1985, Movimento dos Trabalhadores sem Terra (Landless Workers' Movement) became the most successful movement for land reform in Brazilian history.

The onslaught on social movements triggered a political reaction to the authoritarian state led by communist party dissents. The first break in the Partido Comunista Brasileiro (Brazilian Communist Party) had happened in 1962, resulting in the formation of the Partido Comunista do Brasil (Communist Party of Brazil). The members who were dissatisfied with the political orientation of the party general secretary, Luís Carlos Prestes, had created a new party. A new division within the Brazilian Communist Party would occur again in 1967, during the military regime, triggered by the expulsion of members such as Carlos Marighella and other comrades who advocated political resistance through armed struggle. The leaders expelled from the Brazilian Communist Party created left-wing underground organizations such as the Ação Libertadora Nacional (National Liberation Action), the Movimento Revolucionário 8 de Outubro (Revolutionary Movement October 8), and the

Comando de Libertação Nacional (National Liberation Command). These organizations acted on the front line of armed resistance to the civilian-military regime installed by the coup of 1964. The urban guerrilla promoted several actions, but the one with the most significant repercussions was the kidnapping of the United States ambassador Charles Burke Elbrick, who was released in exchange for the freedom of fifteen political prisoners. The Aliança Nacional Libertadora and the Movimento Revolucionário 8 de Outubro organized the kidnapping in Rio de Janeiro on September 4, 1969. The operation reached its immediate objectives, and only three days later the fifteen political prisoners landed in Mexico City. According to some analysts, the kidnapping triggered more violence and terrorism by the state, intensifying political persecution and torture (Resende 2019, 121–29). In the rural area, the Communist Party of Brazil led guerrilla movements in the Ribeira Valley (south of the State of São Paulo) and in Araguaia (Amazon region). Between 1972 and 1974 the army hunted and executed most guerrilla members. In 1971 the former congressman Rubens Paiva was arrested and killed by the state. In 1975 Vladimir Herzog, journalist and director of TV Cultura, was murdered in a location of the repressive state apparatus in São Paulo. Herzog's death sparked a movement calling for the end of torture and terrorism promoted by the state. The following year, 1976, would witness the formation of the Movement for Amnesty.

Two of the military regime's main instruments of political control were removing political leaders working in the country and creating of restrictions for political parties' functioning, which led to an artificial bipartisanship. In 1966 the political parties were forced to reorganize into two blocs: the National Renovating Alliance and the consenting opposition party, the Brazilian Democratic Movement. The bipartisan system ran until 1979, and in 1980 the military regime allowed the registration of new political parties.

Brazilian democracy since the 1960s has been strongly tied to the land issue. Urban reform and land reform were debated in the government of João Goulart, which established some restrictions on private property rights in the countryside and urban areas. Landownership is a central obstacle to expanding the supply of public housing estates in large cities or stopping the rural exodus, increasing access for family-based farming in the countryside. The Brazilian constitutions of 1946 and 1967 already had the language of "social function of property."[17] Eminent domain and expropriation have always been a prerogative of the state, along with the social function as a limitation of property rights. The key obstacle to implementing social limits on property has been the manner in which the state compensate previous owners in cases of expropriation. Conservative governments pushed for expropriations to be paid in cash, severely limiting the ability of the state to reconfigure landownership. The 1988 Federal Constitution included payment with government bonds and certificates of debt as part of the urban policy tools to fulfill the social function of property, inaugurating a new cycle of relations between the urban system and the political process.

5

CITIES DURING THE LOST DECADE OF THE 1980S

At the beginning of the 1980s, social movements expanded to become the critical social forces that put pressure on changing the Brazilian political system with a new urban and rural territorial pact announced by redemocratization debates and solidified by the new constitution ratified on October 5, 1988. Social movements in the 1980s had as main objectives the end of the authoritarian regime and lifting restrictions on political and ideological freedoms to accelerate the movement toward a limited democracy announced under the government of Ernesto Geisel (1974–1979).

Since the 1980s, the dispute over land access has been the central social pressure for restructuring the territorial pact. The main movements still active in Brazilian society appeared in the political arena of democratization in the late 1980s, when the 1987 constituent process opened democratic channels of participation. The Landless Workers' Movement (Movimento dos Trabalhadores sem Terra, MST) and the National Movement for Urban Reform (MNRU) led a wave of invasions of unproductive land and empty buildings in city centers are the symptoms of political wear and tear of the economic model, the concentration of property, and overexploitation of workers.

The crisis was triggered by the foreign debt conundrum of 1981–1982 that increased urban poverty in the periphery of the cities and threatened even the middle-class checkbook. The combination of stagnant wages and yearly inflation at 100-percent levels generated strong labor demands by unions that were finally breaking away from the control of the military regime. The social movements were important protagonists of the nascent democracy established after the fall of the military government. Meanwhile, the poorest urban workers organized to protest against the rise of cost of living and the precarious services in their neighborhoods. The middle class that had been so happy during the 1970s was hit hard by the economic crisis of the 1980s and also took to the streets. To complete the framework of the 1980s, urban growth was followed by stalling infrastructure investment amid the economic crisis. In 1990 Fernando Collor de Mello froze bank deposits for the whole country and still was not able to control inflation. In the end it was his disastrous economic policies that eroded his middle-class support, not so much the exposition of corruption schemes. Make no mistake, the Brazilian Congress pulled the plug and impeached him to save themselves and avoid deeper scrutiny into campaign finance, the main cause of the impeachment process, as we will discuss in the next chapter.

Using our theoretical tripod to synthesize those issues, we argue that the 1980s saw a gradual decrease in police repression in urban conflicts for those on the basis of the social pyramid, but slightly higher crime numbers contributed to a sensation of unsafety for the wealthy, perhaps associated with less repression but certainly associated with the press's being able to report more freely. The 1980s were also a time of gradual labor gains as a result of more union activity and strikes (some still brutally repressed) as well as the rise of the charismatic leader Luiz Inácio Lula da Silva. In terms of land rights, the 1980s witnessed the consolidation of occupancy rights with less forced relocations and gradual improvements in water and electricity connections.

Politics and protests aside, the late 1980s in Brazil held a basic contradiction that produced the contemporary complexity of its metropolitan regions: the necessity of urban investments in the poorest and populated neighborhoods to support the political stability in the transition to the earlier democracy and the profits of the real estate sector focused on the luxury market to support the financial system, squeezing the middle class, which had previously benefited from inequality and now saw the rich getting further away and the poor getting closer.

All those gains for the working class contributed to stagnant wages and job growth for the middle class and help explain the latter's dissatisfaction with Collor de Mello's economic policies, taking to the streets and ultimately forcing his resignation in December of 1992. As we discuss in chapter 6 and the conclusion, those contradictions have not been fixed and still haunt the now-three-decade-old Brazilian "democracy."[1]

THE RISE OF BRAZILIAN URBAN POLICY AND THE TRANSITION TOWARD DEMOCRACY

Despite the period of planning that yielded positive results in Brazilian cities, the housing and urban policies led by the BNH-SERFHAU system were insufficient to face the metropolitan crisis of the 1980s. The BNH produced around 4.5 million units nationwide in twenty-two years of operation, and SERFHAU elaborated more than six hundred master plans for as many cities, until its closure in 1975. However, despite the large number of plans, the BNH-SERFHAU system was heavily criticized for being a political device of the authoritarian regime.

The housing complexes were decried due to the substandard quality of the units, the lack of integration with the city fabric, and the financial system skewed toward the middle classes. These three shortcomings were highlighted by the majority of critics and fully documented by Gabriel Bolaffi (1977) in the late 1970s. SERFHAU's master plans were considered ineffective and authoritarian, leading to the deactivation of the institution in 1975. The BNH would survive until 1986, one year after the end of the dictatorship.

More than twenty years after the closing of SERFHAU, Simone Vizioli (1998) published a rigorous analysis of its successes and failures, focusing more, at that time, on the successes. Another twenty years have passed and new works have revised the accomplishments of the BNH and the SERFHAU in different aspects, drawing new layers to the history of planning in the country. The interest of some authors lies in the integration of federal, state, and municipal levels (a contemporary problem) to ensure that local investments correspond to regional and national development goals, improving rationality in all levels of planning. Another aspect pointed out by Vizioli (1998), Feldman (2005), Ferreira (2007), and Koury (2013b, 2014b) was the interdisciplinary nature of the plans developed by SERFHAU, aggregating many areas of knowledge within the planning board and resulting in broad diagnostics for successful interventions. These authors also remembered the existence of a municipal information system responsible for collecting and systematizing information for urban and local planning during the authoritarian period.

SERFHAU shuttered concurrently with the creation of specific institutions to deal with metropolitan growth. The Comissão Nacional de Regiões Metropolitanas e Política Urbana was created in June of 1974, one year before the closing of SERFHAU, and signaled a power shift toward urban conurbations and the necessity of specific legislation. The urban policies formulated henceforth were an attempt to tackle the metropolitan complexity. We should remember that before 1988 municipalities had much less autonomy. In 1977 the National Commission of Urban Policy released a proposal that would limit the rights of private urban landownership.[2] Later, in 1979, the Comissão Nacional de Regiões Metropolitanas e Política Urbana became Conselho Nacional de Desenvolvimento Urbano (Decreto no. 83.355, April 20, 1979). This group overhauled the 1977 proposal of urban law and submitted Bill 775/83 to Congress in 1983. The final version of this law included further limits of private urban landownership and instruments for urban renewal, such as the extension of the right to build over the basic floor area ratio (FAR) in order to finance public investments and the obligation of urban properties to be used according to the zoning law for the rational development of the city. Those measures tried to control real estate market speculation and incentivize development in certain areas of the major cities. Ricardo Lira (1983) explained at the time that the new proposal adjusted the Brazilian law to the urban reality through specific instruments (solo criado, parcelamento, edificação ou utilização compulsórios, direito de preempção e direito de superfície).[3] Those instruments basically detached the right to develop from landownership, giving cities the legal tools for guiding developments toward the common good.

The proposal did not pass but became the basis of the debates in the Subcommittee of Urban Issue and Transportation during the Brazilian Constituent Assembly (1987–1988). The subcommittee was of great importance in proposing housing and urban policy to be inscribed into the new Brazilian constitution and to bring to the table social movements that were already well organized at that time.

The resulting Federal Constitution of 1988 stated the urban policy in article 30, paragraph 8, which attributed to municipalities the responsibility for territorial planning, and through articles 182 and 183, which defined the goals of urban policy and the limits of property rights. Article 182 made master plans mandatory for cities with more than twenty thousand inhabitants. Later, in 2001, the Estatuto da Cidade (Federal Law 10.257) determined that master plans must be developed by participatory process and revised every ten years. The 1988 Federal Constitution also guaranteed the municipalities the right to compulsory construction or progressive taxation when the urban development rules defined by the master plans were not fulfilled. Enhanced municipal ability to purchase land—a historical claim of Brazilian architects engaged with the urban reform since 1963—was included in the constitution, pending regulatory laws. In the remaining years of the twentieth century, the Brazilian Congress did not pass a bill facilitating the acquisition of land by municipalities. As hypothesized by our theoretical tripod, landownership is a tenet of Brazilian inequality, and any attempt to change that was historically fiercely fought by the patrimonial elite.

The Estatuto da Cidade (Law 10.257) that regulated those instruments was approved only on July 10, 2001, more than twelve years after the 1988 Constitution. As we elaborate in the following chapter, the Estatuto da Cidade is a legal framework debated for at least four decades that defined the guidelines for urban policies based on a set of rights such as the right to sustainable cities, understood as the rights to urban land, housing, environmental sanitation, urban infrastructure, transportation and public services, and work and leisure for present and future generations. Following chapters of the statute defined the urban policy's tools, including the master plan, the participatory process, and the arrangement by public and private investments to fulfill the urban development.

The World Bank report "Urban Policy and Economic Development: An Agenda for the 1990s," proposed cooperation between public and private sectors as key to facing urban poverty and lack of public resources. The cooperation was defined by increasing permissions for real estate development to produce profits to be shared with the public sector to finance infrastructure, public services, and housing supply for low-income inhabitants. The World Bank report also pointed out critically the lack of local participation in the urban polices enacted in the 1970s and 1980s (Cohen 1991, 4).

Although it seemed a successful formula for urban policies, the inability of public-private partnerships in improving urban equality would be criticized by several authors in the following decade (Martins 2006). The Estatuto da Cidade tried to engage the neoliberal agenda and the real estate market by controlling urban development toward common good. It was broadly based on "the right to the city," which was thought to rein in urban surplus value and transfer back to society the profits from urban renewal operations led by the private sector.

Participatory processes would play an important role to guarantee the democratic management of urban development, counterweighting the power of real estate speculation and technocratic interventions. Through participatory processes, the urban policy agenda in Brazil tried to combine the neoliberal agenda stated by the World Bank report in 1990 with the community-based initiatives of the 1960s. In summary, participatory processes did little to change structural inequalities, as diagrammed by our theoretical tripod, but they do illuminate one possibility of improvement via transparency and debate around public funding priorities. If institutionalized and supported by all levels of government, participatory processes would have been the least painful way of, if not dismantling, at least reducing the efficacy of the inequality tripod structure (discussed more in chapter 6).

In order to honor the political commitments expressed in the recently approved federal legislation, the Ministry of Cities was created by President Lula da Silva in 2003. The Ministry of Cities was intended as an opportunity to deploy the progressive agenda of the Estatuto da Cidade regarding housing and urban planning to a national scale, and it did just that between 2003 and 2005. After 2005 the Ministry of Cities was controlled by center and right-wing political parties associated with the construction industry, and the progressive urban agenda was abandoned in exchange for congressional votes. The full realization of the Estatuto da Cidade remains a great challenge for Brazilian society.

At the beginning of the 1970s the Brazilian population was already concentrated in cities, but only during the following decade would poverty be understood as an urban issue (Santagada 1990). This was no doubt worsened by the economic recession of the 1980s and by the inflationary process triggered by the payment of external debts and its high interest rates. The economic hardship contributed to tensions inside the Geisel presidency, which had already announced the transition to democracy to address the political anxiety of those years.

Urban social movements would take prominence in the late 1970s in a different format. They now appeared as a collective and diffuse movement that was not reacting to any specific fact or policy but combined various claims and sectors to protest in many of the largest cities. This is the case of the Movimento de Professores e Outros Profissionais da Área de Educação, Saúde e Outros Serviços Sociais Públicos (movement of teachers and other professionals in the area of education, health and other public social services), Movimento dos Transportes Coletivos (movement of public transport), Movimento de Lutas por Creche em São Paulo e Belo Horizonte (movement of struggles for daycare in São Paulo and Belo Horizonte), Movimento dos Trabalhadores sem Terra (landless workers' movement), and Movimento de Favelas (shantytowns movements) (Gohn 1995, 118–21).

In the following presidential term of João Figueiredo (1979–1985), anxiety was rife among Brazilian people who joined organized social movements producing huge urban upheavals. In 1983 the economic crisis sparked massive protests and waves of violence, such as the depredation of trains and looting of commercial establishments in São Paulo and Rio de Janeiro.

In 1984 congressman Dante de Oliveira proposed an amendment for direct presidential elections that mobilized broad segments of the Brazilian population. The movement was called Diretas Já and gained momentum in the largest state capitals, achieving high visibility. Rallies were organized all over the country, and in São Paulo, the gathering at the Anhangabaú Valley in April of 1984 mobilized more than one million people.

The Dante de Oliveira Amendment received a significant vote in the House of Representatives (298 in favor, 65 against, 3 abstentions, and 113 absences), but not enough to reach two-thirds necessary for its approval (Rossi 1984). The 1985 elections were indirect. The street demonstrations strengthened the democratic transition negotiated by the opposition party, the Movimento Democrático Brasileiro, which elected its candidate, Tancredo Neves, with 70 percent of the votes of the national Congress.

At that moment, cities were a hot political issue, and all levels of power had to address them to achieve public support. Planning and urban improvements played a strategic role, with changing goals and procedures along the democratic transition. Research presented by Eduardo Marques and Renata Bichir (2002) gives us some clues on how the struggle for infrastructure unfolded in São Paulo. The authors show that a significant portion of the investments made by the São Paulo municipal government from 1978 to 1998 were made in the poorest parts of the cities, not the wealthiest ones, as had been suggested by most authors until them. As we stated in the beginning of this chapter, the middle classes perceived those improvements as a threat to their status and their privileges and demanded the end of the military dictatorship that had previously benefited them so much.

Marques and Bichir (2002) systematized the investments made by the municipal urban development department in each region of the city from 1978 to 1998, covering the explosive growth of the periphery along the democratic transition. They found considerable consistency of investments in the eastern periphery, a dense part of the city where the working class was traditionally settled. Those investments occurred during the dictatorship but also during democratic rule, and no significant difference was found between terms of mayors to the left and to the right of the political spectrum. Comparing the distribution of the investments with the socioeconomic division of the city they stated the importance of the poorest region for political support. However, the investments were made under completely different plans and approaches, namely large-scale interventions and top-down planning to the right versus alternative ways based on participatory processes and self-managed organization to the left. Participation and self-management formed the agenda of a younger generation who advocated a new process to produce the city.

FROM ADVOCACY ARCHITECTURE TO THE RIGHT TO THE CITY

The critical review of the national developmentalist cycle of housing and urban planning policy in Brazil was led by a younger generation engaged in the architecture and planning debates through the late 1960s and the 1970s. Their criticism triggered a resistance to the authoritarian way of producing the city, proposing instead new patterns of construction that could be managed and carried out by local inhabitants. Their agenda played a key role in housing and urban policy in Brazil after 1985 and fostered architecture and urban experiments that would become the examples of implementation of the right to the city in Brazilian democratic rule.

The Brazilian experiments were part of several initiatives of housing and community planning that took place in Latin America mainly in the 1960s and 1970s. In Latin America in general and Brazil in particular the urban population was increasing much faster than the economy and the result was the growth of informality in labor as well as in the housing market. Thus, slums and substandard housing became a common problem in the region.

The Cuban revolution in 1959 threatened the United States' hegemony in the region, and as a consequence housing and urban growth became a sensitive social issue during the Cold War period. In 1960 the International Agency for Development was created to support housing supply in Colombia, Venezuela, Peru, Chile, and Mexico. The agency brought together employers to form savings and loans associations with the intention of financing low-cost housing (OAS 1967, 187–98). In this period a number of North American and British scholars started to study urban poverty, shanty towns and slums in Latin America. Antony Leeds in Brazil and John Turner in Peru became the most important references of that time. They had open minds for new theoretical approaches to urban poverty in Latin America, pointing out variations of spatial arrangements for housing the urban poor based on their sensitivity toward local communities.

On the other side of the Cold War the industrialization and mass production of housing estates were disseminated in Latin America by the Soviet Union and its heavy system of precast panels. Two factories were donated by the Soviet Union, one to Cuba after Hurricane Flora in 1963 and a second to Chile after an earthquake in 1971 (Alonso and Palmarola Sagredo 2013). However, the prefab systems were highly debated and criticized, with most experts preferring local management and self-help construction as the natural solution for the urbanization challenges in Latin America. Nevertheless, the design experiments in housing applied in Latin America were complex, with several cases using a mix of industrialized and self-help techniques expecting to achieve better results. One remarkable case is the Proyecto Experimental de Vivienda ("experimental housing project"), a social housing complex built in Lima, Peru, in the early 1970s that had "several pilot projects that ranged from contractor-built houses (Pilot Plan 1) to self-built ones (Pilot Plan 3)" (Carranza and Lara 2014; Gyger 2019). Cuba also applied a mixed system combining community development and self-help methods with a wide range of mass production systems (Segre 1991).

In the same way, Uruguay developed an important social experiment engaging the communities in the construction process using prefabrication combined with traditional systems. The mutual aid housing cooperatives were promoted under the legal frame of the Ley de Vivienda and the leadership of the architect Ildefonso Aroztegui of the Dirección Nacional de Vivienda from 1969 to 1972. The experiment of housing estates produced under this mutual system in Uruguay reached great visibility in Brazil. Architects such as Hector Vigliecca and Juan Villà had worked there and would later move to Brazil to become influential in social housing design. Architects from Brazil also visited the experiments and brought inspiration to propose new ways of integrating technical innovation in the social system to produce housing estates in Brazil (Craciun et al. 2014, 162–73).

Despite not being under the same demographic urban pressure as its Latin American counterparts, Portugal developed an innovative experiment in the urban community after its return to democracy in 1974, which had great visibility in Brazil. The Portuguese planning program after 1974 was led by architect Nuno Portas, state secretary of housing. The Serviço Ambulatório de Apoio Local was deployed after more than forty years of dictatorship. This program polarized urban movements toward housing but in reality was an experiment in reorganizing the relationship between the state and civil society through local power (Portas 1986).

The Portuguese experiment had particularly fit the Brazilian transition toward democracy. Some points, such as the participatory process included in housing design, technical advice, and direct financial aid to local communities, were soon applied in Brazilian housing experiments in the 1980s. All these experiments brought important solutions for Brazil's gigantic urban policy challenges after the dictatorship. The exiled Brazilian architects had come back to the country after the amnesty law (6.683) of August 1979. Foreign architects also came to Brazil, exiled by dictatorship in their home countries. This Latin American mobility improved the exchange of housing experiments and technologies in these years of a great push for social justice.

Advocacy architecture and planning had identified a possible path toward the new generation's utopia of a democratic future.

The programmatic basis of advocacy architecture in the São Paulo was made by a group called Arquitetura Nova, with members Flavio Império, Rodrigo Lefèvre and Sérgio Ferro, and can be summarized in three texts: "Proposal for the Debate: Possibilities of Architecture" by Sérgio Ferro and Rodrigo Lefèvre in 1963; "New Architecture" by Sérgio Ferro in 1967; and "The Building Site and the Design" by Sérgio Ferro in 1979.

In the first text the authors conceptualized the "poetic of poverty" as the "least useful, least constructive and least didactic," the minimum needs for establishing a new poetic on the basis of the historical reality of peripheral capitalism. Simple and inexpensive materials used with great creativity were considered a path for a peripheral housing production in the country. The second text, "New Architecture," was published after the military coup and clearly explained the radical criticism of Sérgio Ferro toward the mainstream of modern architecture in Brazil. For Ferro and his colleagues, the military coup brought to evidence the failures of the entire cycle of modernization and industrialization of the country. Later, in 1976, the text "The building Site and the Design" ("O Canteiro e o Desenho") became influential for its Marxist critic of work fragmentation in the construction site managed by modern architectural designs.

In 1967 and 1968 Ferro and Lefèvre were teaching at the Faculty of Architecture of Santos, the port city fifty miles from São Paulo. The school advocated an empirical approach toward the reality of underdevelopment such as slums and informal settlements. The pedagogy aimed to introduce students to the urban reality in which they would later work. With this framework, Rodrigo Lefèvre and Sérgio Ferro led a survey in a large slum in Cubatão. They realized most of the units were self-built and owned by their inhabitants. This survey exposed how the city has been produced in the fringes of the industrial capital of São Paulo. The survey was useful for a critical approach in economic theory also. Francisco de Oliveira's (1972) criticism of the Economic Commission for Latin America and Caribbean theories was based on this survey. According to Oliveira, underdevelopment worked very well with the Brazilian unequal pattern of capitalism, which would never really include the backward sectors in the modern economy, thus preventing the rise of a democracy based on a large middle class. The lesson was deeply transformative and inaugurated the critical approach of modernization upon which the democratic rule would be established in the 1980s (Oliveira 2003, 130). According to our theoretical tripod, low wages and lack of property rights are fundamental tenets of Brazilian capitalism, and these can only work with enough police repression to keep the poor away and some cheap transportation to bring them to and from work.

Advocacy architecture would deal with the reality of the peripheral urban growth by improving self-managed organization of building through didactic architectural designs. For Lefèvre and Ferro, architecture is an information system easily appropriated by local inhabitants with local supply—simple materials found in local hardware stores—and by self-production. The "poetics of economy" were basically that: construction with cheap materials such as cinder blocks, development of alternative technologies such as structural vaults, and recognition of the work process on the building site through didactic architectural design. Visible systems of electrical and plumbing conduits, walls left uncovered, and constructive system of domes are not valuable for their isolated characteristics but rather as a building site pedagogy. Instead of focusing on design or technology, they proposed an architecture focused on the inhabitants engaged in the construction of their homes, taking advantage of the building site to propose an entire urban pedagogy for the inclusion of droves of unskilled workers in the São Paulo urban economy (Koury 2003).

Rodrigo Lefèvre (1981) later devised a building site school inspired by Paulo Freire's pedagogy (Marques and Koury 2021). For Lefèvre, as for Paulo Freire, political awareness would trigger major transformations. In this case the main goal was to integrate the migrants from all over the country who were attracted by São Paulo's economic strength in the urban economy. According to Lefèvre (1981, 3), up to 3.6 million migrants arrived in the city between 1970 and 1980, and they did not find shelter or jobs. The proposal was entitled "The Model of Production in a Time of Transition" and would start by dividing the migrants in groups of up to two thousand people who were distributed in temporary shelters provided by the state. In the temporary shelters they would design and build a community center with the technical advice of architects. Collective activities such as training and debating priorities would be hosted in this new structure. After the community center the houses and other buildings would also be produced by the group. The experience of a community building their own neighborhood, led by an architect's technical advice, would train and qualify them for work in civil construction but would also mobilize these social agents and create a political force during the transition to democratic rule. Rodrigo Lefèvre was an important influence for the next generation, which would propose an alternative path for housing and urban policy in the late 1980s based on participatory democracy and urban social movements.

TECHNICAL ADVISORY FOR PERIPHERAL GROWTH

In the early 1980s, concurrent with the democratic revival, several international experiments including housing and public policies were publicized in Brazil. The creation of the Housing Laboratory at Escola de Belas Artes in São Paulo represented a period of high hopes in the 1980s that fostered Lefèvre's and Ferro's experiments, conceived years before in the School of Architecture at Santos. The building site neighborhood school based on the pedagogic theory of Paulo Freire was implemented, and students started spreading technical expertise to social movements in São Paulo. The architects graduated from Belas Artes became community leaders, providing technical advice and developing new technologies to improve the building stock in the fringes of the city (Arantes 2002; Ronconi 2008; Dualibi 2013).

The first experiment of the Housing Laboratory at Escola de Belas Artes in São Paulo took place in Vila Maria in 1982. The tenements dwellers were convinced by engineer Guilherme Coelho to develop a communitarian proposal. Coelho had recently arrived from Uruguay, where he had worked under the cooperative housing movement. Led by him, the Vila Maria Movement developed a participatory design and struggled with the city government for a plot in the neighborhood in which to build a new housing estate. For Nabil Bonduki, a pioneer activist of this generation, the Uruguayan cooperative movements and the Vila Maria experiment inaugurated a new school of thought on housing, one linked with community management (Bonduki 1992, 35–36). Bonduki also highlights the growth of organized movements of dwellers taking place in the south part of the city where they stated a housing policy agenda based on communitarian organization. The dwellers' movement was very confident and hoped to deliver the proposal of a communitarian housing estate to the mayor, but unfortunately they were not even received. It would take a few years for Luisa Erundina to be elected, in 1989, and the community plans to be embraced by the municipality.

The Grajau Community was another housing movement advised by the Belas Artes Housing Laboratory. This group produced eighty-two houses under the community building process and built their own factory to produce cinder blocks. The community had struggled first for the land and later for financial aid to buy building materials. The members were proud of their self-management and of their contribution in the housing process. They decided the minimum standard to be financed by the city government: two rooms with a bath covered by concrete slab and no coating. The technical advice debated the architectural design, and the inhabitants developed a participatory design method that achieved great symbolic power as a strategy of democratic struggle (Bonduki 1992, 97–102; Dualibi 2013, 63–5).

In 1984 the technological innovation in the community production system was improved when Juan Villà and Nabil Bonduki—professors in charge of the Belas Artes Housing Laboratory—visited the Uruguayan cooperative movement. Villà had introduced the reinforced ceramic panels developed by engineer Eladio Dieste for the cooperative movement, but in São Paulo he substituted the ceramic proposed in Uruguay for hollow bricks that were common in Brazilian construction. The change increased the structural thickness and allowed larger panels (hollow bricks are much lighter), prompting a period of technological innovation that was further accelerated when Villà moved from Belas Artes to Unicamp—State University of Campinas—which had better support and research conditions. In 1987 they launched the first building prototype made with hollow brick panels and the next year a two-story design was released. Villà continued improving his experiments with a precast system of hollow bricks, achieving better performance to build longer spans to hold community equipment in the early 1990s (Dualibi 2013, 70–91).

These experiences based on technical advice and peripheral urban movements became a municipal housing program in the São Paulo Municipal Secretary of Housing during the administration of mayor Luiza Erundina (1989–1992). The proposals consolidated an alternative agenda for the housing policy led by Ermínia Maricato in the Housing and Urban Development department and Nabil Bonduki in the Popular Housing department.

The new policy aimed at occupying urban voids to integrate the poor into the city fabric instead of fostering peripheral growth. It meant to guarantee housing estates connected to urban amenities, public transportation, and the commerce of the city. Besides the direct benefits to general life, this new policy helped to connect workers to job locations, avoiding long commutes. As hypothesized by our theoretical tripod, using empty lots in the city center for housing the poor destabilizes the inequality structure by breaking one rod (landownership) and making the transportation knot unnecessary.

The densification of São Paulo was an important issue for the housing policy and was highly debated in the São Paulo master plan of the same period. The Planning Municipal Authority, led by Paul Singer and directed by Raquel Rolnik, made a rigorous diagnostic of the city, determining all land available for public housing. The survey reported 144 million square meters of urban voids, in which 60 million were fully served by infrastructure. According to the report, if properly developed, those voids could house 7.5 million people. The urban voids' occupancy with public housing and the densification policy of the São Paulo master plan proposal of 1991 would allow the city to grow without great investments in infrastructure (Rolnik et al. 1990).

Inserting new housing estates in the urban fabric at that time also meant a change in design, avoiding urban segregation and promoting a continuity of morphology between the neighboring city and the housing estates. Two- or three-story buildings organized around open spaces became more prominent, in substitution of modernist solutions of large vertical blocks considered hostile to the social life of the neighborhood.

Another focus of the new democratic housing policy of São Paulo between 1989 and 1992 were the informal settlements. A significant portion of urban workers lived in informal settlements, and it was impossible to build new housing estates to meet all the demand. Thus, it was of great importance to improve the urban conditions in the informal settlements. The first step to do so was to guarantee the inhabitants' right to stay and eventually legalize ownership. This was also an important issue in the debates around the master plan of São Paulo. The Special Zone of Social Interest (ZEIS) was proposed to improve the conditions in the precarious settlements. The ZEIS, first proposed in Recife, is a planning tool to include informal settlements in the formal city, allowing public investments and avoiding the eviction of their inhabitants (Demplan 1991, 23) One of the obstacles for improving the infrastructure of favelas is the fact that the buildings and lots do not follow municipal codes. The assignment of a ZEIS in the city's zoning map (an attribution of city council) allows building codes in the area to be more flexible, making legalization and infrastructure improvement possible while at the same time diminishing the possibility of forced relocation.

Sewage and drainage systems were the main public works implemented in these areas, and they were designed together with the paving system, green areas, and channeled creeks. To maintain the minimum health conditions in some of the densest favelas, the urbanization was combined with vertical housing blocks to free areas for the necessary infrastructure (Andrade et al. 1993; Bonduki 2000, Lara 2010).

The urbanization works in the housing program were made by a low-cost system based on precast light components produced in a municipal factory. Mayumi Souza Lima in São Paulo and João Filgueiras Lima in Salvador led factories that produced a variety of systems for urban development for each municipality (Marques 2020).

In a broad sense, the new policy aimed to overcome the authoritarian culture in housing policies and to break the stronghold of construction companies and the financial system over housing policy. Most of the housing estates built in Erundina's period were directly funded by the city via neighborhood associations. According to critics of the former period, the direct funding would improve housing quality and reduce costs. No less important is the fact that direct funding would strengthen popular participation in processes of budget management and design decisions—fundamental elements of participatory democracy and design (Andrade et al. 1993; Bonduki 2000; Lara 2010).

The housing policy deployed in São Paulo between 1989 and 1992 became the left-wing housing policy agenda in Brazil thereafter. It was produced in response to urban poverty concentration that also triggered the organization of urban social movements, mainly the urban reform movement and the housing struggle movement. Since the 1990s the illegal occupancy of urban voids and empty buildings in Brazil has become more than an isolated solution for housing; it was considered a legitimate manifestation of the urban poor in the struggle for the right to the city.

At the end of 1980s and beginning of 1990s the largest cities in Latin America had the same framework of urban poverty and the São Paulo housing experiment triggered other initiatives based on self-management and technical advisory throughout the region. The Secretaria Latinoamericana de Vivienda Popular, a Latin American network of self-management popular housing organizations, was founded in São Paulo in 1991.[4] The association disseminated mutual aid as a social device against the neoliberal policies which was deployed by conservative governments after the period of the dictatorships.[5]

URBAN REFORM AND THE RIGHT TO THE CITY IN THE EARLY DEMOCRATIC REGIME

Since the late 1970s urban reform has become an important issue for urban social movements, but its institutionalization only happened in 1987 through the first meeting of the Forum Nacional de Reforma Urbana. The forum was triggered by the announcement of the constituent assembly, as the urban social movements were aware of their struggle in the political arena for promoting transformative changes. The forum would lead several planning initiatives thereafter that led to building a significant number of housing estates.

For instance, the challenge of the first democratic governments in São Paulo was to change the unequal pattern of city growth. Land value was the main point of contention at the 1991 master plan proposal. In order to properly address this, the team in charge of the proposal suggested implementating a unified land use coefficient (floor-area ratio, or FAR) in the whole city. According to the City Planning Authority report, in the past, private investments had concentrated in the wealthiest areas because the zoning law of 1972 had defined high densities in these areas. Thus the 1991 zoning proposal cap the right to build at 100 percent of the lot area (FAR = 1) for the entire city. In the densification zones it would be possible to build more than that by purchasing building rights from the municipal government.

The proposed zoning law hoped to be an instrument to raise funds for improving housing conditions for poor residents, for building public housing estates to favela dwellers, and for promoting other social investments needed to achieve an inclusive urban growth in a moment of acute economic crisis. The proposed zoning reinforced the idea of filling up urban voids, allowing the city to grow without large investments in infrastructure. The same formula would lead the next generations of São Paulo master plans until 2014, which had largely expanded the areas for the densification of the city.

One of the most important issues in this time of transition to democracy in Brazil was the participatory process. Guaranteed by chapter 61 of the 1988 Federal Constitution, which had recognized the right of the citizens to propose laws in Brazil, it was called "right to popular initiative." The experiments in the participatory process after the 1988 constitution started with the proposal and approval of municipal budgets. It was first tried in a large city in Porto Alegre, during Olívio Dutra's term (1989–1992), and soon followed by many other municipalities.

Beyond the participatory budget, the role of civil society in the planning system and the decentralization of planning decisions were intensely discussed in the 1991 master plan of São Paulo. Considering the local specificity of the city, the master plan proposed the decentralization of planning decisions. It would be implemented by the second level of municipal government, the neighborhood administrations (*subprefeituras*).

After following the issue of landownership and land valuation throughout this book, the reader will not be surprised to learn that the 1991 master plan and administrative reform were not approved as proposed by the municipal government under Luiza Erudina. Despite the frustration of the proposal being blocked by the city council, the housing experiments were quite successful, reaching two hundred projects and fifty-five thousand families in the city of São Paulo alone (Andrade et al. 1993). The proposal was also successful in the sense that the 1991 master plan would be the basis for the master plan of 2002, led by Jorge Wilheim during Marta Suplicy's term (2001–2004). The elements of urban and housing policy debated in São Paulo between 1989 and 1992 were part of the leftist agenda for housing policy in Brazil.

Using our theoretical tripod to synthesize this chapter, we argue that the return to democracy in the 1980s created the conditions for addressing all the pillars of Brazilian inequality structure. Labor movements became an integral part of the political process with significant gains for the working class. Police repression decreased and human rights gained space in political discourse and the public imaginary. And in terms of landownership, the 1980s witnessed less construction of social housing (strained public budgets) and significant improvements in infrastructure (water and electricity first, sewage and drainage later) and occupancy rights with all levels of government (executive and legislative first, judiciary later), understanding that relocation and demolition only made matters worse. With improvements in all three pillars of our theoretical tripod of inequality, Brazil entered the twenty-first-century by consolidating all those instruments in the Estatuto das Cidades law of 2001. The following year, the presidential election of Lula da Silva would open a whole new chapter in the history of urban plans and public protests in Brazil.

6

CITIES AND PROTESTS IN LULA'S YEARS AND BEYOND

The sixth and last chapter is devoted to the protests of 2013. What makes those so interesting is that there were so many reasons for the rich and for the poor to protest. June of 2013 marks a turning point that reveals the downfall of the neo-developmentalist project implemented during the Lula and Rousseff governments (2003–2014) as a solution to all ills. As we discuss later in this chapter, the scholarly literature is gradually addressing the Lula and Rousseff governments. Issues such as militarization and segregation addressed by Falhlberg and Vicino (2016), leftist neoliberalism as defined by Saad Filho (2013), and the impact of the mega events such as the FIFA World Cup and Summer Olympics as discussed by Ribeiro and Santos Junior (2017) help us frame the protests of 2013 and the dismantling of Brazilian democracy that followed (Harvey et al., 2015). More specifically, as both Lara (2013) and Koury (and Anelli 2019) have written elsewhere and as we have discussed in this book, there were blind spots of the Lula-Rousseff governments: participatory processes, environmental policies, public safety, and urban mobility. All of these are linked to questions of ownership, control, and exploitation of the land, an evil that has afflicted Brazil in different ways since colonial times.

THE RETURN OF LARGE PROTESTS TO BRAZILIAN STREETS IN THE 1980S

There was no shortage of drama in 1980s Brazil. Inflation was rampant, investment at minimal levels, unemployment the highest since the 1950s. Celso Furtado (1992) labeled the 1980s in Latin America *década perdida* ("lost decade"), and Brazil was no exception. The decade also witnessed a strong presence in the streets demanding presidential elections. Diretas Já brought millions to rallies in all big cities but it was not enough to pass the bill in Congress. The first civilian president after 1960 was elected by Congress. Tancredo Neves, an experienced and moderate politician of the opposition, invited his running mate, José Sarney, who was the leader of Partido Democrático Social (PDS), the main party supporting the military dictatorship. Neves would take office on March 15, 1985. On March 14, after attending mass in the Brasília Cathedral, Neves was hospitalized for an emergency surgery for a severe intestinal inflammation. José Sarney attended the inauguration ceremony; the departing general Figueiredo did not. Neves died a month later, and Sarney governed for six years. His government applied several economic shocks to the economy but ultimately failed to curb inflation. The major accomplishment of the late 1980s was the writing of a new constitution.

The 1987–1988 constitutional assembly was the first time urban policy was treated as a constitutional matter and would become an important pillar to fostering an urban planning agenda toward the right of the city as stated by instruments such as ZEIS (Special Zoning for Social Interest) and by federal laws such as the Estatuto das Cidades, both discussed later in this chapter. In terms of urban policy the 1988 constitution had two major innovations: the idea that property must fulfill a social function and the means to exert pressure on landowners.

Other aspects of the 1988 constitution were also influenced by the right to the city. Article 14 inscribed into the constitution the many ways in which the population can directly participate beyond voting. The institutions of plebiscite, referendum, and popular initiative were made constitutional and regulated ten years later. Plebiscite and referendum may be called by the executive and legislative branches, while popular initiatives, as the name implies, come directly from citizens, provided that they collect signatures of 1 percent of the Brazilian electorate. These additions opened space for the participatory processes included in the master plans by the Estatuto da Cidade.

Article 5 established the idea of social function of property. Landownership is guaranteed (it is a capitalist society, no doubt), but ownership rights end where social needs begin. Paragraph 22 in article 5 establishes property as a right, while the following paragraph (23) mandates that property must fulfill

Figure 6.1. Ulisses Guimarães and the 1988 constitution. Agencia Brasil.

its social function. Articles 182 and 183 then detail how the social function of property should be legislated.

Article 6 established social rights such as education, health care, work, social assistance, and protection to those most vulnerable. Housing was included as a social right in 2000, fostering the agenda toward the right to the city.

Article 182 defines that municipalities are the main instance of urban policy legislation and implementation, inscribes the obligation of master plans (*planos diretores*) for cities with more than twenty thousand inhabitants, and establishes the master plan as the main reference for the fulfillment of the social function of property. Article 182 also determines that the public sector has the right to impose penalties against properties not fulfilling their social function (meaning empty or underdeveloped in areas already served by infrastructure) that could range from progressive taxation to mandatory parceling. Article 183 establishes that anyone occupying less than 2,500 square feet (250 square meters) for at least five continuous years should have ownership rights provided that there is no challenge to that occupation and the person owns no other property.

Together those constitutional provisions had the potential to act directly on the structural roots of spatial inequality as hypothesized by our theoretical tripod. The results were at once significant and limited, and as we write these lines the extreme right government of Jair Bolsonaro is proposing all kinds of amendments to scale back and block such provisions.

PROTESTS BRACKETING THE 1980S

In 1989 Brazilians voted for president for the first time in thirty-nine years. The election was polarized between Fernando Collor de Mello, a politician from Alagoas, running as anti-political and modern, and two leftist leaders:, seventy-seven-year-old Leonel Brizola and forty-four-year-old Luiz Inácio Lula da Silva. Brizola had been governor of Rio Grande do Sul in the 1960s, when he was one of the few to articulate a military resistance against the 1964 coup, and was in 1989 governor of Rio de Janeiro.[1] Lula da Silva was a metalworkers' union leader and a charismatic politician who would become the face of the new left in Latin America after his successful years as president (2003–2010).[2] The first round of 1989 voting was won by Collor, with 30.47 percent, followed by Lula da Silva with 17 percent and Brizola with 16 percent. For the second round all the conservative forces aligned behind Collor and the leftist forces behind Lula. The campaign became nasty when the pools indicated that the result was too close to call. Collor used all kinds of tricks to stir fear in the conservative Brazilian electorate, mentioning abortion and socialization of property as if Lula would turn Brazil into Cuba. The final televised debate, heavily edited by Rede Globo, tipped the balance for Collor, who was elected with 53 percent of the vote.

Once in office, Collor opened the economy, lowering importation tariffs, and tried to curb inflation with the strike of a pen. His economic plan, announced one day after taking office, attempted to control inflation by severely diminishing the amount of money in circulation. Bank deposits were sequestered for eighteen months, and Brazilians could only cash a small amount. That measure was extremely unpopular, and after accusations of corruption very close to the president himself were publicized in 1991, Collor suffered an impeachment process and renounced the presidency on December 29,1991.

Bracketing those two dramatic political events were large street protests. At the front end was the Diretas Já movement, discussed briefly in the previous chapter. Between March of 1983 and April of 1984, people took to the streets of every Brazilian city to demand direct voting for president. The Diretas Já movement failed to reach the mandatory two-thirds necessary for its approval in congress, despite huge popular support. Almost three hundred representatives voted for it and only sixty-five against, but 113 did not show up that day, killing the amendment.

The large street protests of the 1990s were the Caras-Pintadas marches of

Figure 6.2. Diretas Já protest, Goiânia, 1983.

1992. On August 13, 1992, President Collor de Mello spoke on national TV to defend himself against corruption charges and called on Brazilian citizens to take to the streets dressed in green and yellow. The result was that hundreds of thousands of students marched on Sunday, August 16, dressed in black and with their faces painted with dark stripes. The media called them Caras-Pintadas, a reference to Hugo Chávez's failed coup of February 4, 1992, in Venezuela and another failed coup in Argentina, in 1987, the first one leftist and the second ultra-right-nationalist.[3] Despite the obvious differences between the Brazilian anti-Collor, anti-corruption movement and its extremist neighbors to the north and south, the label stuck. The Movimento Caras-Pintadas grew throughout 1992, bringing 750,000 people to a night vigil in São Paulo on September 18. On September 29 the chamber of representatives voted 448–38 for opening an impeachment process against Collor de Mello. On December 29 the president resigned, hours before the Senate was expected to confirm his ousting.

Those two protests are very important in the recent history of Brazil, and much as in the protests against Dilma Rousseff's government in 2015, it was the middle class who participated, not the poor. Going back to our theoretical tripod, those on the middle-upper part of the tripod were the ones taking to the streets to demand change. And what was that change about?

In the case of the Diretas Já movement of 1983–1984, there was a clear understanding of the exhaustion of the military rule and its inability to provide the changes that the Brazilian middle class was interested in. The economic miracle of 1972–1977 was long gone, and the new consensus, pushed by Ronald

Reagan and Margaret Thatcher, was not about import substitution and industrialization but about deregulation and globalization. The military and their economic advisers were late to realize that. Tancredo Neves and José Sarney surfed the wave of discontent about the lack of democracy, but their agenda was to decentralize and facilitate local decision-making. They were very much against planning and regulations, alleviating the private sector of charges and responsibilities ruled by the state. The results in urban issues were devastating. The BNH was extinguished in 1986, and metropolitan coordination abandoned to die of political starvation. Local coronéis were empowered again. The case of Collor de Mello in 1992 was even more intriguing. Collor was elected with the votes of the middle class, almost the same people who would take to the streets two years later to demand his impeachment. What had happened? Collor shocked the Brazilian economy with an arrest of saving accounts and a sharp cut of import tariffs. His proposed policies included broad actions of deregulation from media to landownership, which until today is reserved for Brazilian citizens only. The middle class, seeing what untamed capitalism really looks like, cried corruption as a code for "I want my privileges back," and those privileges included high interest rates for their savings accounts. Using Thomas Piketty's elegant formula of understanding inequality as an equation between investment and interest rates, the Brazilian elites have almost always been on the side of high interest rates, not on the side of investment. For most of the twentieth century investment was done by the government.

The mainstream media turned against Collor when they realized that he was much more ambitious and careless then they expected and that he was not willing to negotiate with local political lords as had been the tradition before him. As a result, he suffered a restless and ruthless negative campaign in the media, with large numbers of young people taking to the streets to demand his impeachment. Ironically, the real charge for impeachment was a humble Volkswagen car bought with money left over from campaign donations, undeclared.

Meanwhile, the city of Rio de Janeiro hosted the United Nations Conference on Environment and Development, popularly known as Rio 92. Representatives of a total of 172 countries, 108 heads of state, and 2,400 NGOs gathered in Rio on June 3–14, 1992. Many improvements were made to receive the UN conference, including an elevated expressway from the south beaches to the international airport, Linha Vermelha.

To provide security for the twenty thousand conference attendees, the Brazilian government devised a quasi-military operation. Police officers, undercover agents, and military personnel were deployed to surveil and control the southern parts of Rio. Images of military vehicles stationed at the entry of the favelas crossed the world along with headlines about the dangers of carbon levels and heat trapping in the atmosphere. Social and environmental sustainability challenges were never so close to each other.

As a result, through the mirror of Rio 92, the long struggle of the Brazilian favelas got the attention of world leaders. The following year the Inter-American Development Bank promised US$300 million for a pilot plan called Favela-Bairro, which marked a paradigm shift in how Brazilians dealt with the lack of infrastructure in their notorious favelas.

While nowadays the majority of the favelas in Brazil have access to water and electricity (90 percent of all urban population in 2000, according to Bonduki 2009),[4] only about half have proper sanitation, the large majority have no property title, and the dwellings are mostly substandard (Instituto Brasileiro de Geografia e Estatística 2013; Rolnik and Klink 2011). In addition to all those physical vulnerabilities, their inhabitants endure the social stigma of marginality, though the large majority of them are low-paid unskilled workers who are victims, not perpetrators, of urban violence (Perlman 2010; McCann 2014).

The economic miracle of the 1970s had given the military the confidence to think that economic growth would eventually reach the poor. Meanwhile, inequality kept increasing, exploding in the lost decade of the 1980s. With the return of civilian rule in 1985, the BNH was extinct, with severe loss of institutional memory and managerial capacity (Bonduki 2009).

The void created by the closing of BNH in 1986 was exacerbated by the 1988 constitution, which dictated that housing and urbanization policy was to be made at the municipal level, with no plan for articulating national and local policies and, worse, no dedicated funds for financing it at the local level. Despite all its mistakes and distortions, the BNH was better than no policy at all. But all was not lost. The 1988 constitution also instituted the concept that land should have a social function. The social function of property purports that the well-being of the community is more important than private property rights, and that the use of urban space must be socially just (Fernandes 2007; Macedo 2008; Friendly 2013). Although the social function dictated by the constitution does not have a direct impact on city planning, its principle guided the writing of federal law 10257/2001, known as Estatuto das Cidades.

ESTATUTO DAS CIDADES

Debated in Congress, in academia, and in public seminars throughout the 1990s, the Estatuto das Cidades law serves as a framework for legally dealing with informal settlements. First proposed in 1989, the *estatuto* was signed by President Fernando Henrique Cardoso in 2001, twelve years later. During those years intense debates ensued, with the law celebrated as a significant step forward on urban policy, framing the means by which municipalities can legislate landownership to achieve a better city for all. Abigail Friendly (2013) elaborated on the evolution of the Estatuto from the debates of 1987–1988, while Avritzer (2009) and Fernandes (2007) discuss the relationship of those debates to other political issues of late twentieth-century in Brazil. Today, twenty years after its signing, many academics are not so sure that the impact has been as positive as they envisioned back in 2001, precisely because the same instruments that give cities flexibility and means to make good interventions can be used for maximizing profits in land speculation.

The Estatuto das Cidades established instruments for inducing urban development, land regularization instruments, instruments for democratizing urban management, and instruments for social management of land valuation. The Estatuto das Cidades also defined instruments for inducing urban development including compulsory parceling and compulsory building, progressive taxation, eviction paid with public debt securities, real estate consortium and consortium urban operations, the surface right, the transfer of buildings rights, onerous license of building rights, and preemptive acquisition.

Part of those instruments were already included in the urban policy through 1988 Constitution (article 182). The compulsory parceling and building can be applied when the municipality perceives that certain properties are underdeveloped and are impeding the optimal function of the city. Compulsory parceling has been applied to areas surrounded by urbanization that were sitting empty, waiting for valuation. Compulsory building is rarely applied and usually works in large urban operations where private capital is made available. As Friendly (2013, 172) correctly points out, "the [statute] is not, in fact, legally binding on municipalities. Such tools are at the disposal of the municipalities which are free to decide" if and when to use them.

Preemptive acquisition gives the municipal government priority for purchasing certain plots of land to be used for common good. It is often used to purchase land already occupied or with contested ownership so that the conflict can be resolved. It should be noted, however, that according to the Brazilian constitution, public land cannot be donated, so those operations are fairly complex legally and financially.

Transfer of building rights has been widely used since 2001. It allows the property owner to build somewhere else the square footage originally determined for a certain property to be left, in perpetuity, undeveloped. Historic preservation has been made easier by this instrument, as old buildings are preserved in exchange for building rights transferred elsewhere. It must be said that this strategy of preservation only works in wealthy parts of the city, where the profits from possible developments are tremendous. In areas where land values are already low, there is no incentive to transfer building rights, and many historic structures are left abandoned.

Onerous license of building rights is being tested in São Paulo as we write these lines. The master plan of São Paulo approved in 2014 established that most of the city would have a floor-to-area ratio of 1. In some areas the master plan prioritized for densification, the developer can purchase building rights, paying the municipal government for the license to build more.

Consortium urban operations are special development plans for large areas (entire neighborhoods) in which a pool of developers comes together with the municipality and neighborhoods associations (expected to have real representation of the community) to fund urban interventions. Usually, the developers get building rights in exchange for improvements on infrastructure and public space that would benefit the existing community. Consortium urban operations were widely used for building the infrastructure for the FIFA World Cup (2014) and Rio Olympics (2016), with meager results in terms of improving the life of local citizens (Ribeiro and Santos Junior 2017).

Among land regularization tools regulated by the Estatuto das Cidades is a special zoning category for favelas. First implemented in Recife in the mid-1980s, the ZEIS allows for making municipal postures flexible in informal settlements (approved by city council and the mayor's office, like any zoning change), which in turn overcome legal barriers to legalization and infrastructure. For instance, even when the lots or the streets do not meet minimum dimensions required by law (and they seldom do in the favelas), the city can provide services such as water, electricity, sewage, and garbage collection if such area is zoned as a ZEIS. More than providing services, the ZEIS also ensures some security of tenure for the area's inhabitants, working as official recognition of those communities and making repossession, expulsion, and development impossible without city council approval of zoning change.

After 1988 many cities (mostly large state capitals governed by left-leaning mayors) started programs to improve infrastructure for the poorest areas, but with the exception of Curitiba, no Brazilian city had efficient plans to manage growth (Irazábal 2008; Moore 2007; Lara 2010). Any attempt to curb peripheral expansion using zoning laws, green belts, and incentives to densify where the infrastructure already existed would be rendered futile by relaxed regulations in a neighboring municipality with more traditional relationships between political leaders and greedy developers.

Nonetheless, two experiences from the mid-1990s, the Favela-Bairro in Rio and the participatory budgeting in Porto Alegre and Belo Horizonte, were important testing grounds for new urban policies that comprised innovative urban experiments to integrate formal and informal city and produce a more equal society in Brazil.

INNOVATIVE URBAN EXPERIMENTS

In 1994 Rio de Janeiro would lead the charge with the Favela-Bairro program by recognizing "the social, cultural and political importance of the favelas in the city, and considering these agglomerations as part of the urban structure and seek their integration into the existing official city" (Duarte and Magalhães 2010; Fiori and Brandão 2010; Ribeiro and Santos Junior 2017). The idea that favela residents have a right to the city would become common in almost all interventions thereafter (Friendly 2013).

As we discussed in chapter 3, by 1948 informal settlements housed 7 percent of Rio's population, or 139,000 people. This number would rise to 10 percent in 1960 and 13 percent in 1970. At that point the favelas had become a major issue, and the conservative governments appointed by the military dictatorship would evict 175,000 people from the southern areas of Rio, relocating them to the western outskirts of the metropolis (Valladares 2005; Perlman 2010; McCann 2014). The infamous Cidade de Deus, whose story was made into a movie in 2002, was one of these relocations. Nevertheless, during the lost decade of the 1980s, Rio's favelas would grow even faster, reaching 16 percent of the city's population by 1990 and 19 percent in 2000, breaking the barrier of one million inhabitants in six hundred settlements (Valladares 2005).

It was against this scenario of poverty and social vulnerability that the city hosted the United Nations Conference on Environment and Development in June of 1992—the Rio Summit. Within the conference the conversation was mostly about environmental sustainability, but out on the streets the issue of social sustainability loomed over all, visitors and hosts alike. The Brazilian army was deployed to control the favelas, and soldiers could be seen patrolling the boundaries between the hills (*morros*) and the "asphalt" as the informal and the formal parts of the city are commonly referred to in Brazil.

Coincidence or not, the following year the city would announce a new housing policy, based on integration, accessibility, and improved public space: the Favela-Bairro program. A competition was called in 1994 for ideas on how to intervene in midsize informal settlements, those between 500 and 2,500 households, which housed 600,000 people or 60 percent of Rio's informal settlements (Conde and Magalhães 2004). The idea was that larger favelas like Rocinha or Complexo do Alemão would require more complex master plans, while smaller settlements would not yield as many results. Thirty-two local firms submitted proposals, and fifteen were selected (one for each of fifteen areas prioritized). The first phase of Favela-Bairro had a multi-sectoral integrated approach, in which accessibility and connectivity would be addressed by building roads and public space infrastructure to improve drainage and sewage connections, relocating as few families as possible from risky areas and building new housing for those inside each community. In some cases, the projects contemplated community centers and even commercial facilities when a lack of such was deemed an important factor. Those improvements were supposed to be followed by tenurization and legalization but these have not yet happened in the large majority of the cases (Fiori and Brandão 2010; Fernandes 2007).

The implementation was financed at first by the city and later by a loan from the Inter-American Development Bank. Other funding sources were the Brazilian Federal Credit Union in 1997 (Caixa Econômica Federal) and the European Union and the Brazilian federal government in 1998. In its first format, Favela-Bairro had a total investment amounting to US$300 million, which benefited a half-million people in 146 settlements by improving 500 miles of roads and sidewalks and constructing 160 miles of new sewage connections and 5 million square feet of sports facilities.[5]

But like so many other urban infrastructure projects, Favela-Bairro suffered from political setbacks. The success of its first phase from 1994 to 1997 catapulted Luiz Paulo Conde from planning secretary to the mayor's seat, in defiance of his "mentor" and previous mayor César Maia. Four years later Maia was elected again and slowed down Favela-Bairro significantly, despite the fact that he was the mayor who launched it in 1993. The main problem was that several of the projects initiated by Maia in 1994–1996 were inaugurated by Conde in 1997–2000, and a strong identity was formed between Conde and Favela-Bairro.

INNOVATIVE URBAN INVESTMENT

Large-scale upgrades of informal settlements would have to wait for the second presidential term of Lula da Silva to be resurrected. Between 2005 and 2009 the federal government invested US$200 billion in infrastructure, half of it in sanitation and public space improvement, throughout the country.[6] The PAC Program (Programa de Aceleração do Crescimento, or "accelerated growth program") brought US$2 billion to the city of Rio de Janeiro, six times the original Favela-Bairro budget (Camara 2011). While the first version did not address housing needs of individual residents, larger interventions such as the one financed by the PAC Program at Complexo do Alemão did include housing for hundreds of families relocated inside the same community. The second program was also much better articulated with transportation policies, with the implementation of cable cars and bus corridors integrated with public space and amenities.

The new version of Favela-Bairro, renamed Morar Carioca, came with other important improvements, such as the mandate that construction companies hire 40 percent of their labor force from the community where work is being carried, a strategy that pours money into the local economy and facilitates a dialogue (often tense) between the construction crews and the inhabitants. In parallel with the PAC-financed infrastructure upgrade comes the security strategy, Unidade de Polícia Pacificadora (UPPs, Pacifying Police Units) were implemented in Rio between 2008 and 2013. These were designed to tame the old tradition of confrontation between policemen and favela inhabitants. To make these possible, an initial phase of occupation would expel drug dealers and establish territorial control. Once the community is secured and stabilized, newly trained police officers would engage in a series of initiatives to foster collaboration, partnering with NGOs and religious groups that already had a presence in the favelas. The goal was to break the cycle of police repression, confrontation and mistrust. As analyzed by Falhberg and Vicino (2016), the UPPs worked well in areas with strong presence of NGOs and other service providers, but not at all in more vulnerable areas like Complexo do Alemão. Falhberg and Vicino also highlight the fact that securitization became top priority for the state, dislodging the previous emphasis on infrastructural improvements. As expected, this worked well only in areas that already had infrastructure.

While Rio was improving the infrastructure of their favelas, another novelty was taking root in Brazil, starting with Porto Alegre in 1989 and Belo Horizonte in 1993: the participatory budgeting process. The participatory budgeting process (PB) would become the flagship of the PT (Worker's Party) administrations, especially from 1993 to 2004 (Hunter 2010). It must be said that those institutional processes of participation were never implemented in Rio (Cardoso 2009). The experience in Rio demonstrates that while architectural competitions are surely the best process for achieving design quality, the implementation of such designs fall short if the community is not engaged (Crewe 2001). Most of the scholarship written about Favela-Bairro so far (Duarte and Magalhães 2010; Fiori and Brandão 2010; Soares and Soares 2005) corroborates such shortcomings.

INNOVATIVE URBAN MOBILIZATION

Between 1993 and 2008 the city of Belo Horizonte was governed uninterrupted by mayors from either the PT or its ally at the time, the PSB (Socialist Party). Such continuity allowed the participatory budget experience to evolve and mature, reaching some of its best results. The participatory budget process works with the city allocating public works' funds to be ranked in a series of assemblies attended by the general population (Nylen 2002; Avritzer 2009; Lara 2010). The implementation of the participatory budget has coincided with the strengthening of a municipal agency that specifically deals with favela infrastructure. The Companhia Urbanizadora de Belo Horizonte (URBEL) was created in 1961 to manage city land properties and has therefore engaged the favelas in one way or another for the previous thirty years, mostly promoting relocations.[7] In 1993 the PT administration made URBEL responsible for executing city housing policy and managing all interventions in the favelas. At that time URBEL also inherited a number of well-designed plans that had been developed by the metropolitan autarchy PLAMBEL (1975–1996) but never fully implemented for lack of political will.[8]

In 1994 Belo Horizonte started small interventions based on the idea of right to the city, relying on its own budget. By starting small with a participatory model, Belo Horizonte had time to plan, test, and fine-tune processes before moving to large-scale intervention, which might have been a blessing after all.

Between 1994 and 2004 URBEL elaborated 55 comprehensive plans (PGEs) benefiting 77 favelas and 283,000 inhabitants (Lara 2011). Since the PGE is a prerequisite for any project to be funded by the participatory budget, it is of interest to every community association to request and support the elaboration of a plan for its favela.

A PGE includes a detailed survey of the settlement and the elaboration of a series of thematic GIS maps that detail existing infrastructure, household socioeconomic data, and of course all kinds of problems from open sewage to garbage dumping to drug-dealer-controlled areas. The elaboration of a PGE is the work of an interdisciplinary team of no less than a dozen professionals, including engineers, architects, sociologists, health workers, economists, and social workers. The process involves numerous meetings with community leaders and several assemblies with the area population to make sure that every problem is addressed and the priorities are set properly. The process usually takes a few years from approval to completion. After the PGE is completed and approved by the city (with reviews by URBEL and other related city agencies) it becomes the guiding plan for the area. Any intervention proposed for the PB voting process, as well as projects funded by other sources, should comply with the local PGE.

From 1994 to 2006 R$174 million (US$100 million) from the participatory budget has been allocated to Belo Horizonte's favelas, generating 326 projects, 219 of them concluded as of 2010. The execution of those projects demanded another layer of community involvement, for any construction implies changes in people's routine and sometimes even changes to their house structures. Administrative continuity is therefore a key element in the process, allowing URBEL to manage each of those three hundred projects that often span over many years and different mayors' terms. The positive impact of the participatory budget in the lives of Belorizontinos can be seen when the city plotted all the improvements funded against the areas classified as informal (*vilas e favelas*), with the match being very clear. The large majority of participatory budget works are inside or right at the edges of the favelas.

However, as much as those US$100 million allocated via participatory budget are a welcome novelty in Brazilian public policy, they pale in comparison to the projects funded by a partnership of the city and the federal government between 2006 and 2012. The PAC program has made more than US$200 billion available for infrastructure projects, and the city of Belo Horizonte raised R$580 million (US$340 million) to a favela infrastructure project labeled Vila Viva. There is no doubt that the proximity of Belo Horizonte's mayor, Fernando Pimentel, to Dilma Rousseff (the minister responsible for PAC at the time) was a factor in procuring those funds, but Belo had all the plans well developed from the participatory beginning all the way to the budgeting and bidding phases.

Between 2006 and 2010 Vila Viva built major interventions in the city's largest favelas. At the Serra agglomerate, for instance, an informal settlement of 48,000 inhabitants, the Vila Viva project opened miles of roads and relocated 1,100 families who lived in areas prone to floods or mudslides. From those 1,100 families, 900 decided to stay in the community in apartment buildings constructed near the new roads.

The construction of four-story apartment blocks is the most criticized point of the intervention. As the literature in urban design and defensive planning indicates, the common areas in buildings for low-income populations are prone to conflict, jeopardizing the well-being of the entire complex. Interviews with city officials conducted in 2008 and 2009 indicate that construction companies were resistant to the idea of row houses or more elaborate typologies, and the administration fell for their arguments.

The high point of the intervention is the management of the waterways that now run free, allowing for the creation of a tri-branch park, providing recreation facilities and much-needed green areas in a neighborhood whose density is more than three hundred inhabitants per hectare.

As much as the planning has been well considered and the participatory channels well implemented, the bidding process was the Achilles' heel of Belo Horizonte's favela upgrade. Once URBEL finishes the plans, design and construction are contracted from the lowest bid. If the winning construction company brings a good architect (as was the case of Fernando Maculan at Beco São Vicente, Carlos Teixeira at Parque das 3 Águas, or Horizontes group at Pedreira Prado Lopes—all three award-winning designs) the design quality is high and the results optimal (Lara 2011). But if the construction company brings a mediocre architect (which is unfortunately the case in the majority of Vila Viva interventions) the results are dismal. On several occasions URBEL refused to go along with poorly conceived designs, either forcing the construction company to hire another architect or creating an addendum to existing contracts to hire the architects themselves. This process is costly, prone to delays, and, worse, open to lawsuits from all sides, with no guarantee that the result will be as good as planned.

More worrisome is the report by community associations and local activists that the participatory processes were sidelined once the scale (and mostly the budget) of the interventions were magnified by the PAC financing (Azevedo 2019). What started as excessive ambition under Mayor Fernando Pimentel became an open battle after 2009, given Mayor Marcio Lacerda's inability (to say the least) to deal with social movements (Inez 2016).

Meanwhile, the participatory budget process that was once celebrated all over Brazil was gradually sidelined. The slow death of the PB is made evident by how difficult it has been to find published data on its numbers. If in the first decade of the twenty-first century the cities administered by the PT flashed the participatory budgeting numbers in all party publications (print and online), collecting such information now requires a substantial amount of data-mining.[9] The reason becomes clear when we finally find some data, deep in the city website, which shows declining participation and stagnant (at best) funds. In Belo Horizonte the participatory budget process once mobilized 44,000 people, in 2001, and ten years later that number are below 35,000. Between 1997 and 2008 the participatory budget funded more than 100 projects per year; this number had decreased to 25 in 2015. In terms of funding amounts, the PB, which had R$85 million between 2001 and 2002, was kept practically stable at R$87 million in 2011–2012, while the overall city budget grew 275 percent (from R$2.8 billion to R$7.7 billion). Sixteen years of progressive administration and participatory processes were dismantled for the sake of governability by the same PT that created it all (Wood and Murray 2007; Brasil 247 2012).

Going back to our theoretical tripod, it becomes clear that once it gained control of the federal government, the PT focused its efforts on the labor rod, effectively diminishing wage inequality by pushing for yearly increases of the minimum wage above inflation (Hunter 2010). Meanwhile, the land rod was mostly ignored (no major policy here except the ill-designed Minha Casa Minha Vida, discussed later in this chapter), and police repression actually worsened, both in the favelas with the emphasis on occupation and securitization and on the "asphalt" (as formal parts of city are commonly called in Brazil) with repression of protests and social movements. Worse yet, the same wage increases that fueled consumption (including of course automobiles and motorcycles) and brought down the outrageous Brazilian Gini coefficient, contributed to a real estate inflation that pushed the working class further away from downtown jobs and services, and created a transportation crisis with significant consequences (Lara 2013, 2014). According to Instituto de Pesquisa Econômica Aplicada, average commuting time in 2013 reached fifty minutes each way in São Paulo and Rio, an increase of 20 percent over the previous decade (Krause, Balbim and Linke 2016). The data also show that a wealth increase of only 20 percent allows a reduced commute time.

URBAN CRISES AND THE 2013 SHAKEUP OF BRAZILIAN DEMOCRACY

It is not a coincidence that public transportation was the catalyzer for massive protests that swiped Brazilian streets in June of 2013 (Saad Filho 2013; Anelli and Koury 2019). The FIFA World Cup was scheduled for June and July 2014 and the Confederations Cup, a small tournament that FIFA uses to test the World Cup infrastructure, for one year before. Two weeks before this small but highly visible event, the city of São Paulo enacted a 5 percent raise in the price of bus tickets, from R$3.00 to 3.20. Those twenty cents sparked a first round of protests that was brutally repressed by the police. Both the protests and the repression follow our hypothesis squarely. Another round of protests called days later attracted large crowds of young people. One more week, and the protests had spread to all major cities, the participants numbered in the hundreds of thousands, and the protests were no longer about the twenty cents. The demands now were as diverse as the country and somehow converged around insufficient public services (wanting hospitals and schools with FIFA standards) and a diffuse rally against corruption. When the Confederations Cup started on June 15, the country was on fire and the political system, from all levels and all parties, cornered.

However, before we look into the 2013 protests, we must ask ourselves why the Brazilian media (and some scholarship) characterized the years between 1992 and 2013 as "calm" in contrast to the "turmoil" of 2013–2015. Not that protests did not happen. When president Fernando Henrique Cardoso privatized the mining giant Vale do Rio Doce in 1998, the protests against the sale turned violent and were brutally repressed. In 1999 one hundred thousand

Figure 6.3. Passe Livre protest, June 2013. Agencia Brasil.

people marched against corruption in his government. In 2005 the Revolta da Catraca brought Florianópolis to a halt in another protest against tariff hikes.

What we see clearly now, in hindsight, is that the media constructed for the 1990s and early 2000s a narrative of order and progress to borrow from the Brazilian flag. The usual protests against police repression and transportation costs were labeled as "disturbances," as were the protests against the neoliberal reforms of Cardoso (1994–2002). Meanwhile the middle-class protests of 1984 and 1992 were celebrated over and over as broader, inclusive, and representative of Brazilian society (Saad Filho 2013, 658). Once again, the media (and part of the intelligentsia also) understood Brazilian society as white, middle-class, college-educated residents of central areas, in contrast with marginal dark-skinned people who live on the outskirts and insist of disrupting traffic with their "old grievances about police repression and crowded buses" (Ribeiro and Santos Junior 2017, 914).

One of the most interesting and most intriguing features of the protests of 2013 is that they started as a fight against transportation costs and police repression and evolved into something else. Saad Filho (2013, 658) described how the media bolstered the protests under the pretense of coverage. Fahlberg and Vicino (2016) and Glebbeck and Koonings (2016) analyze the fact that a repressive structure was not only in place but had been strengthened by policy decisions of the first decade of the twenty-first century. And again Fahlberg and Vicino (2017) elaborate on the right to the city dimension of 2013 protests in taking up physical space, something we discuss throughout this book.

Our theoretical tripod structure was severely stressed in 2013. Labor wages were stagnating after a decade of steady rise and the working class was worried about not being able to maintain the consumption levels of the Lula years. Land rights were at the lowest point of the twenty-first century with the obliteration of the participatory process and the forced evictions carried out for mega-event infrastructure. The transportation infrastructure was saturated, both in terms of public systems (buses in most cities and subways and surface rail in a few) and private (an increase in automobile sales were not accompanied by better road infrastructure). Those were reasons enough for large and conflicting groups of Brazilian society to feel unease and take to the streets, and the repressive police apparatus was ready to bring down, violently, any kind of dissent.

The result, as we now know, was devastating to all Brazilian institutions.

SEARCHING FOR (IN)CONCLUSIONS

It is very difficult at this point to determine with certainty what led to the abandonment of participatory processes precisely when Luiz Inácio Lula da Silva governed Brazil and reached unquestionable success in fighting inequality. It is clear that the beginning of the end happened as early as 2003 with the creation of the Ministry of the City, which replaced the urban-base democracy led by the Workers Party since the eighties with a technocratic sphere of power. It became worse in 2005 with the changes in the Ministry of the City as a result of the *mensalão* scandal (Saad Filho 2013, 662). Between 2006 and 2013 the developmental emphasis, which ameliorate income distribution and employment, left serious scars in Brazilian cities (Lara 2013, 2014), and we need to discuss the relationship between those scars and the protests of 2013.

The literature has already made clear the relationship between the *mensalão* scandal and the changes in the Ministry of Cities. In response to the political crisis that followed the accusations of congressman Roberto Jefferson in 2005, the Lula government promoted a drastic change in the Ministry of Cities.[1] The departure of Minister Olívio Dutra and his team marked the abandonment of the participatory processes at the federal level. Dutra had been a great champion of participatory processes since he was mayor of Porto Alegre between 1989 and 1993. In a diametrically opposing position, the Ministry of Cities was led by leaders of the Republican Party and the Progressive Party, which had nothing at all progressive or republican in their agendas, being traditionally linked to construction industry interests.

Instead of participatory decisions and small-scale localized interventions, the Lula government embarked on gigantic infrastructure projects, bundled together under the umbrella of the Programa de Aceleração do Crescimento. Saad Filho (2013) uses the term *leftist neoliberalism*, and its apparent contradiction is indeed a very good summary of the main issues.

Articulated by Minister Dilma Rousseff, the PAC plan made hundreds of billions of dollars available for construction projects in roads, ports, energy generation, and urban mobility. Later, in 2010, when Brazil secured the opportunity of hosting the 2014 FIFA World Cup, the PAC–Copa do Mundo was created to improve airports and mobility infrastructure related to that event (Ribeiro and Santos Junior 2017). The total amount of all PACs in nine years (2006–2014) amounts to R$1.9 trillion, or about US$800 billion.

The side effect of the PAC model was that at every level it privileged the automobile and the spreading of the cities in search of cheap land, triggering the mobility crisis and worsening environmental degradation. In those years the Brazilian construction industry was in such frenzy that a real estate bubble was inevitable. As a consequence, our theoretical tripod was skewed in those years. Brazilian workers survived the twentieth century with low wages, long hours in deficient transportation, and police repression. Now one of the rods was being dramatically shortened: the labor costs were rising faster than productivity and economic growth. People had more money in their pockets. While working on infrastructure projects in the favelas one of the authors of this book once had an opportunity to ask an elderly lady what had changed in her life. Her answer was shocking: "I have my fridge stacked with yogurt for my grandkids. I spent my life dreaming about yogurt but it was too expensive. Now my grandkids eat as much as they want" (interview by F. Lara, Complexo da Serra, Belo Horizonte, July 2011).

That something as simple as having yogurt in the fridge can represent the difference between the Lula and Rousseff governments and the fifty years before them is both striking and precise. But the same economic model that put yogurt in her fridge created a real estate valuation that pushed families like hers further from services and opportunities. Worse yet, the abandonment of negotiation channels championed by the participatory budget strategies made it easier for construction companies and real estate interests to abuse the power to dislodge people from their homes. Brazil's urban land is infamously undertitled and underregistered, and while this often help the working class build their homes closer to jobs and infrastructure (our tripod has land ownership as one of the main pillars of Brazilian inequality), it also makes them vulnerable to forced relocation.

The labor leg of our tripod had been shortened, with higher minimum wage and a significant increase in employment with full benefits (less informality). Meanwhile, the land leg of our tripod had lengthened—the poor were being pushed further out by the real estate bubble combined with forced relocation associated with the fast pace of building infrastructure. The resulting instability, felt mostly by the middle class, was no doubt a major component of the protests of 2013.

It is not that the federal government had forgotten about the housing deficit. It simply had an insufficient and problematic answer to it: the Minha Casa Minha Vida (MCMV) project. The MCMV works with the federal government, through the Caixa Econômica Federal, lending construction companies a certain amount of money to build social housing and guaranteeing the purchase of the houses back (with a profit, of course) to be mortgaged, with or without subsidies, for the working class.[2]

The MCMV program is rife with problems. It gives construction companies no incentive to improve design or construction because with a set price being paid per unit, profit is made by building as cheaply as possible. It also induces the occupation of the cheapest land available, inevitably at the outskirts of the city where there is minimal infrastructure or in areas previously zoned for environmental protection.

Minha Casa Minha Vida standardizes the housing typology of a late-Fordist influence (Krause, Balbim, and Lima 2013). Even more serious is the transfer of funds from the Fundo Nacional de Habitação de Interesse Social (National Social Housing Fund) to MCMV, restricting the resources available to other solutions. This generates another negative impact: only the smaller cities with less dynamic economies have cheap land that justify MCMV construction (Cardoso and Aragão 2013). The larger cities, where social housing solutions should be built in consolidated areas or areas of decreasing density, are completely neglected by the current policy, which prioritizes a specific program, Minha Casa Minha Vida, above a state policy, the National Housing Plan (PlanHab). Cleandro Krause, Renato Balbim, and Vicente Correia Lima Neto (2013) concluded correctly that MCMV was a program to generate jobs and economic growth, not to guarantee the right to the city.

The emphasis on car ownership that came along with the PAC plan was fraught with problems. It subjugates residents into crowded buses and massive traffic jams, isolates the poorest from the infrastructure that is still concentrated in the central areas, and confuses urban quality of life with title deeds. Take the market test: compare the rent value of the houses of Minha Casa Minha Vida with that of favelas in the central areas of any Brazilian city, and the answer will tell you where people live better.

One of the most perverse issues of the program is the abandonment of participatory processes in direct opposition to PlanHab, which had encouraged local participation and diverse solutions in response to a wide range of urban problems across the country. In the long run the process is even more perverse. Vicente Fox promised to build five million homes when elected in Mexico in 2000, pumping money into an existing program called INFONAVIT that closely resembles MCMV. The goal of five million units was achieved during the term of his successor Felipe Calderon. The large majority of those units were built on the farthest outskirts of Monterrey, Chihuahua, Ciudad Juárez, Guadalajara, and Tijuana, and today, two decades later, a much as 40 percent of these homes are abandoned and any relation to the alarming rate of violence is not mere coincidence (Shirk 2014; Díaz Montemayor 2019). In the Brazilian case we have *City of God* as an example; the film by Fernando Meirelles showed the world what can happen when a community is removed to areas completely isolated from the rest of the city.

The protests of June 2013 brought the urban question again to the center of national debate. The main claim of the demonstrations was that public transportation would transform the urban structure and land value (Harvey et al. 2015). With efficient transportation, the periphery would become more valuable, making a revolutionary transfer of income and a great improvement in quality of life for millions of Brazilians.

The case of Vila Autódromo in Rio de Janeiro is exemplary. What was once a fishing village became an informal community in the 1980s, when the city of Rio built a racetrack over a swamp area. For thirty years Vila Autódromo grew with minimal infrastructure, and electricity and water were connected only after decades of protest and political pressure. A sewage system was never built. In 2010, in preparation for the 2016 Olympic Park to be built over the racetrack, Vila Autódromo was supposed to gain protection and, finally, a sewage system. Or at least this is what was delineated in the Olympic master plan competition won by Aecom in 2011. However, the real estate investors that financed the housing towers that would host athletes and later be sold to the public were adamantly against the neighboring favela. With support from city officials and state police, they applied an aggressive strategy to buy and force people out (Megaeventos 2011; Estado 2011). When some families sold their homes to the city, the structures were demolished, but the rubble was left on-site to make life miserable to the ones resisting. Out of 700 families living there in 2010, only about 20 remained during the 2016 Olympic Games, but the economic crisis ravaging Brazil since 2015 on top of the new COVID-pandemic-induced recession will surely induce new growth. Meanwhile, out of 3,400 units built for the athletes, only 250 had been sold as of 2019 (Duarte 2019).

This historical context of the urban question illuminates in part the 2013 protests. The acceleration of infrastructure works and the political and economic space gained by general contractors and construction groups, together with the deterioration in public and private transportation and the real estate bubble, has created widespread frustration and a new urban social movement (Ribeiro and Santos Junior 2017; Fahlberg and Vicino 2016). Unfortunately, the developmentalist obsession that took over the PT in the federal government became the trademark of Rousseff's government, which kept pouring more asphalt and concrete as a solution to all problems.

In 2015 Brazil would experience another set of large-scale protests, this time asking for the impeachment of President Dilma Rousseff. The trigger for this book was the large-scale protests of June 2013. We watched closely the dramatic events of those weeks around the FIFA Confederations Cup, naively optimistic about the fact that young Brazilians were taking to the streets to demand change. Eight year later, we have little reason to be optimistic. The presidential campaign of 2014 was the most polarized and vicious in recent Brazilian history, with the added drama that Eduardo Campos died in a plane crash two months before the election, when he was second place in the polls. The conservative candidate Aécio Neves da Cunha never accepted his loss to President Dilma Rousseff and started sabotaging her government the day after the second round of the election. Conspiring with a Congress that was perceived to be the most conservative in decades, Aécio Neves da Cunha helped elect Eduardo Cunha (no relation) as Speaker of the House and together they enacted a program they called a "bomb agenda": a series of irresponsible measures that added expenses to a budget deficit, making a bad financial crisis even worse. At the background of all this political catfight was a corruption investigation that stained several members of Rousseff's cabinet and made all members of Congress run for their lives. The year 2015 saw a disjointed government trying to impose austerity measures against their leftist base and a conservative Congress devoted to spending as much as possible to make sure the government would fail.

When Dilma Rousseff and the Workers Party, at that point the main target of the investigation, refused to vote to protect Eduardo Cunha, the Speaker of the House accepted one of many popular initiatives to begin the presidential impeachment process. What followed was an explosion of discontent with the progressive policies of the Worker's Party, with middle-class and wealthy people filling the streets to protest corruption. Interestingly enough, there were no corruption charges against President Rousseff; she was prosecuted for an accounting maneuver that was routinely made by elected officials in the previous decades, including many shouting for her removal.

The parallels with 1963 and 1964 are striking, as Perry Anderson (2019) has discussed. In the words of Fernando Haddad, mayor of São Paulo at the time, the middle class saw the rich pulling ahead and the poor closing in behind them and took to the streets to fight for the dismantling of the wage distribution and affirmative action policies of Lula (2003–2010) and Rousseff (2011–2015). The year 2016 started with robust upper-class demonstrations (not many Blacks, minorities, or even working-class Brazilians were seen in those protests) and a bizarre vote in the House of Representatives on April 17, 2016. The senate confirmed the ousting of President Rousseff on August 31, 2016. Michel Temer, vice president, took office that day and quickly imposed an extreme program of legislative reform aimed at cutting as much labor rights and social services as possible. Government spending on education and health was frozen for twenty years, a murderous act on such unequal society. Labor laws such as US right-to-work have been proposed, and severe cuts in unemployment legislation disproportionately affecting the poor were approved in Congress in 2017.

Since then, we have seen the progressive movements very disorganized and unable to articulate streets protests or legislative maneuvers. When this regressive agenda was proposed, we saw large protests taking to the streets, but nothing large enough or articulated enough to enact real pressure on the government. During the 2018 presidential campaign, with the favorite candidate Lula da Silva in jail despite flimsy evidence against him and extreme right-wing retired army major Jair Bolsonaro leading the polls, the progressive social movements went back to the streets with a large protest #EleNão ("not him"). The large-scale media made sure not to feature any of those protests prominently, precisely the opposite of the approach toward the protests for ousting Rousseff, which were televised ad nauseam.

We know by now that the middle class that took to the streets in 2014 and 2015 were not much bothered by corruption but more by a feeling that the poor were catching up on them. This has been confirmed by qualitative research and reconfirmed by the fact that the same middle class did nothing in 2017, when several members of the Temer government, including runner-up candidate Aécio Neves da Cunha were recorded in audio and video negotiating bribes for a variety of interferences, all of them real impeachable crimes. Furthermore, such indifference toward corruption on the right was corroborated in 2018, when 70 percent of the Brazilian elite in the South and Southeast voted for Bolsonaro, electing a candidate that repeatedly and publicly defended torture and expressed racist judgment, homophobic values, and blatant misogyny, not to mention the dozens of corruption scandals affecting himself, his family, and all his closest advisers.

It is difficult to explain such hypocrisy except when we perceive a desperate desire to keep the structure of our conceptual tripod intact. People often protest to change something, but sometimes specific groups protest against change. The key is to ask who was taking to the streets? It is clear now, eight years after 2013, that the middle-class standard of living has not improved. Nevertheless, middle-class Brazilians stopped protesting the moment Dilma Rousseff was ousted, indicating that they do not care about corruption, provided that things do not change. In 2020 the country was again engulfed by accusations of corruption against Bolsonaro and his sons, ending with the ousting of justice minister Sergio Moro, who had jailed Lula on dubious evidence while he negotiated his participation in the Bolsonaro government. In a series of small-scale events in support of Bolsonaro after he took office in 2019, the participants have mostly claimed for an idyllic past in which women and people of color did not "bother" them with complaints and protests. As we write these lines in 2021, the Supreme Court ruled that Moro broke the law to put Lula da Silva in jail and annulled all convictions. Meanwhile, the country is facing the worst COVID outbreak in the world, with Bolsonaro insisting that masks and social distancing are useless and refusing to purchase the number of vaccine doses that could make things better. Change may be the concept that scares the middle class the most, for this group has traditionally taken to streets to prevent changes in social structure, not to promote them. Throughout 2020 and 2021, while COVID killed in the periphery, a significant part of the Brazilian upper classes partied and traveled as if there was no pandemic. It was only when the private hospitals ran out of ICU beds in February of 2021 that they started to question Bolsonaro's lack of health policy.

But what about working-class Brazilians? They surely are the ones who lost the most with the political and economic disarray of 2013–2021 (and counting). Why have they not taken to the streets yet? Why have so many of them voted for a candidate that promised to roll back their rights?

In June of 2017, with the Temer government accused of corruption from all sides (the president himself was taped discussing bribes with the CEO of JBS, the world's largest meat producer), scholars started discussing the idea of "protest fatigue" to explain the passivity of Brazilian society. On the contrary, it is our understanding that there is no protest fatigue. The middle class stopped protesting because there was a strong indication that the pace of change in

Brazil would slow to a halt, which was their goal from the beginning. The working class, on the other hand, is still taking to the streets on a daily basis as they always did, protesting relocations, police brutality, inadequate transportation, and to a lesser extent labor conditions (Sandler 2020). With unemployment at 14 percent before the COVID pandemic, and now hovering around 25 percent, the maneuvering space for labor demands is minimal. The scenes from Brazilian hospitals in 2021 are shocking. COVID patients are dying for lack of oxygen; cardiac patients are dying because there are no ICU beds for them. It is indeed hard to explain why the country has not yet exploded with massive protests due to the COVID pandemic.

Once again, our theoretical tripod helps explain the occurrence (or not) of protests and how they differ if voicing for maintaining or for transforming the social structure. Let's take the issue of police repression or police brutality, one of the main pillars of our diagram. The protests of 2013 started against a hike in bus fares, and it was only after the police brutalized the protesters that the movement grew to a nationwide scale not seen in decades. Since 2013 we have witnessed an intriguing phenomenon. In middle-class protests for the ousting of Rousseff's government, the police were extremely kind, working to preserve the "peaceful" nature of the protests and make sure they had as much space as possible. The protests of 2015–2016 will be forever represented by the fact that millions of people took selfies with the police. Dressed in full militarized anti-riot gear, police officers were photographed hugging and smiling with upper-middle-class protesters. Meanwhile every protest called by social movements or organized labor was confronted by the police with very little patience or space for conversation. Images of the police beating K-12 teachers in Curitiba on April 29, 2015, or indigenous people in Brasília on April 24, 2015, are two of the most famous, and bloody, repressions that were publicized around the world. But police brutality is something that happens every day in Brazil: ten people are killed by the police every single day, hundreds beaten.[3]

Those sad numbers are not new. Police repression of the working class is a feature of Brazilian social structure, and this feature is very precisely spatialized: it happens in the periphery of the largest cities and more intensely in the informal settlements. What is new is the pornographic exposure of this unequal treatment in the form of wealthy white Brazilians taking selfies with the police, who by the way are not members of the elite and every day go back to their own homes in the periphery.

In 2018 several candidates were elected on the promise to unleash the full power of police deadly repression on *vagabundos*, including the governor of Rio de Janeiro, Wilson Witzel (impeached on corruption charges in 2020), and President Jair Bolsonaro. Violence was made into a natural component of this society. If you happen to live in the periphery, you either suffer or impose violence, very often both. The issue of violence has permeated the latest protests (since 2013) also because of the presence of *black-blocs*, groups of masked young men that engage in vandalism during the protests. Those groups are sometimes formed by gangs from impoverished areas that use violence as an identity, much like *torcidas organizadas* at soccer games. But other times, there is enough evidence to support that masked men were undercover policemen working to "provoke" the troops and therefore justify brutal responses.

This was clear in Brasília on May 24, 2017, when a peaceful major protest was happening on the north side of the Esplanada dos Ministérios, surrounded by security forces, while on the south side, behind the police blockade, buildings were vandalized by masked men. At some point that evening a small part of the police force moved south to repress the "black-blocs" (with quotation marks to emphasize their dubious origin) while at the same time the bulk of the police contingent marched toward the peaceful protesters, dispersing them with significant violence. Any responsible person in charge of public safety that day would have ordered the arrest of the masked men attacking government property while making sure that the peaceful protesters be allowed to disperse calmly. The fact that the police routinely brutalize protests from the left while taking selfies with protesters from the right reinforces our theoretical tripod, with the rod of public safety being widely different at the bottom than the top. It seems that Bolsonaro appealed to both the top and the bottom with his blatant defense of violence as the primary way to maintain order.

Another rod of our tripod that helps explain the unique nature of street protests in Brazil concerns the issue of labor. Unlike public safety, labor did change quite a bit in the first two decades of the twenty-first century. Starting with a deliberate policy of raising the minimum wage above inflation, the Lula government induced a major transfer of wealth toward the working class. In 2002, the last year of the Cardoso government, the Brazilian minimum wage hit its lowest value in US dollars: 63.88. That's US$63 for a full month of work. Our readers can imagine how little it can purchase even after dividing the price of food and housing by a factor of 3 or 4 to approximate the purchasing power of the Brazilian real. Let's assume a very high purchasing power of around US$300 per month—a misery wage, no doubt. Purchasing power aside, the same minimum wage hit US$348 in 2012, a fivefold increase in a decade. The Brazilian working class understood this policy very well, voting overwhelmingly for Lula's reelection in 2006 and Dilma Rousseff in 2010, less overwhelmingly for Rousseff reelection in 2014. Economists are still discussing the extent to which the Brazilian economic growth of that same decade was fueled by internal consumption or the Chinese thirst for commodities, but there is no question that those were the two pillars of that exuberant performance. Add to this wage rise the 2013 law that extended general labor rights to domestic workers (Estatuto das Domésticas) and you have significant changes to our labor rod.

We can debate if the working class understood the extent of those changes as a result of deliberate leftist policies or, as some recent polls indicate, as the consequence of individual efforts on schooling and training that resulted in better employment. But there is no doubt that the middle class understood this very well and turned sharply against such policies. The well-being of middle-class Brazilians had been for decades supported by an army of women that leave their home every morning to take care of somebody else's. *Domésticas*, as they are called, are the most visible and most underpaid and undervalued of all Brazilian workers. Overwhelmingly female and Black, they are the bottom of the labor pyramid, but they are not the only ones: there are doormen for every apartment building, security guards for every business, construction workers for every home improvement project, supermarket clerks for every purchase, motorcycle riders for every delivery.

The rise of their wages during a time of full employment scared the hell out of the Brazilian middle class. It was common in 2012–2013 to overhear people saying in restaurants and shopping malls that it was "impossible" to find a good maid or a good doorman now that "everybody" thought they could go to college or go to the beach during their newly awarded thirty-day vacation, leaving desperate housewives behind.

It is now clear that the middle-class Brazilians who took to the streets in 2015–2016 were protesting those changes and were not at all bothered by corruption. Corruption was just a convenient excuse to enact still another coup. However, with one rod of our theoretical tripod firmly standing (police) and another just slightly shaking (labor rights and cost), the Brazilian elite would still be comfortably installed in their privileged position, provided that the third rod—land—held steady.

As we discuss throughout the book, the structure of landownership in Brazil did not change at all during the twentieth century. Moreover, when we had income distribution and labor gains between 2003 and 2012, the issue of land was not part of the equation. Much to the contrary, as discussed, the Ministério das Cidades had been operating under the leadership of politicians affiliated with construction companies and developers since 2005. The land rod was supposed to be as safe as the police rod. Ironically, the same protests in 2013 that worked toward the destabilization of the Rousseff government also brought urban issues back to the forefront. Debates around urban policy in general and mobility in particular were exhaustively held in 2013 and 2014.

In parallel to this national discussion was the revision of the master plan of the city of São Paulo. The largest and wealthiest city in Brazil was undergoing a review of its master plan and zoning under a leftist mayor: Fernando Haddad, who also happens to have a very well-developed sensibility for urbanism. We might credit Haddad's knowledge of urbanism to some of his closest advisers in city hall: Fernando Mello Franco, secretary of urbanism; João Sette Whitaker Ferreira, secretary of housing; and Gustavo Partezani, president of SP Urbanism (municipal real-estate investment fund). Together they helped Haddad respond to the challenges of mobility and land planning in the twenty-first century. His administration closed main avenues on Sundays, bringing people to the streets to bike, rollerblade, run, or just stroll. It created hundreds of miles of bike lanes, taking away parking spots and making cycling a bit safer. It created hundreds of miles of bus corridors, once again taking away space dominated by automobiles in order to speed up public transportation. And it lowered the speed limit of the Marginais expressways, reducing the number of accidents with victims. All those actions infuriated the São Paulo middle class, which responded by demonizing Haddad and voting him out.

But nothing scared the Brazilian elite more than the new master plan of São Paulo. Approved in 2014 after many months of negotiations at city council, the 2014 master plan was an important step toward giving the city more control over land use and development. The 2014 master plan marked several corridors that should be densified, bringing more homes closer to public transit and therefore making the whole city more sustainable. The logic had been very successful in Curitiba and need not carry ideological connotations, for it is indeed very simple: those who need public transportation should live in smaller apartments close to transit corridors, while those who can afford to have cars should live farther away. With miles and miles of underused real estate in São Paulo, the public sector should be able to increase density where there is enough infrastructure already, or along the subway or bus corridors.

The issue of allowing the city to induce development over here in exchange for controlling investment over there became highly politicized. The 2014 master plan imposed a floor-area ratio (the amount of construction you can do in relation to the size of your property) of 1.0 for the entire city. Along densification corridors developers would be able to purchase construction rights from the city and build 1.5, 2.0, or even 4.0 times the area of their property.

You can imagine that lowering the floor-area ratio of the entire city would not much change the overall value of the land. If anything, it would make land more expensive for everybody by potentially diminishing the supply of new units. But Brazilian urban land value was never about supply and demand. As of today, the country has a housing deficit estimated at seven million units, while another six million units sit empty. It has never been about market forces adjusting supply and demand for housing, or for infrastructure, even for labor. Brazilian urban land is about making sure that the working poor, who happen to be overwhelmingly Black and *mulato*, would never get close to the wealthy areas except to work as maids or doormen or any other low-paid low skilled jobs. When the 2014 São Paulo master plan gave city hall more power to dictate where developers should build more and where they should build less according to principles of social and environmental sustainability, hell broke loose. The 2014 master plan induced two very different kinds of protests, in line with our main hypothesis of both the upper middle class and the working poor being connected but positioned at the extremes of theoretical tripod. At the periphery people protested the lack of participatory processes and the imposition of bus corridors over their commercial strips that would be tremendously impacted by demolitions. Koury's work at Itaim Paulista, at the eastern periphery of São Paulo, demonstrate that people know very well the impact suffered by their communities and protest accordingly (Koury and Cavallari 2018).

Meanwhile, in the wealthier areas, the protests were subtle and more emotionally effective. Placards read "Out with the Cuban Model" or "Down with the Ticket Industry." The "Cuban model" is a well-rehearsed code for any regulation imposed on capital that might challenge the functioning of the city as a machine for exclusion. Any initiative that threatens centuries of exclusion, such as affirmative action or paid vacation for maids, is labeled "Cuban" and therefore fought as foreign imposition of communist ideology. The other code tested in focus-groups and successfully applied in mayoral campaigns of 2016 is the idea of "ticket industry"—the state using traffic violations to raise money. In São Paulo the new bus corridors were quite effective in improving public transportation by making it faster than cars, taxis, and ridesharing services. The city also reduced speed limits in the Marginais expressways. Both initiatives were fought in the media and talk-show radio as a scheme to increase city revenue. Locked in traffic for hours on end while the buses drove by freely, the average paulistano was bombarded with radio hosts saying that they were being targeted by a ticketing industry.

In 2017 a new mayor restored higher speed limits, and the number of victims of traffic accidents rose immediately. So far, the bus corridors have not been dismantled and the number of tickets remain the same, but nobody is talking about a ticket industry anymore. In 2019 the Bolsonaro government approved higher speed limits and less radar, a move that delighted his right-wing political base. The land column of our theoretical tripod was shaken just a little in 2013–2014, but it was enough to bring the middle class to the streets to make sure that the pace of change stalled.

Unfortunately, it worked. The coup of 2016 served to reinforce the inequalities that we explained in this book with our theoretical tripod. Labor laws and retirement policies that protected the workers since Getúlio Vargas's term are still being dismantled in Congress. Other labor laws, such as one against subcontracting main business activity, were changed in 2020, using the COVID pandemic as an excuse to make labor rights flexible. The police repression apparatus was emboldened, and the president elected in 2018 promises to be tough on crime against any hint of human rights. Progressive land proposals have no future right now, Congress passed a new law of land regularization (Law 13465/17) that does not differentiate if codes were broken by the poor or by the wealthy. Such law criminalizes low-income informal residences (which usually do not follow building codes) while giving a pass to high-income informality that tends to happen with large lots, low density, and wide setbacks.

In summary, the rods of our theoretical tripod that operate as well as a machine to create inequalities have cracked a little in the first two decades of the twenty-first century, only to be reinforced again by regressive policies implemented after the coup of 2016. Ironically, street protests pushed both ways.

Streets do matter.

NOTES

INTRODUCTION

1. The catchphrase Padrão FIFA was widely publicized on social networks such as Acerto de Contas and Diário do Centro do Mundo, and referenced by mainstream newspapers such as *O Globo*. See, respectively, http://acertodecontas.blog.br/atualidades/queremos-escolas-e-hospitais-padrao-fifa-nao-se-trata-de-r-010/; https://www.diariodocentrodomundo.com.br/queremos-um-pais-padrao-fifa/.

2. BRICS is a Goldman Sachs acronym coined in 2001 to describe the rising powers of Brazil, Russia, India, China, and South Africa. Those five countries went beyond just being bundled together for economic analysis and created a BRICS summit in 2009 and a BRICS development bank in 2012. As the events of the years since demonstrate, we should have focused more on the troubled aspect of these countries and less on their rise.

3. Gini coefficient is a statistical measure of distribution developed by the Italian statistician Corrado Gini in 1912. The Gini coefficient is widely used as a gauge of economic inequality, measuring income distribution or, less commonly, wealth distribution among a population.

4. How different is the scenario now, in 2021, with an extreme-right government pushing for the dismantling of anything public, allowing fast deforestation, and preaching hate and violence with an economy in shambles and the COVID pandemic out of control.

5. It is interesting to note that Arturo Escobar, along with other leaders of the decolonial movement—Anibal Quijano, Walter Mignolo and Enrique Dussel—departed from both CEPAL dependency theory (Quijano) and liberation theology (Dussel) to arrive at a complete debunking of the idea of development as empowering and transformative. By elaborating on "The Dark Side of Modernity" (Mignolo 2011) they prove that colonization is inherent to any modernization, a topic that is central to our motivation of telling the history of planning in parallel to the history of urban protests.

6. We are referring to the works of Carlos Andrade (1991), Cristina Leme (1999), Virgínia Pontual (2001), Sarah Feldman (2005), Adrian Gorelik (2005), Gouvêa (2005), Célia Ferraz Souza (2008), Renato Anelli (2011), Ana Fernandes (2012, 2014), and Vera Rezende (2012).

1: IN THE BEGINNING, THERE WAS LAND

1. See Martins and Lage 2004.

2: URBANISM OF CORONÉIS, TENENTES, AND BACHARÉIS

1. May 1 is Labor Day all over the world in honor of the Haymarket protest on May 1, 1886, in Chicago and the Bay View massacre three days later. The United States of America is the only country that celebrates Labor Day on a different day (the first Monday of September), in a deliberate attempt to erase that tragic event from the history of this country.

2. *Pelego* is a term used to designate union leaders that align themselves with elite politicians and capitalist bosses, betraying the labor movement.

3: URBAN POLICY UNDER GETÚLIO VARGAS

1. There is a huge debate on the formation of the Brazilian labor Market. An introduction on this debate can be found in Barbosa 2008. Specifically on the urban labor, see Hall and Garcia 1989, 161–91, and Barbosa 2008, 188–239.

2. Alfredo Gordo's Act 1907 was approved to face the anarcho-syndicalist movement, which was growing with the São Paulo state industry. The workers, mainly from Italy, started to organize a strong unionist movement to protect their interests. To prevent this movement, the act legislated the deportation of the striking workers (Levine 1998, 313). See French 2006.

3. Wolfe (1993, 50) also added the workers were tortured and killed in Cambuci's prison.

4. See Leal 1997 [1949], 85–86, 91–92.

5. Of 1,494 workers associations, only 364 were officially part of the national system (Levine 1998: 316).

6. According to Hall and Garcia (1989, 171), the development of labor regulation would be complete in 1943 but its political features were working out since the beginning of the revolutionary government.

7. See Harding 1973, 101.

8. See Fernandes 2007, 59–64.

9. "A Assembléia Constituinte de 1933–1934, que reviveu o debate público sobre a organização social e política e endossou o princípio corporativista de representação classista, trouxe a restauração do governo constitucional em

julho de 1934 e um significativo aumento dos conflitos trabalhistas" (Levine 1998, 316).

10. The Communist activities were Coligação dos Sindicatos Proletários, a Liga Comunista Internacionalista, o Comitê das Mulheres Trabalhadoras, o Comitê da luta contra as Guerras Imperialistas, a Reação e do Fascismo (Levine 1998, 317).

11. About the communist party in Brazil see Brandão 1997.

12. Previously the state contributed to the system only by transferring a portionof the fare to the funds controlled by the private companies.

13. The work accident insurance was supported by employers, and there was no unemployment insurance in Brazil in that time (Sussekind 1955, 162–63).

14. Letter from Rômulo de Almeida to the Vice-President of the National Social Welfare Commission (Josué de Castro), December 23, 1952, forwarding and presenting the report on the work of the Subcommittee on Housing and Favelas; Report of the Subcommittee on Housing and Slums, CPDOC: Getúlio Vargas Archive, classification: GV c 1952.12.23, December 23, 1953.

15. In 1939 Act 1.843 protected jobs for Brazilian citizens. Companies had to employ Brazilians for at least two-thirds of their workforce.

16. The investments in housing made by the institutions for their workers were regulated in 1937 with Decreto no. 1.749, June 28, 1937.

17. A broad survey about favelas in Brazil was written by Valladares (2005).

18. The definition was itemized in 1960 census and was the same as the one applied in the 1950 census (Guimarães 1953, 18; Censo Demográfico 1968, VI).

19. Favela is the name of hill in a little town called Monte Santo near the Arraial de Canudos, where Republican soldiers were defeated by Antônio Conselheiro's defenses—see Canudos chap. 1 (Mattos 2008, 49).

20. It is sad to realize that the exact same shock over the destruction power of the mob and the brutality of police repression could be repeated with the exact same words when commenting on the protests of June 2013, almost seven decades later.

21. Original Portuguese: "O 1º de agosto não foi apenas um protesto contra um precário e insuficiente sistema de transportes e o eventual aumento no preço das passagens, . . . foi também uma manifestação contra as condições de moradia, contra a deficiência no atendimento da saúde pública, contra a ausência de escolas, contra as péssimas condições de salubridade urbana e os péssimos salários e outras carências, porque essas eram experimentadas, pelas classes populares. . . . Se esse conflito aberto emergiu relacionado ao tema dos transportes públicos é porque para ele confluíam todas as demandas urbanas de uma população que se percebia abandonada."

4: DARK CLOUDS OVER THE CITIES

1. Report from Comissão de Mobilização Econômica (1943); Report from Comissão de Investigação Econômica e Social da Assembleia Constituinte (1946); Letter from Rômulo de Almeida to the Vice-President of Comissão Nacional de Bem-Estar Social (Josué de Castro), December 23, 1952, submitting the report of Subcomissão de Habitação e Favelas. RELATÓRIO DA SUB COMISSÃO DE HABITAÇÃO E FAVELAS (8 anexos). CPDOC Archive: Getúlio Vargas Classificação: GV c 1952.12.23 dated December 23, 1953 (88pp.).

2. Since the Portuguese arrival and the subsequent death of 90 percent of the natives in the sixteenth century, the population of Brazil has been concentrated on the Atlantic shore. Early movements of occupying and developing land in the interior were pushed by colonial booms such as the gold rush of Minas Gerais in the eighteenth century and the coffee plantation economy of São Paulo in the nineteenth century. The construction of Brasilia, planned by the federal government since 1890s, was a major planned effort of continuing this process toward the center savanna and the northwest rainforest areas of the country.

3. Oliveira, Beltrão, and David (1998) presented the amounts in June 1998 currency (CZN $162,078,273.05). The conversion for the 1961 currency was made by us through the O Estado de São Paulo currency converter: https://economia.estadao.com.br/ferramentas/conversor-de-moedas.

4. The pioneering works that relate the political process and the urbanization are by Milton Santos and Nestor Goulart Reis Filho in the late sixties. In 1975 the Ceprap—Brazilian Center for Analysis and Planning—carried out a research on the periphery of São Paulo registered and analyzed in several publications by Lúcio Kowarick, Vinícius Caldeira Brant and José Álvaro Moisés, and Paul Singer, among other authors who later focused mainly on analysis of the urban political phenomenon in Brazil.

5. "Essa maciça redistribuição da população modificou o perfil da própria população urbana. Em 1970, mais da metade da população urbana já residia em cidades com mais de cem mil habitantes, e um terço naquelas acima de quinhentas mil pessoas. Em 2000, cerca de 60% da população urbana residia em cidades com mais de cem mil habitantes, mostrando que urbanização e concentração da população em grandes cidades foram processos simultâneos no Brasil" (Britto 2006, 224).

6. On urbanization and political process see Moisés 1978, 1981; Conniff 1981.

7. Poor workers' neighborhoods in Brazil were called *vilas* at that time.

The Portuguese original reads:"o terreno fértil para que o povo sentisse que Jânio, se não o representava pelo menos expressava um anseio de base, foi a descoberta da temática urbana pelo candidato. Jânio, na época, simbolizou o reconhecimento por parte dos que jogavam a grande cena política, de que além da reivindicação operária (que bem ou mal o PC e o PTB expressavam) existia uma ampla reivindicação da periferia urbana, eram as vilas, sem água, sem esgoto, sem calçamentos, sem transportes adequados que irrompiam na política. Duas décadas de desenvolvimento urbano-industrial, acelerado na época da guerra, com fortes correntes de migração interna, trouxeram para São Paulo centenas de milhares de nordestinos, mineiros, paulistas do interior que, mesmo antes de reivindicarem no sindicato . . . necessitavam como moradores de alguma atenção."

8. Another austerity plan would enact the same worsening of living standards and erode political support, leading to the coup against Dilma Rousseff in 2016.

9. Sandra Cavalcanti succeeded José Arthur Rios, the former secretary of social service of Guanabara state. Rios made the transition from the SERFHA, which was created in 1956 to improve the favelas, and the new institution created under Lacerda.

10. Original Portuguese: "Em 1964, a gravidade da questão urbana levou Sandra Cavalcanti [Secretaria do Estado da Guanabara] a redigir Memorando ao Presidente Castelo Branco, com Projeto de Lei (18/IV/1964) (1) para criação do Banco Nacional de Habitação [BNH]. Em seu Memorando Sandra recomendou a criação de Banco como 'órgão central' para que 'houvesse uma moeda sadia circulando no Sistema de Habitação' que ficasse infensa a inflação que vigia. Apontou também para importância de revisão da lei do inquilinato, para futura participação do Banco 'nas áreas de saneamento básico e transporte de massa,' para necessidade de dotar os conjuntos com 'água, luz, esgoto, policia, e transporte' bem como sugeriu a criação de 'Serviço para pesquisas e estudos de urbanismo e habitação, para ver se nossas cidades se organizam melhor e se a nossa industria de construção civil sai de sua fase artesanal e rudimentar' e disse que a população favelada exigia atenção especial—'gente que tem um poder aquisitivo mínimo, mas é gente.'"

11. Pereira was linked with the Urban Research Center of University of São Paulo (Centro de Pesquisas Urbanas) and had attended the Urban Reform Seminar in 1963.

12. See Law 4380 of August 21, 1964, chap. 4 (Do Banco Nacional da Habitação) art. 22 and art 25, accessed April 14, 2017, https://www.planalto.gov.br/ccivil_03/leis/l4380.htm.

13. On the BNH phases, see Valladares and Figueiredo 1981, 31.

14. According Lucchese (2009, 272–73), it was drafted earlier in 1966 in the article he published in *Arquitetura*, "Uma política de desenvolvimento urbano o grande objetivo."

15. Ferreira (2007) has analyzed Franca's Integrated Plan of Development and shown how the main export economic sector of the city nowadays, the shoe industry, was planned in a clear industrialization strategy for the interior of the state of São Paulo.

16. He would make the master plan for São Paulo city only in 1984 as director of municipal planning secretary under Mario Covas.

17. Constitution of 1946, Art 147—O uso da propriedade será condicionado ao bem-estar social. A lei poderá, com observância do disposto no art. 141, § 16, promover a justa distribuição da propriedade, com igual oportunidade para todos. (The use of the property will be subject to social welfare. The law may, in compliance with the provisions of art. 141, § 16, promote the fair distribution of property, with equal opportunity for all). Constitution of 1967, Art 157—A ordem econômica tem por fim realizar a justiça social, com base nos seguintes princípios: [. . .] III—função social da propriedade. (The economic order is intended to bring about social justice, based on the following principles: [. . .] III—social function of property).

5: CITIES DURING THE LOST DECADE OF THE 1980S

1. As we edit the book manuscript in 2021, following the legislative coup against Dilma Rousseff in 2016 and the election of Jair Bolsonaro in 2018, we are not sure if we can call the current functioning of Brazilian institutions a democracy.

2. According to Lira 1983 the proposal was published in *Jornal da Tarde* on May 24, 1977.

3. The instruments included in the 1988 Constitution—solo criado, parcelamento, edificação ou utilização compulsórios, direito de preempção e direito de superfície—translate as transfer of building rights, subdivision, compulsory building, compulsory use, preemption rights, and surface rights.

4. More information about Secretaria Latinoamericana de Vivienda Popular can be found at http://selvip-america.blogspot.com.br/.

5. It was reported by Professor Nestor Jeifetz (architect of the cooperative housing projects and social organization MOI) on March 15, 2017, in the Urban Voids Meeting in Buenos Aires, organized by professors Ingrid Breckner (HafenCity University-Hamburgo) and Alicia Gerscovich (Universidad de Buenos Aires).

6: CITIES AND PROTESTS IN LULA'S YEARS AND BEYOND

1. Leonel Brizola (1922–2004) was the heir of João Goulart's *trabalhismo*. He was elected state representative in 1947 and married Goulart's sister in 1950. In 1954 he was elected to Congress and in 1958 as governor of Rio Grande do Sul. Both in 1961 with a parliamentarism attempt and 1964 he organized a movement to support Goulart's presidential term. Exiled in Uruguay in 1964, he came back in 1977 and was elected governor of Rio de Janeiro in 1982.

2. Luis Inácio Lula da Silva was a metalworkers' union leader in São Paulo. He was labeled as a *pelego* (union leader who sells his constituents in exchange for benefits for himself) by the left, still positioned as in resistance to dictatorship. His positions, always in favor of negotiation, would play an important role in the role of centrist deals (from right and left) and the PT foundation in the 1980s. Lula da Silva was elected president in 2002 and reelected in 2006, ending his term with 87 percent approval. An important political articulator during Dilma Rousseff's government, Lula da Silva was prosecuted by Lava-Jato taskforce and sentenced to twelve years in prison in 2017, on flimsy evidence. Meanwhile, the judge who sentenced him, Sergio Moro, seriously damaged his credibility by accepting a position in Bolsonaro's cabinet in 2019. In November of 2019 Lula da Silva was released from prison. In March of 2021 the Brazilian Supreme Court ruled that Sergio Moro broke the law to force Lula's sentence, annulling all convictions.

3. The attempted coup in Venezuela in 1992 was led by Hugo Chávez, who would be elected in 1998 with the same platform of a Latin American version of socialism for the twenty-first century. The *carapintadas* revolt in Argentina in 1987 was a mutiny of officers unhappy with the prosecution of crimes committed during the dictatorship (1976–1983).

4. See also IBGE data on housing, available at http://brasilemsintese.ibge.gov.br/habitacao.

5. It has been difficult to find precise quantitative data on Favela-Bairro, as different authors use very different numbers. The sums presented here were taken from Conde and Magalhães 2004, 147–55.

6. Numbers for the PAC and PAC-2 programs were available at http://www.brasil.gov.br/pac but the Bolsonaro government disconnected the webpages. Now those numbers are only available in publications such as *Zuanazzi, Pedro Tonon, Gustavo Inácio de Moraes, Milton Andre Stella*, and *Pedro Henrique Vargas Cabral*. 2015. *Avaliação e Evolução do Programa de Aceleração do Crescimento (PAC 1 e PAC 2)*. Porto Alegre: PUCRS/SESCONRS.

7. It is striking to note that city maps from as late as 1982 do not depict

major favelas and instead show approved parceling projects as if they were on empty land ready to be developed.

8. PLAMBEL was created in 1975 to articulate a metropolitan urban policy beyond the municipal limits of Belo Horizonte but was disenfranchised after the 1988 constitution gave individual mayors much more autonomy. The autarchy was dismantled in the early nineties and its well-trained technicians absorbed by different departments, mostly at the state level.

9. There are several publications by the city of Belo Horizonte about the participatory budget from the mid-1990s to 2008. After 2009 the city website only hosts citations with no real numbers. Some numbers are available at http://www.pbh.gov.br/comunicacao/pdfs/publicacoesop/revista__15anos_portugues.pdf.

SEARCHING FOR (IN)CONCLUSIONS

1. Congressman Roberto Jefferson accused the Lula government of bribing him and other congressmen to approve bills proposed by the executive. The accusation was widely explored by the media and got the nickname of *mensalão*, for monthly payments allegedly paid to congressmen. A congressional investigation ensued, with Jefferson being stripped of his mandate in 2015 and several leaders of the PT, such as José Genoino and José Dirceu, sentenced and jailed.

2. The subsidy for lowest income bracket was used here for the first time in Brazil, allowing the MCMV program to reach some of the poorest Brazilians.

3. For an analysis of police brutality in Brazil see Smith 2016, Levine 2016, and Ceccato et al. 2018.

REFERENCES

Abreu, Alzira Alves. 1984. *A revolução de 1930: Dicionário histórico biográfico Brasileiro*. 1st ed. Accessed January 26, 2021. http://cpdoc.fgv.br/acervo/dhbb.

Abreu, Maurício de A. 1987. *Evolução urbana do Rio de Janeiro*. Edited by J. Zahar. Rio de Janeiro: IPLANRIO.

Albuquerque, Wlamyra R. de. 2006. *Uma história do negro no Brasil*. Salvador: Centro de Estudos Afro-Orientais; Brasília: Fundação Cultural Palmares.

Almeida, Caliane Christie Oliveira de. 2008. "O engenheiro-arquiteto Rubens Porto e os Institutos e Caixas de Aposentadorias e Pensões (IAPs/CAPs): Contribuições para a formulação de uma política pública habitacional no Brasil na década de 1930." *Revista Risco* 2, no. 8: 35–48.

Almeida, Rômulo de. 1946. Primeiras Observações sobre o projeto da Fundação da "Casa Popular." *Observador Econômico*, 111–15.

Almeida, Rômulo de. (1980) 1990. "Statement" (interview conducted in 1980). *História Oral*. Rio de Janeiro, Fundação Getúlio Vargas / CPDOC Archive.

Alonso, Pedro Ignacio, and Hugo Palmarola Sagredo. 2013. "A Panel's Tale: The Soviet I-464 System and the Politics of Assemblage." In *Latin American Modern Architectures*, edited by Patricio Del Real and Helen Gyger, 153–69. New York: Routledge.

Anderson, Perry. 2019. *Brazil Apart: 1964–2019*. London: Verso.

Andrade, Carlos Roberto Monteiro de. 1991. "O plano de Saturnino de Brito para Santos e a construção da cidade moderna no Brasil." *Espaço e Debates* 34:55–63.

Andrade, Carlos R. Monteiro de, Nabil Bonduki, and Rossella Rossetto. 1993. *Arquitetura e Habitação Social em São Paulo, 1989–1992, Catálogo da mostra 2ª*. Bienal Internacional de Arquitetura de São Paulo. São Paulo: Fundação Bienal.

Andrade, Manuel Correia de. 1963. *A Terra e o Homem e no Nordeste*. 1st ed. São Paulo: Brasiliense.

Anelli, Renato Luiz. 2010. "O projeto de arquitetura na pesquisa acadêmica: especificidades, limites e desafios. In *IV Projetar. Projeto como investigação: Antologia*. São Paulo: Alter Market.

Anelli, Renato Luiz. 2011. *Plano e conformação de base da metrópole: Redes de mobilidade Paulistanas.* Porto Alegre: Marca Visual.

Anelli, Renato, and Ana Paula Koury. 2019. "Junho de 2013: A participação no impasse da política urbana." *Arquitextos* 19, no. 226. http://www.vitruvius.com.br/revistas/read/arquitextos/19.226/7337.

Arantes, Pedro Fiori. 2002. *Arquitetura nova: Sérgio Ferro, Flávio Império e Rodrigo Lefèvre, de Artigas aos mutirões.* São Paulo: Editora 34.

Arantes, Pedro Fiori. 2009. "Em busca do urbano: marxistas e a cidade de São Paulo nos anos de 1970." *Novos Estudos CEBRAP* 83:103–27.

Arquitetura, 1963. "O Plano Trienal e a Habitação" Revista to IAB-GB, no. 8, February 1963, 2. Rio de Janeiro: IAB Guanabara.

Atas da Subcomissão da questão urbana. 1988. available at http://www2.camara.leg.br/atividade-legislativa/legislacao/Constituicoes_Brasileiras/constituicao-cidada/o-processo-constituinte/comissoes-e-subcomissoes/comissao6/subcomissao6b

Avritzer, Leonardo. 2009. *Participatory Institutions in Democratic Brazil.* Baltimore: Johns Hopkins University Press.

Azevedo, Aroldo de. 1956. *Vilas e cidades do Brasil colonial: ensaio de geografia urbana retrospectiva.* Saõ Paulo: Secçaõ Gráfica da Faculdade de Filosofia, Ciências e Letras da Universidade de São Paulo.

Azevedo, Sérgio de, and Luis Aureliano Gama de Andrade. 1982. *Habitação e poder da Fundação da Casa Popular ao Banco Nacional da Habitação.* Rio de Janeiro: Zahar Editores.

Azevedo, Uatumã Fattori. 2019. "Análise do declínio do número de implementações e do aumento do abandono das experiências de orçamento participativo no Brasil (2004–2016)." PhD dissertation, Unicamp.

Barbosa, Alexandre de F. 2008. *A formação do mercado de trabalho no Brasil.* São Paulo: Alameda.

Batalha, Claudio H. M. 2000. *O Movimento Operário Na Primeira República.* Descobrindo O Brasil. Rio de Janeiro: Jorge Zahar Editor.

Benchimol, Jaime Larry. 1992. *Pereira Passos: um Haussmann Tropical; A renovação urbana da cidade do Rio de Janeiro no início do século XX.* Rio de Janeiro: PMRJ.

Bernardini, Sydney Piochi. 2016. "Os planos da cidade. As políticas de intervenção urbana em Santos. De Estevan Fuertes a Saturnino de Brito." Master's thesis, Universidade de São Paulo.

Blay, Eva Alterman. 1978. *A luta pelo espaço: textos de sociologia urbana.* Petrópolis: Editora Vozes.

Bolaffi, Gabriel. 1977. "A casa das ilusões perdidas: Aspectos socioeconômicos do plano nacional de habitação." *Caderno CEBRAP* 27.

Bonduki, Nabil, and Ana Paula Koury. 2010. "Das reformas de base ao BNH: as propostas do seminário de habitação e reforma urbana." *Arquitextos* 2. http://www.vitruvius.com.br/revistas/read/arquitextos/10.120/3432.

Bonduki, Nabil, and Ana Paula Koury. 2014. *Inventário da produção pública no Brasil 1930–1964. Os Pioneiros da Habitação Social*, vol. 2. São Paulo: Edunesp.

Bonduki, Nabil. 1992. *Habitação e Autogestão: Construindo territórios da utopia*. Rio de Janeiro: Fase.

Bonduki, Nabil. 1994. "Origens da habitação social no Brasil." *Análise Social* 29, no. 127: 711–32.

Bonduki, Nabil. 1998. *Origens da habitação social no Brasil: Arquitetura Moderna, Lei do Inquilinato e Difusão da Casa Própria*. São Paulo: FAPESP/Estação Liberdade.

Bonduki, Nabil. 2000. *Habitar São Paulo: Reflexões sobre a gestão urbana*. São Paulo: Estação Liberdade.

Bonduki, Nabil. 2009. "Política habitacional e inclusão social no Brasil: revisão histórica e novas perspectivas no governo Lula." *ARQ URB, Revista Eletrônica de Arquitetura* 1: 70–104. Available at http://www.usjt.br/arq.urb/numero_01.html.

Bonduki, Nabil. 2010. "Habitação Social na vanguarda do movimento moderno no Brasil." In *Textos Fundamentais sobre História da Arquitetura Moderna Brasileira*, vol. 2, edited by Abílio Guerra. São Paulo: Romano Guerra.

Brandão, Marçal. 1997. *A esquerda positiva: as duas almas do Partido Comunista, 1920–1964*. Rio de Janeiro: Editora Hucitec.

BRASIL 247. 2012. "Em BH orçamento participativo vira só papel." Online news on April 23, 2012. http://www.brasil247.com/pt/247/minas247/55659/Em-BH-Or%C3%A7amento-Participativo-vira-s%C3%B3-papel.htm.

Brito, Saturnino. 1944. *Urbanismo*. Rio de Janeiro: Imprensa Oficial.

Bruhn, Kathleen. 2008. *Urban Protest in Mexico and Brazil*. Cambridge: Cambridge University Press.

Buarque de Holanda, Sérgio. 1995. *Raízes do brasil*. São Paulo: Companhia das Letras.

Cabral, Castilho. 1962. *Tempos de Jânio e outros tempos*. Rio de Janeiro: Editora da Civilização Brasileira.

Caldeira, Teresa. 1984. *A política dos outros: O cotidiano dos moradores da Periferia e o que pensam do poder e dos poderosos*. São Paulo: Brasiliense.

Caldeira, Teresa. 2000. *City of Walls: Crime, Segregation, and Citizenship in São Paulo*. Berkeley: University of California Press.

Caldeira, Teresa, ed. 2011. *Ruth Cardoso: Obra reunida*. São Paulo: Mameluco.

Camara, Andreza A. F. 2011. "Políticas Públicas e o programa de aceleração do crescimento: Análise das intervenções no estado do Rio de Janeiro." *Revista Brasileira de Políticas públicas* 1, no. 3 (December 2011): 147–78.

Camargo, C. P. F. D., F. H. Cardoso, L. Kowarick, and V. C. Brant. 1976. *São Paulo, 1975: crescimento e pobreza*. São Paulo: Loyola.

Cardoso, Adauto, and Themis Aragão, 2013. "Do fim do BNH ao Programa Minha Casa Minha Vida 25 anos da política habitacional no Brasil." In *O programa Minha Casa Minha Vida e seus efeitos territoriais*, edited by Adauto Cardoso, 17–65. Rio de Janeiro: Letra Capital.

Cardoso, Fernando Henrique. 1980. "Partidos Políticos." In *São Paulo: O povo em movimento*, edited by P. Singer and V. C. Brant, 177–206. São Paulo: Vozes-Cebrap.

Cardoso, Isabel C. 2009. "O Orçamento Participativo do Rio de Janeiro e as Políticas de Planejamento Urbano Estratégico." *Revista Em Pauta* 6, no. 24 (December 2009).

Carone, Edgard. 1978. *A República Velha I Instituições e classes sociais, 1889–1930*. São Paulo: Difel.

Carranza, Luis E., and Fernando Luiz Lara. 2014. *Modern Architecture in Latin America: Art, Technology, and Utopia*. Austin: University of Texas Press.

Carvalho, Jose Murilo de. 1987. *Os bestializados: O Rio de Janeiro e a República que nao foi*. São Paulo: Cia. das Letras.

Carvalho, Jose Murilo de. 2003. *A Construção da Ordem/Teatro de sombras: A politica imperial*. Rio de Janeiro: Civilização Brasileira.

Carvalho, Maria Alice Rezende de. 1998. *O Quinto Século: André Rebouças e a Construção do Brasil*. Rio de Janeiro: Editora Revan, IUPERJ.

Castells, Manuel, ed. 1973. *Imperialismo y urbanizacion em America Latina*. Barcelona: Gustavo Gilli.

Castells, Manuel. 1984. *The City and the Grassroots: A Cross-Cultural Theory of Urban Social Movements*. Berkeley: University of California Press.

Castro Gomes, Angela. 2004a. "O aumento do salário mínimo e a saída de Jango do Ministério do Trabalho." In *A trajetória política de Jango*, edited by Célia Maria Leite Costa and Suely Braga da Silva. Rio de Janeiro: CPDOC.

Castro Gomes, Angela. 2004b. "O Vice de JK." In *A trajetória política de Jango*, edited by Célia Maria Leite Costa and Suely Braga da Silva. Rio de Janeiro: CPDOC.

Castro Gomes, Angela Maria de, and Maria Celina D'Araújo. 1989. *Getulismo e Trabalhismo*. São Paulo: Editora Ática.

Cavalcanti, Nereu. 2003. *O Rio de Janeiro Setecentista: a vida e a construção da cidade da invasão francesa até a chegada da corte*. Rio de Janeiro: Zahar.

Ceccato, Vania, Silas N. Melo, and Tulio Kahn. 2018. "Trends and Patterns of Police-Related Deaths in Brazil." In *The Palgrave Handbook of Criminology and the Global South*, edited by K. Carrington, R. Hogg, J. Scott, and M. Sozzo, 521–50. Cham: Palgrave Macmillan.

Censo Demográfico de 1960. 1968. Favelas do Estado da Guanabara. Fundação Instituto Brasileiro de Geografia e Estatística.

Chalhoub, Sidney. 1986. *Trabalho, Lar e Botequim: O cotidiano dos trabalhadores no Rio de Janeiro da Belle Époque*. São Paulo: Brasiliense.

Chalhoub, Sidney. 1996. *Cidade Febril: Cortiços e Epidemias na Corte Imperial.* São Paulo: Companhia das Letras.

Cohen, Michael A. 1991. *Urban Policy and Economic Development: An Agenda for the 1990s.* Word Bank Policy Paper, Washington, DC.

Conde, Luis Paulo, and Sergio Magalhães. 2004. *Favela-Bairro: Rewriting the History of Rio.* Rio de Janeiro: ViverCidades.

Conniff, Michael L. (1981) 2006. *Política Urbana no Brasil: A ascensão do populismo, 1925–1945.* Rio de Janeiro: Relume-Damará.

Correia, T. B. 1998. *Pedra: Plano e cotidiano operário no sertão.* Campinas: Papirus.

Costa, Fernando Nogueira da. 1978. *Bancos em Minas Gerais, 1889–1964.* Master's thesis. Instituto de Economia, Universidade Estadual de Campinas.

Craciun, Martin, Santiago Medero, Mary Méndez, Emilio Nisivoccia and Jorge Nudelman. 2014. *La aldea feliz: Episodios de la modernización en Uruguay.* Catalogue of the Uruguayan Exhibition at the XIV Venice Architectural Bienale.

Crewe, Katherine. 2001. "The Quality of Participatory Design: The Effects of Citizen Input on the Design of the Boston Southwest Corridor." *Journal of the American Planning Association* 67, no. 4: 437–55.

Davis, Mike. 2007. *Planet of Slums.* London: Verso.

Dias, Everardo. 1977. *História Das Lutas Sociais No Brasil.* São Paulo: Editora Alfa-Omega.

Díaz Montemayor, Gabriel. 2019. "Recovering Subsidized Housing Developments in Northern México: The Critical Role of Public Space in Community Building in the Context of a Crime and Violence Crisis." *Sustainability* 11, no. 19: 5473.

Dualibi, Jackson. 2013. "Arquiteto Joan Villà: A construção de cerâmica armada." Master's thesis, Universidade Presbiteriana Mackenzie.

Duarte, Adriano Luiz. 2005. "O dia de São Bartolomeu e o carnaval sem fim: o quebra-quebra de ônibus e bondes na cidade de São Paulo em agosto de 1947." *Revista Brasileira de História* 25, no. 50: 25–60.

Duarte, Angelo. 2019. "Legado em Ruínas: O 'Porto Maravilha' e o Parque Olímpico representam ruínas do presente?" Paper presented at 42nd Congresso Brasileiro de Ciências da Comunicação. Accessed May 14, 2020. http://portalintercom.org.br/anais/nacional2019/resumos/R14-2110-1.pdf.

Duarte, Cristiane, and Fernanda Magalhães. 2009. "Upgrading Squatter Settlements into City Neighborhoods: The Favela-Bairro Program in Rio de Janeiro." In *Contemporary Urbanism in Brazil: Beyond Brasilia,* edited by Vicente Del Rio and William Siembieda, 266–90. Gainesville: University of Florida Press.

Dudeque, Irã Taborda. 2010. *Nenhum dia sem uma linha: Uma história do urbanismo em Curitiba.* São Paulo: Studio Nobel.

Dussel, Enrique. 1995. *The Invention of the Americas: Eclipse of the Other and the Myth of Modernity.* Translated by Michael D. Barber. New York: Continuum.

Egas, Eugenio. 1927. *Galeria dos Presidentes de São Paulo: Período republicano, vol. 3.* São Paulo: Editora do Estado.

Escobar, Arturo. 1995. *Encountering Development: The Making and Unmaking of the Third World.* Princeton: Princeton University Press.

Escobar, Arturo. 2018. *Designs for the Pluriverse: Radical Interdependence, Autonomy, and the Making of Worlds.* New Ecologies for the Twenty-First Century. Durham: Duke University Press.

Estado de São Paulo. 2011. "Relatora vê remoção forçada para Copa e PAC." available at http://www.estadao.com.br/noticias/impresso,relatora-ve-remocao-forcada-para-copa-e-pac,701838,0.htm.

Fahlberg, Anjuli, and Thomas J. Vicino. 2016. "Breaking the City: Militarization and Segregation in Rio de Janeiro." *Habitat International* 54: 10–17.

Faoro, Raymundo. (1958) 1991. *Os donos do poder: Formação do patronato político brasileiro.* 9th ed. São Paulo: Editora Globo.

Fausto, Boris. 1984. *Crime e Cotidiano: a Criminalidade em São Paulo.* São Paulo: Editora da Universidade de São Paulo.

Fausto, Boris. 2016. *Trabalho Urbano e Conflito Social.* São Paulo: Companhia das Letras.

Fausto, Britto. 2006. "O deslocamento da população brasileira para as metrópoles." *Estudos Avançados* 20, no. 57: 221–36.

Feldman, Sarah. 2005. *Planejamento e Zoneamento: São Paulo, 1947–1972.* São Paulo: Editora da Universidade de São Paulo/Fapesp.

Fernandes, Ana. 2012. "Urbanismo como política—1930–1945: Formulações e experiências." In *Urbanismo na Era Vargas: a transformação das cidades brasileiras,* edited by Vera Rezende, 59–64. Niteroi: Editora da UFF, Intertexto.

Fernandes, Edésio. 2007. "Constructing The Right to the City in Brazil." *Social & Legal Studies* 16, no. 2: 201–19.

Fernandes, Florestan. (1974) 1987. A revolução burguesa no Brasil: ensaio de interpretação sociológica. 3rd ed. Rio de Janeiro: Editora Guanabara.

Ferreira, Marieta de Moraes. 2013. "As reformas de base." In *A trajetória política de Jango,* edited by Célia Maria Leite Costa and Suely Braga da Silva. Rio de Janeiro: CPDOC.

Ferreira, Mauro. 2007. "Planejamento Urbano nos tempos do SERFHAU: O processo de construção e implementação do Plano Diretor de Desenvolvimento Integrado de Franca." PhD Dissertation, Instituto de Arquitetura e Urbanismo, Universidade de São Paulo at São Carlos.

Ferro, Sergio. 1967. "Arquitetura Nova." *Teoria e Prática* 1.

Ferro, Sergio. 1979. *O canteiro e o desenho.* São Paulo: Projeto Editores Associados.

Fiori, Jorge, and Zeca Brandão. 2010. "Spatial Strategies and Urban Social Policy: Urbanism and Poverty Reduction in the Favelas of Rio de Janeiro." In *Rethinking the Informal City*, edited by Felipe Hernandez and Peter Kellet. London: Bergham.

Fischer, Brodwyn. 2008. *A Poverty of Rights: Citizenship and Inequality in Twentieth-Century Rio de Janeiro*. Stanford: Stanford University Press.

Francisconi, Jorge Guilherme. 2013. "Seminário de Quitandinha e Q+50: resultado, avaliação e desafios atuais." *Arquitextos* 160, no. 4 (September 2013). http://www.vitruvius.com.br/revistas/read/arquitextos/14.160/4880

French, John D. 2006. "Proclamando leis, metendo o pau e lutando por direitos: A questão social como caso de polícia, 1920–1964." In *Direitos e justiças no Brasil: ensaios de história social*, edited by Silvia Hunold Lara and Joseli Maria Nunes Mendonça, 379–416. Campinas: Editora da Unicamp.

Freyre, Gilberto. 1933. *Casa-Grande e Senzala*. Rio de Janeiro: Maya and Schmidt.

Freyre, Gilberto. 1936. *Sobrados e Mocambos: decadência do patriarcado e desenvolvimento do urbano*. São Paulo: Global Editora.

Freyre, Gilberto. 1979. *Oh de Casa! Em torno da casa brasileira e de sua projeção sobre um tipo nacional de homem*. Recife: Arte Nova.

Friendly, Abigail. 2013. "The Right to the City: Theory and Practice in Brazil." *Planning Theory and Practice* 14, no. 2: 158–79.

Furtado, Celso. 1962. *A pré-revolução Brasileira*. Rio de Janeiro: Fundo de Cultura.

Furtado, Celso. 1992. *Brasil: A construção interrompida*. São Paulo: Paz e Terra.

Gadelha, Regina Maria d'Aquino Fonseca. 1989. "A lei de terras, 1850: E a abolição da escravidão; Capitalismo e força de trabalho no Brasil do século XIX." *Revista de História*, no. 120 (July 1989): 153–62.

Garcia Canclini, Nestor. 1995. *Hybrid Cultures: Strategies for Entering and Leaving Modernity*. Minneapolis: University of Minnesota Press.

Gohn, Maria da Glória Marcondes. 1982. *Reivindicações populares urbanas: um estudo sobre as associações de moradores em São Paulo*. São Paulo: Editora Autores Associados.

Gohn, Maria da Gloria Marcondes. 1995. *Historia dos movimentos e lutas sociais: A construção da cidadania dos brasileiros*. São Paulo: Edições Loyola.

Gorelik, Adrian. 2005. *Das vanguardas a Brasília: cultura urbana e arquitetura na América Latina*. Belo Horizonte: UFMG: Humanitas.

Goulart, João. 1963. "Mensagem ao Congresso Nacional." Brasília, March 1963. http://www.biblioteca.presidencia.gov.br/publicacoes-oficiais/mensagem-ao-congresso-nacional/mensagem-ao-congresso-nacional-joao-goulart-1963.

Gouvêa, Ronaldo Guimarães. 2005. *A questão metropolitana no Brasil*. São Paulo: Fundação Getúlio Vargas.

Guimarães, Alberto Passos. 1953. *As Favelas do Distrito Federal e o Censo Demográfico de 1950*. Rio de Janeiro: Instituto Brasileiro de Geografia e Estatística.

Gyger, Helen. 2019. *Improvised Cities: Architecture, Urbanization, and Innovation in Peru*. 1st ed. Pittsburgh: University of Pittsburgh Press.

Haddad, Fernando. 2017. "Sofri na pele o que li nos livros." *Revista Piaui*, June 2017.

Hall, Michael M., and Marco Aurélio Garcia. 1989. "Urban Labor." In *Modern Brazil: Elites and Masses in Historical Perspective*, edited by Michael Conniff and Frank McCann, 161–91. Lincoln: University of Nebraska Press.

Hamilton, Alexander. 1791. "Final Version of the Report on the Subject of Manufacture." Accessed September 15, 2021. http://founders.archives.gov/documents/Hamilton/01-10-02-0001-0007.

Harding, Timothy Fox. 1973. "The Political History of Organized Labor in Brazil." PhD dissertation, Stanford University.

Harvey, D. 1976. "Labor, Capital, and Class Struggle around the Built Environment in Advanced Capitalist Societies." *Politics and Society* 6, no. 3: 265–95.

Harvey, David, Ermínia Maricato, Mike Davis, Ruy Braga, Slavoj Žižek, Mauro Luis Iasi, Felipe Brito. 2015. *Cidades rebeldes: Passe livre e as manifestações que tomaram as ruas do Brasil*. Boitempo Editorial.

Herzog, Tamar. 2015. *Frontiers of Possession: Spain and Portugal in Europe and the Americas*. Cambridge, MA: Harvard University Press.

Holston, James. 1989. *The Modernist City: An Anthropological Critique of Brasília*. Chicago: Unversity of Chicago Press.

Holston, James. 1993. "Legalizando o illegal: propriedade e usurpação no Brasil." *Revista Brasileira de Ciências Sociais*, February 1993: 69–89.

Hunter, Wendy. 2010. *The Transformations of the Worker's Party in Brazil, 1989–2009*. Cambridge: Cambridge University Press.

Ianni, Octávio. 2009. *Estado e Planejamento Econômico no Brasil*. Rio de Janeiro: Editora da UFRJ.

IBGE (Instituto Brasileiro de Geografia e Estatística—Brazilian Census Bureau). 1930. *Recenseamento do Brasil 1872–1920*. Rio de Janeiro: Directoria Geral de Estatística.

IBGE (Instituto Brasileiro de Geografia e Estatística—Brazilian Census Bureau). 1997. *Contagem da população 1996*. Rio de Janeiro: Instituto Brasileiro de Geografia e Estatística, vol. 1.

IBGE (Instituto Brasileiro de Geografia e Estatística—Brazilian Census Bureau). 2001. *Resultados relativos a sexo da população e situação da unidade domiciliar*. Rio de Janeiro: Instituto Brasileiro de Geografia e Estatística, vol. 7.

IBGE (Instituto Brasileiro de Geografia e Estatística—Brazilian Census Bureau). 2007. *Estatísticas do Século XX*. Rio de Janeiro: Instituto Brasileiro de Geografia e Estatística.

IBGE (Instituto Brasileiro de Geografia e Estatística—Brazilian Census Bureau). 2011. *Sinopse do censo demográfico: 2010*. Rio de Janeiro: Instituto Brasileiro de Geografia e Estatística.

Inez, Ana Claudia. 2016. "Repertórios De Ação Coletiva e Performance na Dinâmica de Afirmação Pública do Movimento Føra Lacerda." PhD dissertation, UFMG, Pós Graduação em Comunicação Social. https://repositorio.ufmg.br/bitstream/1843/BUBD-AANQLA/1/disserta__o_ana_claudia_inez.pdf.

Instituto Brasileiro de Geografia e Estatística. 2013. "Pesquisa de Aglomerados Subnormais." Accessed April 18, 2017. http://biblioteca.ibge.gov.br/visualizacao/periodicos/552/cd_2010_agsn_if.pdf.

Irazábal, Clara, ed. 2008. *Ordinary Places, Extraordinary Events: Citizenship, Democracy and Public Space in Latin America*. London: Routledge.

Jacobi, Pedro. 1993. *Movimentos Sociais e políticas públicas: Demandas por saneamento básico e saúde 1974–1984*. São Paulo: Cortez Editora.

King, Anthony. 1990. *Urbanism, Colonialism, and the World Economy: Cultural and Spatial Foundations of the World Urban System*. International Library of Sociology. London: Routledge.

Koury, Ana Paula. 2003. *Grupo Arquitetura Nova*. São Paulo: Romano Guerra, Edusp e Fapesp.

Koury, Ana Paula. 2013a. "A política urbana e a questão social: Quitandinha, o que restou?" *Arquitextos* 14, no. 159.03. http://www.vitruvius.com.br/revistas/read/arquitextos/14.159/4846.

Koury, Ana Paula. 2013b. "Construção Social e Tecnologias Civis (1964–1986): Contribuição para um debate sobre política habitacional no Brasil." *Revista Brasileira de Estudos Urbanos e Regionais* 1, no. 15: 167–82.

Koury, Ana Paula. 2014a. "Rômulo Almeida e a política habitacional brasileira." *Anais do X Encontro de Economia Bahiana*. Salvador: Planejamento e estratégias de desenvolvimento.

Koury, Ana Paula. 2014b. "Decifra-me ou devoro-te: O enigma da política habitacional e urbana e o sistema BNH." In *Habitação e Cidade*, edited by Luis Octavio de Faria and Ruben Otero Silva, vol. 5, 67–75. 1st ed. São Paulo: Escola da Cidade.

Koury, Ana Paula, and Maria Luiza Freitas. 2014. "Olaria, racionalidade construtiva e urbanismo monumental nas cidades-jardins dos comerciários." In *Os Pioneiros da Habitação Social* vol. 3, edited by Nabil Bonduki and Ana Paula Koury. São Paulo: Edunesp.

Koury, Ana Paula, and Talita Veiga Cavallari. 2018. "Desenvolvimento urbano em áreas de fronteira: o caso do Itaim Paulista." *Urbe, Revista Brasileira de Gestão. Urbana* 10, no. 3: 663–76.

Kowarick, Lúcio. 1975. *Capitalismo e Marginalidade na América Latina*. Coleção Estudos Latino-Americanos, vol. 3. Rio de Janeiro: Paz e Terra.

Kowarick, Lúcio, ed. 1994. *Social Struggles and the City: The Case of São Paulo*. New York: Monthly Review Press.

Kowarick, Lúcio. 2012. *Espoliação Urbana*. Rio de Janeiro: Paz e Terra.

Kowarick, Lúcio, and Clara Ant. 1994. "One Hundred Years of Overcrowding: Slum Tenements in the City." In *Social Struggles and the City: The Case of São Paulo*, 60–76. New York: Monthly Review Press.

Krause, Cleandro, Renato Balbim, and Vicente Correia Lima Neto. 2013. *Minha Casa Minha Vida, nosso crescimento: Onde fica política habitacional?* Texto para discussão no. 1853. Brasilia: IPEA.

Krause, Cleandro, Renato Balbim, and Clarisse Linke. 2016. *Cidade e movimento: mobilidades e interações no desenvolvimento urbano.* Brasilia: IPEA.

Lafer, Celso. 1970. "O Planejamento no Brasil: Observações sobre o Plano de Metas 1956–1961." In *Planejamento no Brasil*, edited by Betty Mindlin Lafer, 29–50. São Paulo: Perspectiva.

Lara, Fernando. 2010. "Beyond Curitiba: The Rise of a Participatory Model for Urban Intervention in Brazil." *Urban Design International* 2, no. 15 (Summer 2010): 119–28.

Lara, Fernando. 2011. "Arquitetura Quae Sera Tamem," Cadernos PROARQ no. 17, 9–21.

Lara, Fernando. 2012. "O paradigma do Asfalto." *Revista Forum: um outro mundo em debate*, no. 106 (January): 42–44.

Lara, Fernando. 2013a. "Free Pass Movement and Other Blind Spots of the Brazilian Left." *Llilas Benson* (blog). https://sites.utexas.edu/llilas-benson-blog/2013/10/04/free-pass-movement-and-other-blind-spots-of-the-brazilian-left/.

Lara, Fernando. 2013b. "Favela Upgrade in Brazil: A Reverse of Participatory Processes." *Journal of Urban Design* 18, no. 4 (September): 553–64.

Lara, Fernando. 2014. "Cidades na Era Lula, o lento abandono dos processos participativos." *Revista do IEB—Instituto de Estudos Brasileiros*, no. 58 (June): 218–35.

Latini, Sydney A. 2007. *A implantação da indústria automobilística no Brasil: Da substituição de importações ativa à globalização passiva.* São Paulo: Alaúde Editorial.

Leal, Victor Nunes. (1949) 1997. *Coronelismo, enxada e voto: O município e o regime representativo no Brasil.* Rio de Janeiro: Editora Nova Fronteira.

Lefèvre, Rodrigo B. 1981. "Projeto de um acampamento de obra: Uma utopia." Master's thesis, Faculdade de Arquitetura e Urbanismo da Universidade de São Paulo.

Lefèvre, Rodrigo B., and Sérgio Ferro. 1963. *Proposta inicial para um debate: Possibilidades de atuação.* São Paulo: Cadernos Encontros, Grêmio da Faculdade de Arquitetura e Urbanismo.

Leme, Maria Cristina da Silva, ed. 1999. *Urbanismo no Brasil, 1895–1965.* São Paulo: Studio Nobel, Faculdade de Arquitetura e Urbanismo da Universidade de São Paulo.

Levine, Robert M. 1982. "Brazil: The Dimensions of Democratization." *Current History* 81 (472): 60–87.

Levine, Robert M. 1998. *Father of the Poor? Vargas and His Era*. New York: Cambridge University Press.

Levine, Robert M. 2016. *Brazilian Legacies*. London: Routledge.

Linhares, Hermínio. 1977. *Contribuição à História das Lutas Operárias no Brasil*. 2nd ed., vol. 13. São Paulo: Editora Alfa-Omega.

Lippi, Lucia. 1984. "A Revolução e suas versões." In *A Revolução de 1930: Dicionário Histórico Biográfico Brasileiro*. 1st ed. Accessed January 26, 2021. http://cpdoc.fgv.br/acervo/dhbb.

Lira, Ricardo Pereira. 1983. "O uso do solo urbano e o seu controle: Alguns aspectos do Projeto de Lei Federal No. 755/83." *Revista do Direito Administrativo* 154 (October/December 1983): 1–28.

López-Durán, Fabiola. 2018. *Eugenics in the Garden: Transatlantic Architecture and the Crafting of Modernity*. Austin: University of Texas Press.

Low, Setha M., ed. 1999. *Theorizing the City: The New Urban Anthropology Reader*. New Brunswick, NJ: Rutgers University Press.

Lucchese, Maria Cecília. 2009. "Em defesa do planejamento urbano: Ressonâncias britânicas e a trajetória de Harry James Cole." PhD dissertation, Instituto de Arquitetura e Urbanismo, USP São Carlos.

Macedo, Joseli. 2008. "Urban Land Policy and New Tenure Paradigms: Legitimacy versus Legality in Brazilian Cities." *Land Use Policy* 25: 259–70.

Macedo, Roberto B. M. 1970. "Plano trienal de Desenvolvimento Econômico e Social, 1963–1965." In *Planejamento no Brasil*, edited by Betty Mindlin Lafer, 51–68. São Paulo: Perspectiva.

Machado, Gilmar. 2011. "Dos Mananciais para as Freguesias: a distribuição de agua no espaço urbano do Rio de Janeiro no decenio 1850–1860." *Anais do Encontro da ANPUH*. http://www.snh2011.anpuh.org/resources/anais/14/1300850338_ARQUIVO_DosMananciaisparaasFreguesiasadistribuicaodeaguanoespacourbanodoRiodeJaneironodecenio1850-1860.pdf.

Malloy, James. 1979. *The Politics of Social Security in Brazil*. Pittsburgh: University of Pittsburgh Press.

Manoel, Sálua Kairuz. 2004. "Fundação da Casa Popular: projeto frustrado de construção de uma política habitacional no Brasil." Master's thesis. Escola de Engenharia de São Carlos, Departamento de Arquitetura e Urbanismo-USP, São Carlos.

Maranhão, Ricardo. 1981. "O Estado e a Política 'Populista' no Brasil 1954–1964." In *O Brasil Republicano*, edited by Boris Fausto, 257–94. São Paulo: Difel.

Marques, Ana Carolina Buim Azevedo, and Ana Paula Koury. 2021. "A pedagogia de Paulo Freire no Acampamento Escola de Rodrigo Lefevre." *Arquitextos* 22, no. 256.

Marques, André. 2020. *Lelé: Dialogues with Neutra and Prouvé*. São Paulo: Romano Guerra and Nhamerica Press.

Marques, Eduardo, and Renata Bichir. 2002. "Investimentos públicos, infra-estrutura urbana e produção da periferia de São Paulo." *Revista Espaço e Debates* 42: 9–30.

Martinez Estrada, Ezequiel. (1933) 1996. *Radiografía de la pampa*. San José: Editorial Universidad de Costa Rica.

Martins, Jeová Dias. 2006. "As Regras da Metrópole: o campo urbanístico e a ordem social na Região Metropolitana de São Paulo." PhD dissertation, Universidade de Brasília.

Martins, Paulo Emílio Matos, and Allene Carvalho Lage. 2004. "Canudos e o Movimento dos Trabalhadores Rurais Sem Terra (MST): Singularidades e nexos de dois movimentos sociais brasileiros." *Proceedings of the VII Luso-Brazilian Congress of Social Sciences*. Coimbra: Universidade de Coimbra.

Mattos, Romulo Costa. 2008. "Pelos Pobres! As campanhas de Habitações populares e os discursos sobre as favelas na primeira república." PhD Dissertation, Universidade Federal Fluminense.

McCann, Bryan. 2014. *Hard Times in the Marvelous City*. Durham, NC: Duke University Press.

Medeiros, A. E., and N. L. O. Campos. 2010. "Cidade projetada, construída, tombada e vivenciada." In *Brasília 50 anos: da Capital a Metrópole,* edited by A. Paviani. Brasília: Editora UnB, 137–61.

Megaeventos e Violações de Direitos Humanos no Brasil (Violations of human rights in mega events in Brazil). 2011. Dossier prepared by Articulação Nacional dos Comitês Populares da Copa. http://www.ippur.ufrj.br/index.php?option=com_content&view=article&id=451:laboratorio-etternippur-publica-dossie-megaeventos-e-violacoes-de-direitos-humanos-no-brasil-&catid=67:outros&Itemid=7.

Mendonça, Sérgio E. A. 2002. "A experiência do DIEESE em pesquisa e conhecimento." São Paulo Perspec 16, no. 3: 54–59. http://www.scielo.br/scielo.php?script=sci_arttext&pid=S0102-88392002000300008&lng=en&nrm=iso.

Mignolo, Walter. 2011. *The Darker Side of Western Modernity: Global Futures, Decolonial Options*. Durham: Duke University Press.

Mitchell, Don. 2003. *The Right to the City: Social Justice and the Fight for Public Space*. New York: Guilford Press.

Moisés, José Alvaro, ed. 1978. *Contradições Urbanas e Movimentos Sociais*. Rio de Janeiro: Paz e Terra.

Moisés, José Alvaro, and Verena Martinez Alier. 1978. "A revolta dos suburbanos ou patrão o trem atrasou." In *Contradições Urbanas e Movimentos Sociais*, 13–63. Rio de Janeiro: Paz e Terra.

Monis, Edmundo. 1978. *A Guerra Social de Canudos*. Rio de Janeiro: Civilização Brasileira.

Moore, Steven. 2007. *Alternative Routes to the Sustainable City: Austin, Curitiba, and Frankfurt*. Lanham: Lexington.

Morangueira, Vanderlice Souza. 2006. "Vila Maria Zélia: visões de uma vila operária em São Paulo, 1917–1940." PhD dissertation, Programa de Pós-Graduação em História Econômica, Universidade de São Paulo.

Mota, Juliana Costa. 2007. "Uma análise da criação e da atuação do SERFHAU." *Anais do XII Encontro da ANPUR*, May 2007, 1–20.

Motta, Marcia. 1998. *Nas fronteiras do poder: Conflitos de terras e direito agrário no Brasil de meados do século XIX*. Rio de Janeiro: Vicio de Leitura.

Needell, Jeffrey D. 1987. "The Revolta contra Vacina of 1904: The Revolt against 'Modernization' in Belle-Époque Rio de Janeiro." *Hispanic American Historical Review* 67, no. 2: 233–69.

Neto, Lira. 2012. *Getúlio1 (1882–1930)*. São Paulo: Companhia das Letras.

Neves, Eduardo. 2006. *Arqueologia Da Amazônia*. Rio de Janeiro: Jorge Zahar Editor.

Nylen, William. 2002. "Testing the Empowerment Thesis: The Participatory Budget in Belo Horizonte and Betim, Brazil." *Comparative Politics* 34, no. 2: 127–45.

OAS. 1967. *The Alliance for Progress and Latin-American Development Prospects: A Five Years Review 1961–1965*. Baltimore: Johns Hopkins University Press.

Ofício do Arcebispo D. Luís. 1882. http://www.portfolium.com.br/Sites/Canudos/conteudo.asp?IDPublicacao=153.

Oliveira, F. E. B de, Kaizô Iwakami Beltrão, and A. C. de A. David. 1998. *A Dívida da União com a previdência social: Uma perspectiva histórica*. Rio de Janeiro: IPEA.

Oliveira, Francisco de. 1972. "A Economia Brasileira: Crítica à razão dualista." *Estudos Cebrap*, 4–82.

Oliveira, Francisco de. 2003. *Crítica à Razão Dualista: O ornitorrinco*. São Paulo: Boitempo Editorial.

Oliveira, Francisco de. 2006. "O vício da virtude. Autoconstrução e acumulação capitalista no Brasil" *Novos Estudos* 74 (March 2006), 67–85.

Outtes, J. 1994. "Disciplining the Society through the City: Town Planning Genesis in Brazil and Argentina (1905–1945)." *Bulletin of Latin American Research*.

Paviani, A., ed. 1987. *Urbanização e Metropolização*. Brasília: UNB.

Perlman, Janice. 2010. *Favela: Four Decades of Living on the Edge in Rio de Janeiro*. New York: Oxford University Press.

Pinto, Luiz A. Da Costa. 1953. *O negro no Rio de Janeiro*. São Paulo: Companhia Editora Nacional.

Plano Trienal de Desenvolvimento Econômico e Social. 1962. Distrito Federal: Imprensa Nacional.

Pontual, V. 2001. *Uma cidade e dois prefeitos: Narrativas do Recife das décadas de 1930 e 1950*. Recife: Editora Universitária.

Portaria do MT. 1939. *SCM 177*. November 10, 1939. Rio de Jeneiro: Ministério do Traballho Industria e Comércio.

Portas, Nuno. 1986. "O processo SAAL: entre o Estado e o poder local." *Revista Crítica de Ciências Sociais* 18/19/20 (February 1986): 635–44.

Porto, Rubens. 1938. *O problema das casas operárias e os Institutos e Caixas de Pensões*. Rio de Janeiro: Ministério do Trabalho, Indústria e Comércio.

Prado, Caio, Jr. (1935) 1983. *A cidade de São Paulo: Geografia e história*. São Paulo: Brasiliense.

Prado, Caio, Jr. (1942) 2006. *Formação do Brasil Contemporâneo*. São Paulo, Brasiliense.

Prado, Caio, Jr. (1966) 1977. *A Revolução Brasileira*. São Paulo: Brasilense.

Quijano, Anibal, and Immanuel Wallerstein. 1992. "Americanity as a Concept, or the Americas in the Modern World." *International Social Science Journal* 44 (4): 549–57.

Quijano, Aníbal. 1977. *Dependencia, Urbanización Y Cambio Social En Latinoamérica*. Lima: Mosca Azul Editores.

Ramos, Jovelino. 1974. "Interpretando o fenômeno Canudos." *Luso-Brazilian Review*, 11 (1): 65–83.

Ramsdell, Lea. 1990. "National Housing Policy and the *Favela* in Brazil." In *The Political Economy of Brazil: Public Policies in an Era of Transition*, edited by Lawrence S. Graham and Robert H. Wilson, 224–53. Austin: University of Texas Press.

Rego, Alcides Marinho. 1942. *A Vitória do Direito Operário no Governo de Getúlio Vargas*. Rio de Janeiro: Departamento de Imprensa e Propaganda.

Reid, Michael. 2014. *Brazil: The Troubled Rise of a Global Power*. New Haven: Yale University Press.

Reis, Nestor Goulart. 1996. Notas sobre a organização das Regiões Metropolitanas. *Cadernos de Pesquisa do LAP* no. 12. April/May 1996. São Paulo: Faculdade de Arquitetura e Urbanismo da Univerisdade de São Paulo.

Relatório da Sub Comissão de Habitação e Favelas. 1953. 8 vols. Archive no. GV c 1952.12.23 Centro de Documentação da Fundação Getúlio Vargas.

Resende, Pâmela de Almeida. 2019. "Ser um embaixador não é um mar de rosas: o sequestro de Charles Burke Elbrick no Brasil em 1969." PhD dissertation. Faculdade de Filosofia, Letras e Ciências Humanas, Universidade de São Paulo. doi:10.11606/T.8.2019.tde-16092019-151925.

Rezende, V. L. F. M. 2012. *Urbanismo na Era Vargas: a transformação das cidades brasileiras*. Niterói: Intertexto/Editora da UFF.

Ribeiro, Darcy. 1995. *O povo brasileiro: a formação e o sentido do Brasil*. São Paulo: Companhia das Letras.

Ribeiro, Luiz Cesar de Queiroz, and Orlando Alves dos Santos Junior. 2017. "Neoliberalization and Mega-events: The Transition of Rio de Janeiro's Hybrid Urban Order." *Journal of Urban Affairs* 39(7): 909–23.

Rich, Jessica. 2019. *State-Sponsored Activism: Bureaucrats and Social Movements in Democratic Brazil*. Cambridge: Cambridge University Press.

Rodrigues, Jose Albertino. 1968. *Sindicato e Desenvolvimento no Brasil*. São Paulo: Difusão Europeia do Livro.

Rodrigues, Rute Imanishi. 2013. *Os "parques proletários" e os subúrbios do Rio de Janeiro: Aspectos da política governamental para as favelas entre 1930–1960*. Rio de Janeiro: IPEA.

Rolnik, Raquel, and Jeroen Klink. 2011. "Crescimento Econômico e Desenvolvimento Urbano: Porque nossas cidades continuam tão precárias?" *Novos Estudos* 89 (March 2011): 89–109.

Rolnik, Raquel, Lúcio Kowarick, Nadia Somekh, and Ana Lucia do Amaral. 1990. *Crise e mudança. São Paulo para todos*. São Paulo: Brasiliense/Editora Prefeitura de São Paulo.

Romeiro, Adriana. 2008. *Paulistas e emboabas no coração das Minas: Idéias, práticas e imaginário político no século XVIII*. Belo Horizonte: Editora da UFMG.

Ronconi, Reginaldo. 2008. *Canteiro Experimental: 10 anos na FAU USP*. São Paulo: Faculdade de Arquitetura e Urbanismo da Universidade de São Paulo.

Rossi, Clovis. 1984. "A nação frustrada!" *Folha de S. Paulo*. April 26, 1984. Accessed March 13, 2021. http://almanaque.folha.uol.com.br/brasil_26abr1984.htm.

Russell-Wood, A. J. R. 1992. *The Portuguese in Africa, Asia and America, 1415–1808: A World on the Move*. Manchester: Carcanet.

Saad-Filho, Alfredo. 2013. "Mass Protests under 'Left Neoliberalism': Brazil, June–July 2013." *Critical Sociology* 39 (5): 657–69.

Sandler, Daniela. 2020. "Grassroots urbanism in contemporary São Paulo." *Urban Design International* 25: 137–51.

Santagada, S. 1990. "A situação social no Brasil nos anos 80." *Indicadores Econômicos* 17, no. 4: 121–43.

Santos, Carlos Nelson Ferreira. 1981. *Movimentos Sociais Urbanos no Rio de Janeiro*. Rio de Janeiro: Zahar.

Schwarcz, Lilia Moritz. 1993. *O Espetáculo Das Raças: Cientistas, Instituições E Questão Racial No Brasil, 1870–1930*. São Paulo: Companhia das Letras.

Seed, Patricia. 1995. *Ceremonies of Possession in Europe's Conquest of the New World, 1492–1640*. Cambridge: Cambridge University Press.

Segre, Roberto. 1991. *Arquitetura e urbanismo da revolução cubana*. São Paulo: Nobel.

Serran, J. R. 1976. *O IAB e a política habitacional brasileira 1954–1975*. São Paulo: Schema Editora.

Shirk, David A. "A Tale of Two Mexican Border Cities: The Rise and Decline of Drug Violence in Juárez and Tijuana." *Journal of Borderlands Studies* 29, no. 4. (2014): 481–502.

Silva, Davi Ramalho Oliveira da. 2015. "Perfil profissional do urbanista Jorge Wilheim." Research report granted by Brazilian National Council of Research. Universidade São Judas Tadeu: São Paulo.

Simonsen, Roberto C., and Eugênio Gudin. (1945) 2010. *A Controvérsia Do planejamento Na Economia Brasileira.* 3rd ed. Brasília: Ipea.

Singer, Paul, and Vinicius Caldeira Brant. 1980. *São Paulo: O povo em movimento.* São Paulo: Vozes, Cebrap.

Skidmore, Thomas. (1967) 1982. *Brasil: De Getúlio a Castelo.* Rio de Janeiro: Paz e Terra.

Smith, Christen A. 2016. *Afro-Paradise: Blackness, Violence, and Performance in Brazil.* Urbana: University of Illinois Press.

Smith, Nigel J. H. 1999. *The Amazon River Forest: A Natural History of Plants, Animals, and People.* New York: Oxford University Press.

Soares, Claudete Gomes. 2000. "Teologia da Libertação no Brasil." PhD dissertation, IFCH, Unicamp.

Soares, Fabio, and Yuri Soares. 2005. "The Socio-economic Impact of Favela-Bairro: What Do the Data Say?" Office of Evaluation and Oversight Inter-American Development Bank, Washington, DC.

Sorj, B. 2008. *A construção intelectual do Brasil contemporâneo: da resistência à ditadura ao governo FHC.* Rio de Janeiro: Centro Edelstein de Pesquisas Sociais.

Souza, C. F. 2008. *Plano Geral de Melhoramentos de Porto Alegre: O plano que orientou a modernização da cidade.* Porto Alegre: Armazém Digital.

Souza, Luiz Felipe Machado Coelho de. 2014. *Irmãos Roberto arquitetos.* Rio de Janeiro: Rio Books.

Street, Jorge, and Evaristo de Moraes Filho. 1980. *Idéias Sociais de Jorge Street.* Ação E Pensamento Da República 4. Brasília: Rio de Janeiro: Senado Federal; Fundação Casa de Rui Barbosa, MEC.

Sussekind, Arnaldo. 1955. *Previdência Social Brasileira.* Rio de Janeiro: Livraria Freitas Bastos.

Suzigan, Wilson. 1986. *Indústria Brasileira: Origem e desenvolvimento.* São Paulo: Brasiliense.

Tavares, Jeferson. 2014. *Projetos para Brasília, 1927–1957.* Brasília: Iphan.

Teixeira, Palmira Petratti. 1990. *A Fábrica do Sonho: Trajetória do Industrial Jorge Street.* São Paulo: Paz e Terra.

Telles, Pedro Carlos da Silva. 1984. *História da Engenharia no Brasil.* Vol. 2, *Século XX.* Rio de Janeiro: Clavero Editorações.

Trindade, Alexandro Dantas. 2011. *André Rebouças: Um Engenheiro do Império,* Pensamento Político-Social 4. São Paulo: Editora Hucitec : FAPESP.

Trindade, Mário. 1971. *Habitação e desenvolvimento.* São Paulo: Vozes.

Unites States Government. 1816. *Tariff, or rates of duty, after the thirtieth of June 1816, on all goods, wares and merchandise, imported into the United States of America.* Accessed September 15, 2021. https://www.loc.gov/item/08021092/.

Valladares, Lícia Prado. 2000. "Qu'est-ce qu'une favela?" *Cahiers des Amerique Latines*, no. 34, 61–72.

Valladares, Lícia Prado. 2005. *A invenção da favela: Do mito de origem a favela.com.* Rio de Janeiro: Fundação Getúlio Vargas.

Vasconcelos, Pedro. 2016. *Salvador: Transformações e Permanências (1549–1999).* Salvador: EDUFBA.

Velho, Gilberto. 1980. "O antropólogo pesquisando em sua cidade: sobre conhecimento e heresia." In *O desafio da cidade: novas perspectivas da antropologia brasileira.* Rio de Janeiro: Campus.

Victor, Mário. 1965. *Cinco anos que abalaram o Brasil: de Jânio Quadros ao Marechal Castelo Branco.* Rio de Janeiro: Editora da Civilização Brasileira.

Villaça, Flavio. 1978. *Uso do solo urbano.* São Paulo: Fundação Prefeito Faria Lima, Centro de Estudos e Pesquisas de Administração Municipal.

Villaça, Flavio. 1998. *Espaço intra-urbano no Brasil.* São Paulo: Studio Nobel.

Vizioli, Simone H. T. 1988. "Planejamento Urbano no Brasil: a experiência do SERFHAU enquanto órgão federal de planejamento integrado ao desenvolvimento municipal." PhD dissertation, Faculdade de Arquitetura e Urbanismo da Universidade de São Paulo.

Weffort, Francisco. 1972. *Participação e conflito industrial: Participação e conflito industrial: Contagem e Osasco, 1968.* São Paulo: Cebrap.

Weinstein, Barbara. 1996. *For Social Peace in Brazil. Industrialists and Remaking of the Working Class in São Paulo, 1920–1964.* Chapel Hill: University of North Carolina Press.

Wilheim, Jorge. 1963. *São Paulo Metropole 65, subsídios para o seu plano diretor.* São Paulo: Difusão Europeia do Livro.

Wolfe, Joel. 1993. *Working Women, Working Men: São Paulo and the rise of Brazil's Industrial Working Class, 1900–1955.* Durham: Duke University Press.

Wood, Terence, and Warwick Murray. 2007. "Participatory Democracy in Brazil and Local Geographies: Porto Alegre and Belo Horizonte Compared." *European Review of Latin American and Caribbean Studies* 83 (October 2007): 19–41.

Zaluar, Alba, and Marcos Alvito. 1998. *Um século de favela.* Rio de Janeiro: Fundação Getúlio Vargas.

INDEX

Note: Page numbers in *italics* indicate figures.